Vinegar Joe's War

Vinegar Joe's War

Stilwell's Campaigns for Burma

Nathan N. Prefer

PRESIDIO

To those who served

"Heroism, the Caucasian mountaineers say,
is enduring for one moment more."

George F. Kennan
Letter (1921)

Copyright © 2000 by Nathan N. Prefer

Published by Presidio Press, Inc.
505 B San Marin Drive, Suite 160
Novato, CA 94945-1340

Library of Congress Cataloging-in-Publication Data

Prefer, Nathan N.
    Vinegar Joe's war : Stilwell's campaigns for Burma/
Nathan N. Prefer.
      p. cm.
    Includes bibliographical references and index.
    ISBN 0-89141-715-X
      1. Stilwell, Joseph Warren, 1883-1946. 2. World War,
1939–1945—Campaigns—Burma. 3. Generals—United States—
Biography. I. Title
D767.6 .P78 2000
940.54'25—dc21

                                  00-039170

All photos are courtesy of the National Archives

Printed in the United States of America

Contents

Acknowledgments   vii
Introduction   1
1. Mukden to Quebec   8
2. A Call for Volunteers   26
3. First Mission: Walabum   50
4. Second Mission: Shaduzup   78
5. Siege at Nhpum Ga   100
6. Third Mission: Myitkyina   128
7. New Galahad   149
8. From Galahad to Mars   180
9. Tonkwa   197
10. The Burma Road   207
11. The Last Battles   223
Epilogue   253
Appendix 1: Orders of Battle   260
Appendix 2: Combat Awards   266
Appendix 3: Medal of Honor Citation   269
Appendix 4: United States Army Forces, CBI Theater   270
Appendix 5: Chronology: CBI Theater, 1944–1945   276
Appendix 6: Colonel Hunter's Letter to General Stilwell   281
Chapter Notes   284
Bibliography   297
Index   303

Acknowledgments

No history such as this one can be written without the considerable assistance of many people. In the case of the two Burma campaigns I was fortunate in that there are several very active and very interested veteran's associations that did everything in their power to assist me in this project. The first of these is Merrill's Marauder's Association, Inc. and its president, Ray Lyons. Another is the China-Burma-India Veteran's Association and its president, Dwight O. King. The Jewish War Veterans of the USA, Inc. and its president Mr. Steve Shaw were equally cooperative. Equally important in providing information and personal recollections was Mr. W. ("Woody") B. Woodruff Jr. and his Mars Task Force Mountain Artillery Association.

Certainly no book such as this can possibly be written without the assistance and professional guidance of the men and women who preserve our nation's historical heritage at the National Archives and Records Center in College Park, Maryland. In my case I am especially indebted to Ms. Rebecca Collier of the Modern Military Records Branch for her considerable efforts on my behalf during and after my visits there. Another individual who was of considerable assistance was Mr. Robert K. Wright Jr., of the Historical Resources Branch, Center of Military History.

Chief among those who contributed are those who offered gave of their time and memories to willingly and cooperatively provide the information that makes up most of this book. These are the veterans whose personal contributions are the core of any history dealing with campaigns and battles. Once again, I am indebted to Mr. Arthur W. Wilson (Red C/T); Mr. Tom Harris and Mr. Mike Kozisek (253rd QM Troop); Mr. Stanley Silver (898th Heavy Ordnance Co.);

Mrs. Joel (Ruth) Weichbelbaum (1st Tactical Air Communications Squadron); Mr. Solis Finkel (14th AAF); Mrs Lyman (Marjorie) Gueck (253rd QM Troop); Mr. Won-Loy Chan (NCAC); Mr. Joseph Tannenbaum (Chinese 21st Artillery); Mr. Lloyd Messersmith (274th CMP Co.); Stan J. Moloney (12th Chinese Combat Engineers); Mr. O. J. Taylor (1905 Engineer Aviation Bn.); Mr. Alfred Frankel (7th Bomb Group).

Finally, there are those who suffer through it all despite never having experienced it in person. First and foremost among these is my wife, Barbara Anne, who fulfilled the roles of secretary, research assistant, and cheerleader. Then our daughters, Hollie and Amy, who learned far more about World War II than they ever desired. Finally our sons, Douglas, Kevin, Michael, and Christopher, who fortunately have never had to experience the tragedy of war. Without them this book would never have been completed.

Introduction

The story of the United States Army in the Second World War continues to produce numerous histories of campaigns great and small. As the largest part of that army was involved in the European theater, with a lesser portion struggling across the vast Pacific Ocean areas, nearly all of the studies concern the battles of those campaigns. The debate on the reasons for victory, the strengths and skills of the opposing forces, and the interservice and interallied disputes are both interesting and useful for contemplating modern-day situations.

Yet one area remains largely ignored. This is the U.S. Army's involvement in the China-Burma-India (CBI) theater of operations. Because it was a theater in which little hope was placed, even at the time, for a decisive strategic or tactical success, the importance of the performance of the U.S. Army in its first prolonged battle on the continent of Asia is relegated mainly to a footnote in the larger studies of the war. However, the American involvement in the Burma campaign, in particular, is a classic study in refuting some historian's arguments about the skill and professionalism of the U.S. Army in the Second World War.

These historians, usually but not solely European, argue that the Allies, and most particularly the Americans, won that war by applying a mass of material and manpower to overwhelm a more professional but materially weaker enemy. The argument points out that the Americans relied heavily on air supremacy, undisputed logistical support, and a superior supply of manpower to defeat their enemies. Often the case is argued using some of the more spectacular battles of the war. The campaign in Normandy and the battles of Iwo Jima and Okinawa are just some of the examples used to support this thesis.

Yet to brand the American army as inferior to its enemies in personnel competence is unfair, misleading, and grossly incorrect.
The selection of those battles or campaigns to prove the point is
also misleading, for there were many battles in which the United
States Army did not have any of the usual advantages so often at-
tributed to it. The entire U.S. Army ground-force effort in the
China-Burma-India theater of operations is a case in point. But
because of the small number of American ground forces involved,
as well as the frustration of the American effort there, it is usually
overlooked. An American force, technically under Allied command, did in fact fight a campaign without tactical use of air support, without the vaunted logistical support, and with a manpower
shortage that became so bad that the American commander was
forced to return wounded men to the front lines, a situation not
seen in the American army since the defeat at Bataan. Yet this occurred at the supposed height of American military power, in late
1944 and early 1945.

The fact that this force succeeded in its goals makes the study
even more important, for it highlights the strengths of the average
American infantryman of World War II. No special units were involved in the campaign, although one unit did acquire a nickname
bequeathed upon it by the media. These were ordinary American
infantrymen—army draftees and National Guardsmen from all
across the United States—who more by chance than design found
themselves fighting a "forgotten war."

Indeed, their war was forgotten even while it was being fought.
The distance from home, the sparse media coverage, and the overwhelming numbers of Allied troops who carried the main burden
of the campaign all contributed to the ease in which this campaign
faded from the public conscience. Contributing also were the small
numbers, comparatively speaking, of Americans involved. Three
American regiments carried the main burden of the portion of battle fought under American flags. Briefly reinforced in midcam-
paign by two U.S. combat engineer battalions, those regiments represented only a fraction of Allied troops committed to the Burma
campaign. There were no sweeping armored thrusts to report.
There were no great battles of encirclement either. It was battle at

its most primitive, pitting ground soldiers against each other in difficult conditions of climate and terrain with few mitigating factors present. Because of those conditions, these campaigns present excellent opportunities to study the professional skills of the United States Army in World War II.

The professionalism of America's citizen army of World War II in the U.S. Army's Burma campaign is worth a closer look, for it was a very strange war for Americans. These soldiers were committed to a campaign that their own leadership never believed would lead to decisive results. They fought under foreign command led by an American general whose duty lay with a foreign government. That same general openly criticized the foreign government he was supposed to serve, his own American commanders for sending him to such duty, and his most effective allies due to his own anglophobia.[1] It was a war in which the main supply and transportation routes depended on mules and horses. Yet at the same time, supply was often provided by the most advanced air-carrier techniques of the day. It was also an early version of what decades later in Vietnam would be termed "winning the hearts and the minds" of the civilian populace. Like the Vietnam War, it was for the most part an irregular war depending largely upon ambushes and battles of encirclement to defeat the enemy. At a time when the American army was filled mostly with draftees, this campaign was fought mainly by volunteers.

Still another unique aspect of this campaign is the fact that it was the only one fought on the Asian mainland by American troops during World War II. Determined to keep China in the war to divert Japanese assets away from the Pacific theaters, and equally determined to show to the British ally its commitment to keeping them in the Pacific campaigns, the United States sent a token force to, in effect, "show the flag" to its Allies. As a result, American ground forces for the first and only time fought in Burma.

The country of Burma encompasses about 678,000 square miles and in 1942 had a population of about seventeen million. It is bordered on the west by India, and China looms over its north and northeast borders. To the east and southeast, Thailand and Laos complete the encirclement. Only in the south does Burma have an unobstructed outlet to the world, a coastline along the Bay of Ben-

gal and a major port in the city of Rangoon. The other large cultural
and economic locale was the British-developed city of Mandalay in
the center of the country. The major communications network of
the area in 1944 was the Irrawaddy River system, which drained the
greater part of the country and originated in the forested mountains
of northern Burma before traveling 1,300 miles to the sea. Its tribu-
tary, the Chindwin, roughly marked the border with India. Another
river of importance was the Sittang, which was difficult to cross due
to a tidal bore. Much of the land frontiers consisted of rings of hills
and rugged mountains, making overland movement between
Burma and its adjoining states extremely difficult.

In the center of the country are the lowlands. These lie between
a range of mountains called the Arakan Yoma to the west and the
Shan Plateau to the east. Here another large river, the Salween,
flows across the plateau and marks the border with Thailand. The
average elevation in the area is 3,300 feet above sea level, although
in some places the hills are twice that height. Climate is ruled by the
southwest monsoon, which comes in off the Indian Ocean and creates only three seasons: the rainy season, from May to October; a
cool season, from October into February; and a hot season, from
February into late May. Despite the dominance of the monsoon,
rainfall varies greatly between the coast and the interior of the
country, with the latter getting by far the greater rainfall.

In the interior, rivers tend to run from north to south, with
ranges of mountains between each. Rivers, roads, and trails that run
from east to west have to pass through rugged mountain terrain,
making travel difficult. This natural compartmentalization of the
country developed a people free and independent of others, avoiding outsiders when encountered and fiercely proud of their way of
life. In these hills lived the minorities of the country—Chins,
Kachins, and Karens—who neither cared for nor wanted any contact with outsiders. These minority peoples lived in what others considered untamed jungles and desired nothing more. In more developed areas of Burma, primarily along the lowlands, farmers
created cultivated areas that produced rich harvests. Most of the
lowlanders were Buddhists, but numerous other religions existed
throughout the area.

In the late 1930s Burma was undergoing a transformation from British colony to independent state. Several separate factions struggled to be the predominant political party in place to assume power once independence became a reality. In September 1940 Prime Minister Ba Maw was replaced as head of state by Tharrawaddy U Pu. Ba Maw formed a coalition party, the Freedom Bloc, to demand immediate independence in an effort to take advantage of Britain's diversion with the war in Europe. In this he was unsuccessful, and a new prime minister, U Saw, was appointed. U Saw attempted to suppress the Freedom Bloc and have his own Patriot Party take control of the government after persuading the British to grant Burma either full independence or dominion status.

U Saw went to London to argue his case, which was refused by British Prime Minister Winston Churchill. On his way back to Burma, U Saw contacted Japanese agents at a stopover in Portugal. The Japanese consul sent a report of the meeting to Tokyo, and the British, who had broken the Japanese diplomatic code, were soon aware of his intrigue. He was arrested and exiled to Uganda for the duration of the war. As it turned out, Japanese agents had also contacted Ba Maw. Japan's interest in Burma lay in her strategic resources, especially oil, and in the access that Burma provided to support the Chinese armies of Chiang Kai-shek. Japan, which had been at war with China for several years, determined to cut the Chinese supply lines by controlling Burma. Subsequently, Ba Maw and several comrades received military training from the Japanese and formed the Burma Independence Army (BIA). Aiding the Japanese by intelligence gathering, sabotage, and occasional guerilla warfare, the BIA led Japanese forces into Burma in January 1942. By May the primary supply route to China through Burma, the Burma Road, had been cut.

Shortly afterward, the BIA was transformed into the four-thousand-man Burma Defense Army. In January 1943 Japan's prime minister, Tojo Hideki, announced that independence would be granted at the end of that year. Ba Maw was installed as the head of state. Yet little changed. Japan viewed Burma as simply another asset in its ongoing war with the west. Japanese occupation, as elsewhere, was harsh. Thousands of Burmese were put into forced labor battalions. The Kempeitai, or military police, were universally feared. By late 1943 Karen officers of the BNA were in contact with the British Special Operations Executive Force 136, exchanging intelligence about Japanese deployments. Ba Maw, now aware of the Japanese duplicity, refused to cooperate with them. At one point the Japanese occupation forces considered assassinating him, but they never went further than planning an attack. By 1945, when Allied forces had reconquered most of northern and central Burma, the BNA rose up under British control and assisted in the reconquest of the remainder of their homeland.

The Japanese invasion of Burma was intended to acquire its natural resources—oil, tungsten, and rice—while cutting the major supply road to China from India, the Burma Road. This road ran about 750 miles from Rangoon by way of Mandalay to Lashio and then on into China. In actuality it was two roads connected because of the war. The Chinese had built a road from Kunming to the Burmese border at Wanting to join the existing road from Rangoon to Lashio. Over this road came a vast array of war supplies for the Chinese army, then engaged in a devastating war with Japan. The road was vulnerable to weather and became impassable in heavy rains. When the weather favored travel, the terrain often did not. The road passed through hills about three thousand feet high and then proceeded into the Chin Hills, where it crossed mountains eight thousand feet high. Before reaching the Indian border it again crossed the Naga Hills, where peaks were often twelve thousand feet high. Yet once the Japanese had seized Thailand and French Indo-China, that difficult road was the only land artery to supply China, an ally many Americans considered essential in the war against Japan. For the Americans, the campaign in Burma was primarily to open the Burma Road and to support China in the continued war effort against Japan. For the Allies, particularly the British, it was to recover the lost colonies and reestablish their control, however temporary, over Burma. The Indian army, fighting under British command, was repulsing an invasion of its homeland. The Chinese, and eventually the Japanese, fought for survival.

For the Americans a mainland campaign had never been seriously considered. Prewar planners had consistently rejected proposals for an offensive against Japan on the Asian mainland. They viewed it as contrary to public opinion, logistically impossible, and potentially disastrous. Once war came, however, it was President Franklin D. Roosevelt who was convinced that the assets China brought to the war, its millions of people, and its proximity to the Japanese home islands where Allied bombers could be based made an effort on China's behalf worthwhile.[2]

Each for their own reasons, the Allies campaigned to reconquer Burma. It was easily the longest and most difficult campaign of the Second World War. The contribution of the U.S. Army ground forces in the campaign, however insignificant in comparison to its allies, deserves recognition in the professional and effective manner in which this difficult task was accomplished.

1. Mukden to Quebec

T he involvement of the United States Army in China during World War II can be traced back to the war between China and Japan, which began 18 September 1931 with the so-called Mukden Incident. Using a carefully staged incident along the Manchurian border to justify its actions, Japan seized the entire Manchurian area. Finding no more than verbal opposition from the great western powers, Japan continued to look farther afield.

The seizure of Manchuria soon produced a boycott against Japan by China. As China was a principal market of Japan at the time, this was no idle protest. In an effort to break the boycott, Japan launched an expeditionary force against China on 28 January 1932 with the seizure of Shanghai. This time, world public opinion was much more critical, and after several months Japan withdrew its troops.

Watching from offshore, Japan viewed with some concern the increasing unification of China. A unified China was not popular with Japanese military or business leaders. It could turn into a military and economic power equal to its huge potential, overshadowing Japan. To prevent successful unification of China, Japan constantly provoked incidents with China along her borders from 1932 through 1937. China, racked by a civil war between the nationalists under Chiang Kai-shek and the communists under Mao Tse-tung, had little time or resources to put the Japanese in fear of reprisal.

Finally, on 7 July 1937, after getting no satisfaction from a claim that local Chinese troops had kidnapped one of their soldiers, Japanese troops attacked a Chinese garrison near Peiping, in North China. Taken for just another local incident, the fighting did not peter out as before, and both sides refused all attempts at resolution. The fighting soon spread and became general throughout the area. By that time neither the Japanese nor the Chinese were willing to concede anything to the other side. The Sino-Japanese War had begun.

The Chinese Nationalist Army, at that time the largest and holding the vast majority of Chinese territory, had looked abroad for assistance in developing its forces into modern European models. A glance at the United States military convinced them that they were better off seeking help from the more advanced western European armies. The German army had sent a mission as early as 1928, and they were still on the scene. Requests also went out to the Italian and Russian military for professional guidance. Despite the skills of the German and other European advisers, the main Chinese force of thirty modern divisions failed to hold the lower Yangtze Valley, and the Japanese pushed deeper into China.

To explain the defeat of their best forces, the Chinese nationalist government at about this time reported to the press that the reason for its defeats was the lack of modern weapons. This excuse was denied by both the German military mission, which worked with the Chinese and the American military attaché, Col. Joseph W. Stilwell. Instead, these observers cited the neglect of the fundamental principles of strategy and tactics, indifference to military intelligence, inability to adapt to changed conditions, failure to establish a communications network, and failure to maintain equipment.

The defeats continued throughout 1938 and 1939. Two major efforts by the Chinese at a counteroffensive ended as complete failures. In desperation the Chinese turned to diplomacy. China appealed to the western Allies and Russia for aid. Japan, knowing it needed allies as well, joined with Germany and Italy. By the time the Chinese efforts had reached the western powers, however, the attention of those countries had been diverted to their own survival. September 1939 saw the beginning of World War II in Europe.

China approached the United States, not for the first time, in June 1940. Asking for arms and credits for their war effort, the Chinese were warmly received. Although anxious not to provoke Japan, the clearly defined alliances that had hardened with the outbreak of war seemed to endanger United States interests as well. Concerned about its own safety and not anxious to further deplete its meager stock of arms, which were already being siphoned off to aid Great Britain, the United States agreed to a loan but not to arm the Chinese. This rebuff only made the Chinese redouble their efforts. Later that same year Generalissimo Chiang Kai-shek, renewing his pleas through the American ambassador, Nelson T. Johnson, expressed his concern about the Japanese progress toward the Burma Road, the principal supply access from the West now that Russia was maintaining a neutral position. He also asked for American aircraft manned by American volunteers. He suggested that those aircraft could destroy the Japanese fleet at its anchorages, a plan similar to the one that Japan later executed at Pearl Harbor the following year. Again, the United States hesitated, promising to study the request and reply.

Negotiations continued over the next several months, with requests coming from Mao Tse-tung as well as from Chiang Kai-shek. Both wanted aircraft and the crews to fly and maintain them. Finally, in December 1940, after the Japanese had bombed and sunk the U.S. Navy's gunboat *Panay* on Chinese river waters, President Franklin D. Roosevelt approved the request for aid and instructed his advisers to implement the requests of the Chinese government. A group of about one hundred fighter planes with volunteers to fly them was eventually shipped to China. They were placed under the command of an American, former army captain Claire L. Chennault. Retired from the American army due to a physical disability, he had lived in China for several years and had developed a theory of using air power to defeat the Japanese in China.

When President Roosevelt signed the Lend-Lease Act on 11 March 1941 China immediately put forward its requests. Briefly, China wanted a one-thousand aircraft air force, thirty fully equipped modern infantry divisions, and an efficient line of communications to support both. All of these would require American military support, training, maintenance, and supply. But because the United States was not at war with Japan, only volunteers could be sent. Most of the volunteers were pilots or maintenance crews to support the aircraft sent under lend lease. In the meantime, the army identified officers within its ranks who had experience in

China, could speak Chinese, or were otherwise qualified to participate in the growing number of studies of the problems of China.
Some of those officers were sent in study groups to China to report
back on the true situation of the Chinese war effort.

The study groups found that the Chinese army was modeled on
that of its enemy rather than on Western armies. Like the Japanese
army, the Chinese used the triangular (three regiment) division. It
had no equivalent of the army corps but instead used the term
"armies," which usually consisted of three divisions and army
troops. Three Chinese "armies" made up a "group army." Generally speaking, the concept of three ran throughout the Chinese
army structure. Loyalty was the most serious problem in the Chinese army. Consisting of over three million troops divided into
more than three hundred divisions, only a handful owed alle-
giance to the central government. Most were loyal to their local war
area commanders, not unlike the former Chinese warlords. As was
expected, cooperation between war areas was difficult when not
impossible.

For the balance of the year before the bombing of Pearl Harbor,
China continued to request additional assistance and more American studies of Chinese capabilities. When the Japanese brought
the United States into the active war, China became an ally of the
U.S. and direct assistance was possible. Chiang Kai-shek's immediate response to Pearl Harbor was to offer China as a base of operations for the Allies to defeat Japan. President Roosevelt agreed to
discuss plans over the next few months. Several conferences were
planned by the leading Allied war powers to decide on the course
of their war.

Because the Japanese had created a China war theater for the Allies, the Americans now had to make the necessary arrangements to
include that theater in its war efforts. As they had with their other
allies, the Americans wanted to establish a combined planning staff
for future operations in the China theater. To establish such a staff
an American officer had to be selected to represent the United
States in China. Selected for this position was the senior American
line officer with combat experience, Lt. Gen. Hugh A. Drum. Born
19 September 1879 in Fort Brady, Michigan, Hugh Aloysius Drum

was commissioned from the ranks as an infantry officer in 1898, and
he graduated from the Army Staff College in 1912. During World
War I he fought in France and served as chief of staff of the First
(U.S.) Army. Promoted to brigadier general in 1922, he went on to
hold several important commands, including Commanding General of First Army, the Hawaiian Department, and Second Army. At
the time of his summons to Washington he was again commanding
First Army.

Arriving in Washington expecting to be given command of an active army bound for the main battlefields of Europe, General Drum
was surprised to be told he was to go to China instead. He immediately had several conversations with those who would determine the
process by which the China theater would operate. In meetings
with Secretary of War Henry L. Stimson; Lt. Gen. Henry H. Arnold,
commander of the Army Air Forces; and Brig. Gen. Dwight D.
Eisenhower, assistant to the Army's chief of staff, Gen. George C.
Marshall, General Drum learned that there was much confusion
about just what was to be done with the China theater. Some viewed
it as an active theater of war, while others felt it would be a base for
air operations only. The question of command responsibilities for
an American general officer was extremely unclear.

General Drum drew up a draft of instructions for what he believed his mission to China should be, using the precedent of Gen.
John J. Pershing, who had similarly commanded American troops
under an Allied command in World War I. Just as he completed his
draft, he received the War Department's draft prepared by General
Eisenhower. The two drafts conflicted sharply in that the War Department's version discussed an advisory position while General
Drum's viewed a command responsibility. Additional discussions
followed and at a meeting with General Marshall on 9 January 1942
the discussion drifted to the need for an officer of General Drum's
seniority and experience to conduct an advisory role. General
Drum discounted the need for an officer of his background to advise China on the conduct of its war effort without a substantial
American troop commitment.

Secretary of War Stimson recorded in his diary his reaction to
General Drum's draft memorandum.

He had brought me a paper which he had drawn in which he virtually took the position that he did not think the role in China which I had offered him was big enough for his capabilities. The paper said a good deal more than that but that was what it boiled down to. I told him how much disappointed I was at the attitude that he had taken; that I myself had planned out the position which he was to take and that it seemed to me that it would lead to most important work for his country; that its sphere depended a good deal on his own abilities but that I had had confidence that he would be able to seize the opportunity to expand the importance of the place [China] into a very important sphere. I showed him that he would have had the full support not only of myself but of Marshall and the General Staff. I told him I could not help contrasting the position he was taking with what I considered my own duty when I was offered a position in the Far East which I did not desire and which I felt constrained to accept even in the nonemergent times of peace, because my government had selected me for it. I then closed the interview.[1]

General Marshall viewed General Drum's response as a lack of interest in the position and subsequently recommended against General Drum's assignment to this mission. General Marshall's recommendation was swiftly approved by Secretary of War Stimson. Later it would be stated that General Drum refused to go to China in less than a command position, but this was apparently not the case, because the day after his interview with Secretary Stimson he petitioned to go in any capacity, including as the Generalissimo's chief of staff. However, by then it was too late, and he had lost the confidence of both Secretary Stimson and General Marshall.

In place of General Drum, General Marshall put forward the name of Maj. Gen. Joseph W. Stilwell. Joseph Warren Stilwell was born on 19 March 1883 in Palatka, Florida. Commissioned in the infantry from West Point in 1904, he twice served in the Philippines between the years 1904 and 1912. He then served as Deputy Chief of Staff for Intelligence in IV Corps, American Expeditionary Forces, during World War I. He learned Chinese while assigned to

China between 1920 and 1923. Returning to the United States, he graduated from the Command and General Staff College in 1926. Once again he was dispatched to China, this time to serve with the 15th Infantry Regiment. During his service there he served on a board known as the Board Concerning Measures To Be Taken In Present Emergency. The leader of that board was another major, George Catlett Marshall. While still in China, Stilwell was promoted to Chief of Staff of U.S. Forces, China, and served in that position from 1928 to 1929.

Again he returned to the United States, this time for assignment as an instructor at the infantry school. While there he again served with Lieutenant Colonel Marshall, commanding a group who were later to become well known including, in addition to Stilwell, Majs. Omar N. Bradley and James A. Van Fleet and Capts J. Lawton Collins and Edward M. Almond. Marshall was impressed with Stilwell's ability as a tactician and troop trainer. In his fitness report Marshall wrote that Stilwell was "qualified for any command in peace or war," an unusually complimentary remark not easily received from George Marshall. It was at Fort Benning, while serving under the future army chief of staff, George C. Marshall, that Stilwell received the nickname by which he is widely known. As an instructor at the Infantry School, the colonel was known for his caustic criticism of those students who failed to measure up to his standards. It was after one such critique that one of his officer students drew a caricature of Stilwell rising out of a vinegar bottle labled with three X's and he was forever after known as "Vinegar Joe."

Yet again dispatched to China, this time as military attaché to China and Thailand, Stilwell remained for four years. Returning in 1939 as one of the most knowledgeable officers in the American army on China, he was promoted to brigadier general and given command of the 3d Infantry Brigade, then the 7th Infantry Division. Promoted to major general in October 1940, he received command of II Corps in July 1941. Shortly after the American entry into the war, he was designated to be the commander of the American portion of the North African amphibious assault planned for later in 1942. However, the decision to replace General Drum caused General Marshall, who remembered Stilwell from the infantry school and service together with the 15th Infantry, to call him to Washington for the China assignment. Major General George S. Patton Jr. replaced Stilwell as commander of the North African invasion.

Between 14 and 23 January 1942 Secretary Stimson, General Marshall, and General Stilwell discussed the mission to China. By that time matters had cleared some since General Drum had been considered, and the proposal was that General Stilwell go to China as the senior U.S. officer in the China theater. Although the position was already being viewed as in actuality the post of Chief of Staff to the Generalissimo, that aspect was not under discussion at this point. Asked to go to China, General Stilwell replied that he would go where he was sent. He particularly impressed Secretary Stimson, who recorded,

I was very favorably impressed with him. He is [a] very quick witted and alert-minded man. He knows China thoroughly and for more than two years campaigned with the Chinese armies against Japan in 1937 through 1939. In half an hour he gave me a better first-hand picture of the valor of the Chinese armies than I had ever received before. Of this valor he had a very high opinion. . . . So I went to bed with a rather relieved feeling that I had discovered a man who will be very useful.[2]

The Chinese government soon issued a directive, prepared by Secretary Stimson, that gave Stilwell authority over all Chinese, British, and American units then engaged in the China, and especially the Burma, campaigns. Claire Chennault, now a colonel in the Army Air Corps, would remain the highest ranking air officer. The Chinese were especially interested in keeping the Burma Road open, and the Japanese were already making threatening moves in that direction.

What was later to be termed the first Burma campaign began on 20 January 1942, when about eighteen thousand Japanese troops attacked southern Burma from Thailand. Their purpose was to do exactly what the Chinese feared most: cut off communications between the major supply port of Rangoon and mainland China. The Allied defense was a disaster and soon collapsed. Two understrength Japanese infantry divisions, the 33d and 55th, enjoyed victory after victory over Indian, British, and Burmese troops who were untrained, inadequately prepared for jungle warfare, and completely dependent upon motor transport for all supply. By early March the Japanese were marching on Rangoon itself, while the shattered Allied formations were retreating north toward India. The Japanese entered Rangoon on March 6.

Having accomplished their mission of cutting off overland supplies, the Japanese High Command tried to decide what to do next. While considering the next move, the British, who were the main defending force in Burma, called for assistance from the Chinese to hold central and northern Burma. The Chinese agreed to send some divisions south to assist the British. The Japanese soon became aware of this and determined to drive the Allies completely out of Burma and possibly push into India. Additional troops were dispatched for this purpose. The 33d Division, which had only two regiments, received a third regiment to bring it up to full strength. Two additional Japanese infantry divisions, the 18th and 56th, arrived. The Japanese now began to push north.

The Allies, still poorly trained and poorly organized, continued to fall back under enemy pressure. The precious oil fields were lost after being destroyed by the retreating troops. Mandalay fell. By early May the Allies were out of Burma, struggling to prepare India for the coming invasion.

Although the first Burma campaign did little for Allied morale, it did start to reveal the men who would eventually lead the way back. One such man was Maj. Gen. William Joseph Slim. Born in Bristol, England, on 6 August 1891, Slim was a career Indian Army Officer who had enlisted as a private but immediately earned a commission as Britain entered World War I. Wounded at Gallipoli, he was medically discharged from the British army. Somehow he managed to be reinstated, and he served again in the closing campaigns in Palestine, where again he was wounded. However, he managed to remain on active duty until the war ended. Converting to the Indian army, Slim graduated from the Quetta Staff College and served at the usual interwar appointments until ordered to the command of the 10th Indian Infantry Brigade during the campaign in Abyssinia and Eritrea, where once again he was wounded. Here he came into contact with another British officer, Maj. Orde Wingate, whom he would later work with closely in Burma. Slim returned to duty and eventually commanded the 10th Indian Infantry Division in Syria before being recalled to India. Now a lieutenant general, he commanded Burma Corps during the retreat from Burma. When Burma Corps was dissolved he assumed command of XV Corps for the defense of India.

General Stilwell arrived in India on 24 February 1942 and proceeded to New Delhi. There he learned the details of the first Burma campaign, then still in progress. Stilwell traveled on to Lashio, in Burma, where he was introduced to Generalissimo Chiang Kai-shek and Colonel Chennault. The two Americans talked at length and at the conclusion Chennault agreed both to the placement of his aviation forces under Stilwell and to the induction of his volunteers into the Army Air Forces. Stilwell created what he termed Headquarters, American Army Forces, China, Burma, and India. All American forces in any of those areas at that time came under his command. The physical headquarters was established at Chungking on 4 March 1942.

Stilwell soon learned of the political morass into which he had been sent. The British were upset because they had expected that their senior commander, Gen. Sir Harold R. L. G. Alexander, would receive the overall command, including command of the Chinese. However, the Chinese acted deceptively. Stilwell soon found that his orders were being ignored while those of the British were being obeyed. At a meeting with Chiang Kai-shek on 1 April, Stilwell said that if the generalissimo did not want his subordinates to obey him but rather to obey the British, he should be relieved and sent home. This was the first of many such requests Stilwell was to make over the next two years. The generalissimo replied that he, Stilwell, was in command and provided him with what he described as the seal of the commander of Chinese forces. Stilwell, who knew a great deal about the Chinese, quickly discerned that the seal was in fact that of the chief of staff, not of the commander of Chinese forces. Unknown to Stilwell, one Chinese general, Tu Lu Ming of the Chinese Fifth Army, had told the British governor of Burma, Sir Reginald

Dorman-Smith, "the American General only thinks he is commanding. In fact he is doing no such thing. You see, we Chinese think that the only way to keep the Americans in the war is to give them a few commands on paper. They will not do much harm as long as we do the work!"[3]

Stilwell attempted to bring order out of chaos with the Chinese forces placed at his disposal. But it was too late. Allied forces were already in retreat, and little could be done to prevent the loss of Burma. Stilwell had planned to make a stand in northern Burma, but Chinese withdrawal and the unpreparedness of some of the British forces canceled that idea. Attempting to fly to eastern Burma, Stilwell's plane failed to arrive, and he instead decided to head for the railroad at Myitkyina. However, the Japanese were soon reported to be on the verge of capturing that town. Having little choice, he took his small headquarters party and marched overland directly west out of Burma. In a march that would later become a part of his legend, Stillwell and his group, which included Lt. Col. Frank D. Merrill, struggled over much of the same ground that he would later send American soldiers across the following year.

For those troops who followed Stilwell out of Burma to the west, there was a respite. The Japanese at that time had no intention of invading India, and so the advancing Japanese columns halted along the border between Burma and India. The surviving British, Chinese, and Burmese forces were given a chance to rest and reorganize. The first Burma campaign was over. It had created in American military lore the image of "Vinegar Joe" Stilwell, the frontline American general who had marched out with the troops and had made no excuses. His statement to the press in which he said, "We got a hell of a beating. It was as humiliating as hell. We ought to find out why it happened and go back" was widely quoted and viewed as an honest appraisal of a campaign gone bad.

Stilwell was right. The campaign had been poorly handled and poorly led. The troops had been untrained and unprepared to fight in the jungles and hills of Burma. The Chinese effort had come too late and was too scattered to do much good. It was time for the second Burma campaign.

While the troops reorganized and trained, both British and American leaders decided on the next steps. For the British the need was to conserve their limited forces while keeping open a line of communication with China across the northern tip of Burma. The ultimate responsibility, however, was the protection of India. Stilwell had generally the same goals except that his ultimate responsibility was to support China, not India. Within days of completing his successful march out of Burma, Stilwell asked both Secretary Stimson and General Marshall to send American combat troops to India. He planned to use them to spearhead a Chinese offensive to retake both Burma and Thailand. General Marshall sent Stilwell's request to President Roosevelt, with the notation that the current line of communications and supply would not permit a positive answer at that time. He recommended instead that another study group be formed to determine the best way to keep China active as a war theater. Marshall, who viewed Stilwell as an "immensely capable and remarkably resourceful individual,"[4] knew of the problems in obtaining Chinese cooperation. The President approved Marshall's suggestion.

Although decisions were postponed, active ground operations continued. During the period between the end of the first Burma campaign and a firm decision about what to do with Burma there were three distinct operations under way to improve the Allied position in the area. The first was a renewed British attempt to seize the area of western Burma along the Bay of Bengal immediately below the Indian border. The second was an idea Stilwell borrowed from the British, to construct a road to replace the Burma Road. This was a road from Ledo to the Chinese border over northern Burma. The third effort was a large-scale British raid against Japanese positions in Burma.

The Arakan operation opened with some success for the British against the two Japanese battalions garrisoning the area. Operations quickly fell apart, however, against determined Japanese defenders and subsequent reinforcements, which negated the early gains. The operation showed that British troops still needed more jungle training and less dependency on road-bound lines of communications. The Ledo Road operation had been drafted by Colonel Merrill, Stilwell's operations officer. It called for the construction of a motor road from Ledo, in Assam Province, India, south and east across northern Burma, to a junction with the old

Burma Road. The new road would support a northern Burma campaign and, once linked with the former Burma Road, would provide a land supply line to China. Merrill chose Ledo because it was close to the terminus of the rail line from Calcutta and because it was the northern end of a caravan route out of Burma. Basically, American army engineers would follow the old caravan route through northern Burma until they connected with the old Burma Road east of Bhamo.[5] Meanwhile, Chinese troops would be trained and equipped to open the way across northern Burma for the road.

The last offensive step was taken by the British and began as something similar to the old cavalry raids. About three thousand men under the command of a British officer, Col. Orde Wingate, were to be airlifted into the deep rear of the Japanese in Burma to pave the way for a larger force invading Burma out of India. As with most things in the China-Burma-India theater of operations, nothing ever went as planned. The troops and aircraft available to the British were insufficient to provide a full-scale invasion of Burma. And so, despite opposition, Wingate prevailed upon his commanders to launch the raid as planned but with a time limit and no expectation of support. Using the code name Operation Longcloth, it was launched into Burma on 13 February 1943 at just the time the British were acknowledging defeat in the Arakan campaign.

Born in 1903, Orde Wingate had a checkered career as a British army officer before arriving in Burma. Considered eccentric by many, crazy by some, he had served in Palestine before World War II and had involved himself in the guerilla war between the Arabs and Jews. Leading antiterrorist strikes against Arab guerrillas had earned him the Distinguished Service Order and a reputation as a passionate advocate of causes. This latter quality got him relieved of his duties and demoted from colonel to major. Although he was an artillery officer, he led guerilla forces during the British campaign in Ethiopia. Success there was followed by an illness that prompted him to attempt suicide. Once again he was sent home in disgrace. However, his passion was remembered, and when the need for specialized operations became apparent in India, the British commander, Gen. Sir Archibald Wavell, sent for him.

Wingate organized his brigade-size force and trained them to his exacting standards while trying to imbue them with his passion for victory. What became known as Wingate's First Expedition crossed the Chindwin to destroy enemy communications, rail lines, and routes of supply, and to generally harass the Japanese in Burma before returning to India. Divided into several columns, the operation enjoyed some success and suffered several disasters. The operation so confused the Japanese as to its size and scope that by the end of March they had directed the majority of three divisions, more than twenty thousand men, to track down and destroy Wingate's forces, which never numbered more than three thousand men. The efforts by the Japanese failed, and most of the British objectives in this operation were attacked, if not destroyed. However, the cost was high, because of the swift and overwhelming enemy reaction, particularly in closing off escape routes to India. Nearly one thousand men had been lost—one-third of the force—but that number included more than one hundred native Burmese who had shed uniforms and blended into the local population. All mules, used for transport, and most of the equipment had also been destroyed or abandoned. The various groups had marched 750 to 1,000 miles. Many of the men were barely alive, suffering from malnutrition, beri-beri, and malaria. Most were temporarily unfit for further active service. But they had given the local Allied high command the first victory of which they could boast to the world. They had also accomplished one other thing: they had embarrassed the Japanese commanders defending Burma. As a result, the plan to invade India, from which the Wingate expedition had come, was revived.

For much of 1944 the British forces in India would be dealing with the Japanese attempt to seize that country. The defense would involve some of the most difficult fighting in British military history, and the success of that defense was swiftly turned into an offensive that would eventually sweep the Japanese out of both India and Burma. But the commitment of the British left little in the way of direct aid that they could provide to Stilwell and his Chinese forces trying to advance the Ledo Road.

The fate of the campaign in Burma was being decided while the British struggled in the Arakan and while Wingate led his small force in northern Burma. As a part of a series of conferences at the highest level of Allied leadership, a joint conference of American and British staffs was planned for August 1943 in Quebec. Although it was included on the agenda, the Burma campaign was by no means a high priority for discussion at that conference. The Americans were much more concerned about the continuing evasiveness of the British regarding a cross-channel attack in Europe. They were determined to avoid further delays by diversions in the Mediterranean and to get the British to commit to a direct assault on German forces in western Europe.

As the conferees assembled at the quaint eighteenth-century Chateau Frontenac, overlooking the St. Lawrence River, things around the world were looking positive. There were rumors of Italian peace feelers; the German submarine campaign in the Atlantic was beginning to show signs of diminishing; due to Allied countermeasures, the Russians were starting to turn the German offensive on the eastern front; and in Alaska, American and Canadian troops had recaptured the islands seized earlier by the Japanese. In the South Pacific the American and Australian offensive continued to gain ground. Only in the CBI theater were things more or less stationary.

Between 14 and 24 August the American and British Joint Chiefs of Staff met to debate worldwide Allied strategy. By far the largest portion of the conference was devoted to the western European operations. Indeed, the British had preferred not to discuss the war with Japan at all at this conference, but circumstances dictated otherwise. Two issues were raised by the Americans for discussion: first, to decide on the main axis of attack against Japan, and second, to decide on Britain's role in that campaign. Although the U.S. Navy representative, Fleet Adm. Ernest J. King, took the lead for the American delegation on discussions concerning the Pacific, General Marshall was careful to preserve U.S. Army interests represented by Gen. Douglas MacArthur in the southwest Pacific and by Stilwell's China mission. Admiral King argued for an increase in the amount of resources dedicated to the war against Japan. He believed that even a small increase of resources could result in increased offensive capabilities, which in turn could bring decisive results. General Marshall repeated the need to combine the Pacific operations with those in Burma and stressed that immediately after the defeat of Germany all available resources should be rushed to the Pacific for the rapid defeat of Japan. This was in accord with the earlier statement by the American Combined Chiefs of Staff in their report issued the previous January, in which they noted, "The only way of bringing material help to China is to open the Burma Road. The reconquest of Burma should therefore be undertaken as soon as resources permit." The British agreed in principle and offered additional resources of air and naval units for the Pacific.

The Americans pressed for an offensive to clear northern Burma, with an immediate follow-up to clear the southern portion, beginning no later than November 1944. The British preferred to clear northern Burma and then bypass southern Burma for an effort to seize Singapore, leaving southern Burma until 1946. As discussions continued, British prime minister Winston S. Churchill unexpectedly sided with the United States in supporting a campaign to clear southern Burma rather than a campaign to liberate Singapore. He felt, as did the Americans, that the delay necessary for regrouping from a northern Burma campaign to a Singapore campaign was too long and too dangerous. He also had his own thoughts, as he often did, on the tactical progress of the war and was interested in a campaign to seize Sumatra. President Roosevelt, however, knew there would be insufficient resources to operate in Burma and Sumatra and therefore discounted the prime minister's pet project.

Yet another factor concerning the planners was the new weapon to be used against Japan, the very-long-range bomber known as the B-29 Superfortress. This weapon would need bases in China to reach targets in Japan, and those bases would need supplies, which would have to travel by sea to China, marking the need to keep China in the war and active as a major belligerent. As the conference came to an end, various agreements were made. The British agreed to the American timetable for the Pacific, including the greater use of Allied air forces in the area. Air support to China was to be increased, and the employment of lightly equipped, air-supported jungle troops would be sought. Forces in the central Pacific would be provided by the United States and those in Southeast Asia by the British, except for special types that could be provided only by the United States, such as engineer and air force units. Operations for northern Burma would be carried out in February 1944, but additional amphibious assault plans remained under study as the result of British reluctance to undertake these proposed operations. President Roosevelt had stipulated that the campaign in Burma not be delayed and even openly considered substituting two American divisions if the British sought to withhold forces and supplies for use in their preferred Mediterranean plans. Both Admiral King and General Marshall had expressed their dissatisfaction with the British delay in sending resources from the Mediterranean to the CBI. Another point of agreement was the decision to begin ground operations as a result of general dissatisfaction with the air offensive thus far. Finally, the American proposal to open up a new line of advance across the Pacific through the Gilbert and Marshall Islands was readily accepted by the British.

One final issue of importance remained to be settled: the appointment of a supreme commander in the CBI. Previous discussions had resolved little, and the opportunity was taken at the Quebec conference to finalize this last vital issue. Prime Minister Churchill had complained earlier that he and his staff had little information from General MacArthur's southwest Pacific theater of operations. General Marshall, after investigating, had decided that communications could be improved, and he made the necessary arrangements. Consequently, the British dropped their demand for the appointment of one of their air marshals, Sir Sholto Douglas, to command their forces in Burma. Instead, they put forth Adm. Lord Louis Mountbatten, then British chief of combined operations, whose record and personality appealed to the Americans. General Marshall agreed with the choice and placed General Stilwell as deputy supreme Allied commander under Mountbatten.

In the written agreement resulting from the Quebec conference the issues concerning Burma were listed at number 37 in order of priority. Among the conclusions agreed to and listed in the agreement were the intent of "keeping China in the war," "intensifying operations against the Japanese," "maintaining increased U.S. and Chinese air forces in China," and "equipping Chinese ground forces." The goal in Burma was summarized in the statement that read:

> We have decided that our main effort should be put into offensive operations with the object of establishing land communications with China and improving and securing the air route. Priorities cannot be rigid and we therefore propose to instruct the Supreme Commander in formulating his proposal to regard this decision as a guide and to bear in mind the importance of the longer term development of the lines of communication.

General Stilwell assumed his new appointment along with all his previous appointments. He was now the Deputy Supreme Allied Commander of the Southeast Asia Command, the Chief of Staff to the Generalissimo, Commander of U.S. Army forces in the CBI, and lend-lease administrator. It was quite a variety of duties.

As Deputy Supreme Commander, Stilwell would satisfy the Chinese aversion to being under British command while coordinating the efforts of the Fourteenth and Tenth Army Air Forces then in China. He would also direct the Chinese forces in Burma to coordinate with British efforts to clear that country.

The British had brought with them to the conference the now-brigadier Orde Wingate, leader of the highly touted behind-the-lines Operation Longcloth. The devotion and dedication of Brigadier Wingate easily won over both the prime minister and General Marshall. Wingate explained how six additional brigades of British troops were even then training for renewed operations. So impressed was General Marshall that he suggested that an American unit of similar capabilities be added to the British operation then planned. As a result, American ground combat troops were soon to be committed to the Asian mainland.[6]

2. A Call for Volunteers

General Stilwell had long yearned for American ground troops to lead a Chinese campaign to reconquer Burma and to push the Japanese out of the China-Burma-India theater. His unsuccessful attempts at getting results out of the Chinese troops under his direct command often frustrated him to the point of vicious outbursts against everything around him. When he learned of General Marshall's agreement to send a specialized force of American ground combat troops to operate with British direction, his reaction was predictable. While in Chungking he noted in his diary on 2 September 1943, "Radio From George Marshall on U.S. units for Stepchild. Only 3,000 but the entering wedge. Can we use them! And how!"[1] Sometime later, when he realized the conditions placed upon the use of these troops, he exploded in a message to General Marshall, decrying the placement of his long cherished American contingent under British control.

Indeed, Marshall was seriously concerned about Stilwell's position at this time. The Chinese government was growing increasingly upset about Stilwell's continuing attempts to revitalize and retrain their armies. He repeatedly insisted on firm commitments from the Chinese as to troops, equipment, and schedules. He had turned the usual methods of paying Chinese troops from lump-sum payments to regimental commanders into individual payments to soldiers who had to be present to be paid, thus cutting off a major source of income for many Chinese officers. The demands to the Chinese government were viewed as insulting, despite the fact that they would have resulted in increased efficiency in the Chinese army. In mid-September, just as Stilwell was rejoicing over the commitment of American troops to his theater, Dr. T. V. Soong, the Chinese foreign minister, made a number of proposals to the American government intended to curb Stilwell's power and authority. When these failed he made additional comments about how poorly things were being handled and by implication laid the blame on Stilwell. This implication was supported by Chennault, now a general, who added his complaints about the poor supply flow and lack of support for his air operations, again implying that the failure was Stilwell's. General Marshall was so concerned about the reaction of the Chinese that he had a draft cable drawn up to recall Stilwell and replace him with Lt. Gen. Brehon Burke Somervell, who was then touring China in his capacity as commander of army service forces. Before Marshall could decide, however, an inexplicable twist of politics occurred when Doctor Soong's two sisters, one of whom was the generalissimo's wife, Madame Chiang, intervened on Stilwell's behalf. General Somerville backed them up, and together they persuaded the generalissimo and Stilwell to patch up their differences, at least on the surface. Marshall's draft cable was never sent.

While all the high-level maneuvering was under way, the implementation of General Marshall's interest in creating a small American task force to assist in Burma was also under way. The first step was to decide on the unit that would participate. It was assumed from the start that the unit would be a new one, not one of the existing U.S. Army regiments. Early plans called for three battalions of one thousand men each. On 1 September 1943 the War Department began recruiting personnel from jungle-trained and jungle-tested troops. General Marshall had directed that about three hundred volunteers come from the Southwest Pacific theater of operations, seven hundred from the South Pacific theater of operations, and one thousand each from the Caribbean Defense Command and the army ground forces in the United States.

The two groups from the Caribbean and continental United States concentrated at San Francisco, while the volunteers from the active war theaters assembled at either Noumea, New Caledonia, or Brisbane, Australia, awaiting pickup on the way to India. The senior officer of the group coming from the United States, Lt. Col. Charles N. Hunter, was appointed commander, with instructions to prepare and organize the troops while en route to the CBI and to keep General Stilwell informed of progress.[2]

Colonel Charles Newton Hunter was a career army officer from Oneida, New York, and a graduate of West Point, class of 1929. He had recently served three years in the Philippines and another two and a half years in the Panama Canal Zone. He had also been an instructor at the U.S. Army Infantry School at Fort Benning, Georgia, where he was chief of the rifle and weapons platoon group of the weapons section of that school. He had a reputation for ability, efficiency, and precision and had recently spent several days in Washington receiving instructions from the operations division of the army's general staff as to what was expected of this new "long-range penetration group." Because each battalion was expected to operate independently, much like Wingate's columns in Operation Longcloth, they were neither thought of nor constituted as a regiment of infantry normal to the American army at the time.

A traditional way of thinking in the American army, as in most armies, was that to ask for volunteers was to ask for trouble. The reasons that men volunteer for such an organization, therefore, are interesting. One such volunteer from the contingent coming from the continental United States was 2d Lt. Charlton Ogburn Jr. Entering the Signal Corps as a photographer, he had found himself assigned to a platoon of telephone-and-wire men trained in everything except photography or radios. He had also noted that September nights in Mississippi could be cold when one was sleeping outside on the ground during maneuvers. He passed on his discomfort to a fellow officer one day while lining up for a meal. His fellow officer responded that he had seen a notice asking for volunteers with jungle training, probably for a job in Panama, he thought.

Lieutenant Ogburn had already been in the army for more than two years and was well aware of the universal military maxim to never volunteer. But he decided to think about it. He began to hear unpleasant rumors about the new unit, but was more concerned about the continuing cold nights in Mississippi. After a couple more uncomfortable nights, Lieutenant Ogburn placed his name on a list of applicants. Expecting to have the usual long wait for anything to happen, he was pleasantly surprised to be ordered out only a few days later. He left his position with the 99th Infantry Division's 99th Signal Company and was ordered to report to Casual Detachment 1688-A at the San Francisco Port of Embarkation (POE).

About 960 officers and enlisted men from the Caribbean Defense Command and another 970 jungle-trained officers and men from the army ground forces, including Lieutenant Ogburn, were converging on San Francisco by mid-September 1943. Many of them came from the army's 33d Infantry Regiment, then stationed in Trinidad. One volunteer from this unit was Maj. George A. McGee Jr., a West Point graduate who would be designated as commander of the 2d Battalion. The future commander of the 1st Battalion, Maj. William Lloyd Osborne, accompanied Colonel Hunter from Fort Benning, where Osborne had been lecturing about his experiences in fighting the Japanese in the Philippines prior to his escape from that doomed battle. Unlike Colonel Hunter and Major McGee, Major Osborne was a reserve officer.

One volunteer from the Caribbean was Phil Smart, who was serving with the 1st Cavalry in Puerto Rico. He wrote:

> This was wartime Puerto Rico where we were serving in a spit and polish 1st Cavalry unit enjoying the beautiful beaches, fiestas, girls and modern army quarters of that island paradise. The only reason I volunteered for the 5307th was the promise that if we survived a short but hazardous mission, we would spend the rest of the war stateside. So I guess it was mainly homesickness, maybe mixed with a little guilt that after volunteering to fight the war we were instead enjoying the life of Riley while others were doing the job.[3]

Some months later, as one of the few survivors of the Marauders' 2d Battalion, Smart would leave Burma wounded and weighing ninety pounds, down from his original weight of 180 pounds.

Upon arriving at Camp Stoneman all the volunteers were detailed as infantrymen, regardless of military occupation specialty. They were further advised that they had volunteered for an extremely "dangerous and hazardous" mission, a redundancy that was lost on most of the men. And as a final bit of encouragement, they were told that those who went with the unit should not be expected to return, another military maxim that the experienced discounted.

Organization was the first priority. A conglomeration of nearly two thousand American soldiers had been literally dumped into Camp Stoneman as Casual Detachment 1688-A or Casual Detachment 1688-B. From these detachments two battalions of infantry had to be formed. In typical army style, Lieutenant Ogburn and a dozen other officers, some of them noncommissioned, were handed the thousand cards representing the personnel of Casual Detachment 1688-A and told to create a battalion of infantry by morning. Another group received the same instructions with the cards of Casual Detachment 1688-B. By the following morning these detachments represented two infantry battalions, at least on paper. To celebrate and instruct the men on the structure of their new organization a parade was held later that day. Lieutenant Ogburn, viewing the assembled group, recalls that the word *pirates* sprang immediately to his mind. His reaction was supported by a nearby officer, who remarked to him that "the only thing stupider than volunteering is asking for volunteers."[4]

One other group of volunteers joined the detachment in San Francisco. These men were possibly the most motivated of all the volunteers who had joined up for this "dangerous and hazardous mission," because they had no other reason but patriotism for volunteering. Fourteen members of the Military Intelligence Service merged with the detachment. These men were all nisei, or Americans of Japanese descent. They included the group's leader, SSgt. Edward Mitsukado, a former Honolulu court recorder; Herbert Y. Miyasaki, who became the unit's leading interpreter; Robert Y. Honda, who took a reduction in grade to join; and Henry Gosho, Ben S. Sugeta, Roy Matsumoto, and Akiji Yoshimura, all of whom had enlisted from internment camps and had then volunteered again to accompany the detachment. They were assigned to Capt. William A. Laffin, destined to become the unit's intelligence officer. Born to a Japanese mother Captain Laffin himself had only recently been repatriated from Japan on the Swedish liner *Gripsholm* in an exchange of American and Japanese nationals. Many of the caucasian volunteers were perplexed by the nisei presence, and Corporal Yoshimura was asked by one, "Say, how are things in your country?" Turning to gaze back at San Francisco, he replied, "It looks good from here."[5]

On 21 September 1943 the two battalions, still officially known as casual detachments, sailed from San Francisco on the transport SS *Lurline*. As much equipment as could also be carried went aboard ship, while the remainder was to be forwarded by shipment to Bombay.[6] With stops at Noumea and Brisbane to pick up the volunteers from the South Pacific, the *Lurline* steamed across the Indian Ocean and up the Arabian Sea to Bombay, arriving on 29 October 1943.

The third battalion had its own volunteers as well. One who stood out early in the operation was Capt. John B. George, a veteran of the Americal Division's campaign on Guadalcanal in the South Pacific. He too saw the directive requesting volunteers for the "deadly and hazardous mission." After the brutal campaign on Guadalcanal, the Americal Division, including Captain George, was deposited on New Caledonia for rest and relaxation. As he later recorded, "Picture a beautiful tropical island. Soft warm breezes stirring the coastal groves, rustling the palm fronds. Grassy volcanic hills rolling up to a high divide. Gentle, smiling natives. Handsome white colonists."[7] Yet when the directive came, calling for volunteers for what was obviously expected to be another Guadalcanal type of campaign, Captain George stepped forward. After years of trying to understand his own actions, he decided that he was simply bored and unsettled that a war went on without his immediate participation.

Then there were those in the third battalion who simply could not stay away from combat. Lieutenant Ogburn noted how Sgt. Russell Hill, from Captain George's unit, was unable to stay out of any fight he heard going on in the vicinity. There were also men who volunteered for reasons that had nothing to do with combat or the army. Lieutenant Logan Weston, a former divinity student at Transylvania Bible School, in Pennsylvania, had already served under the worst of combat conditions when his battalion of the 37th Infantry Division had been cut off and surrounded for weeks on New

Georgia. While resting with his unit he learned that his family had broken up, that his fiancée had changed her mind about marrying him, and that his home had been sold. Hearing of the call for volunteers and believing it was for a suicide mission to the Japanese island of Bougainville, he consulted his Bible and then volunteered.

In the Southwest Pacific theater, things were handled a little differently. Edward A. Wade recalls Lt. Gen. Walter Krueger coming to his field artillery battalion to announce that he wanted 119 volunteers—110 privates, six corporals, and three sergeants—for that same "dangerous and hazardous" mission. Private First Class Wade left the 98th Field Artillery Battalion and soon found himself deep in the Burmese jungles. By coincidence, the entire 98th Field Artillery Battalion became, on 25 February 1944, the 6th Ranger Battalion, making it probably the only unit to contribute major portions to the two American army elite forces in the Pacific.

For all their various reasons the soldiers came together on the SS *Lurline*. Here they learned that they were casual detachments no longer. They were now officially known as Galahad, a name that brought only more confusion and derision. Not until well after they were in training in India would they officially become the 5307th Composite Unit (Provisional).

They were not the first American troops to arrive in the China-Burma-India theater. Prior to receiving Galahad, General Stilwell had under his command the Tenth U.S. Army Air Force. Consisting of a handful of men and planes, the Tenth had participated in the defense of Burma and was then committed to the defense of the air route from India to China. Headquartered at New Delhi, the Tenth Air Force was slowly building up to greater strength. Plans to incorporate the American Volunteer Group (AVG) into the Tenth as the 23d Fighter Group had to be postponed when it was learned that most of the American volunteers could not be retained in service. Instead, a few volunteers and a new 23d Fighter Group had to be activated. As a result of the loss of the AVG, the Tenth Air Force had to deploy its combat units forward into China to replace the air defense previously provided by the volunteers. Officially consisting of the 7th Bombardment Group and 23d and 51st Fighter Groups, many of its planes were diverted to other emergencies, including a major diversion to assist the British in the Middle East. Its airfields and personnel were scattered all over the theater.

Brigadier General Earl L. Naiden commanded the Tenth Air Force at that time, and his problems were overwhelming. Lack of sufficient aircraft, poor airfield sites, the dispersion of assets, the lack of replacement parts including tires and engines, and the threat of Japanese air attack all combined to stretch the very fiber of the Tenth Air Force. When the Japanese seized the airfield at Myitkyina the route over the mountains to China became even more dangerous than before. Enemy aircraft flying from Myitkyina could intercept aircraft flying the route to China, thus creating a need to fly a different and much higher route to China. Pilot strain and gasoline consumption increased accordingly. General Stilwell viewed the situation as serious and recommended to Washington that General Naiden be given the sole responsibility of the air cargo line while another officer, Brig. Gen. Clayton L. Bissell of his own staff, be given overall command of the Tenth Air Force. General Bissell assumed command of the Tenth Air Force on 18 August, but that was too late for General Naiden. The strain had proved too much, and he had to be sent home for hospitalization shortly afterward. Finally, Air Transport Command, which was slowly building up its assets in the theater, took over responsibility for the ferry route, although the Tenth Air Force still provided protection.

The China Air Task Force was another American force then engaged in China against the Japanese. This organization consisted of the 23d Fighter Group, which was detached from the Tenth Air Force; the 16th Fighter Group; and the 11th Bombardment Squadron, Medium, under the command of General Chennault. This group was completely dependent upon air supply and operated out of an area that was nearly surrounded by Japanese forces. Later, as the Japanese advance continued deeper into China, this group would be forced to relocate and eventually participate in the Burma Campaign.

A third force operating in the area was known as India Air Task Force. This group was based at Barrackpore, near Calcutta, and contained the 25th and 26th Fighter Squadrons, and the 9th, 22d, 436th, 491st, 492d, and 493d Bombardment Squadrons. Under the overall command of the Tenth Air Force, this group would also participate in the Burma campaign.

General Chennault disagreed with the way the air effort was being conducted in the CBI theater. Arguing that his theories of air power could better accomplish the defeat of the enemy, he argued consistently for independence from the Tenth Air Force command. The ongoing conflict between General Chennault and General Bissell, who deliberately had been given a one-day seniority ranking as brigadier general over Chennault, went on with the support of Chiang Kai-shek, who was disappointed with what he considered the paltry amount of air support the Americans had sent to China. He also was suspicious of what he believed was British influence over the Tenth Air Force. Using his influence with the generalissimo and knowing of the resentment held by the Chinese leader against the Americans and the British, Chennault pushed for an independent air force under his command. The Americans were opposed to that idea, and the commander of the army air forces, Lt. Gen. Henry H. Arnold, voiced his objections to General Marshall after an inspection trip of the CBI. Arnold cited his concerns over the increased need for men, equipment, and supplies that an additional air force would create.

Meeting with the generalissimo in February 1943, General Arnold was angered that he was lectured to by the Chinese leader on the need for an independent air force under Chennault. Although Arnold refused to return with that message to President Roosevelt, he could not refuse to present the generalissimo's letter to the president, which stated the views to which Arnold so strenuously objected. Despite the fact that both Generals Marshall and Arnold objected, President Roosevelt decided that the wishes of Chiang Kai-shek would be granted. As a result, the Fourteenth Air Force was activated on 10 March 1943 in China. It would eventually consist of men and equipment diverted from the Tenth Air Force or sent from the United States. Chennault was in command to the end of the war, although both General Bissell, also promoted to major general at that time, and General Chennault were subordinated to General Stilwell.

There was another essential American contribution to the campaign. As early as April 1941, when President Roosevelt had authorized lend-lease, American engineers had become involved in the support of China. Although not sent to China at that time, some thirty thousand tons of rails were removed along a 125-mile stretch of abandoned narrow-gauge railway of the former Denver, Rio Grande, and Western line in New Mexico and Colorado. The Army Corps of Engineers dismantled and shipped these supplies to China for the Yunnan-Burma Railroad Authority. Once General Stilwell arrived in India he began additional projects that required engineers. As no American engineers were then in the theater, he used a reverse sort of lend-lease, in which he borrowed British army engineers who would use supplies and equipment provided by the United States to begin his construction programs.

With the use of this method and Indian civilian contractors, progress was slow and unsatisfactory. A call for U.S. army engineers was soon issued. In response, the 45th General Service Regiment, commanded by Col. John C. Arrowsmith; the 823d Aviation Engineer Battalion, led by Maj. Ferdinand J. Tate; and the 195th Engineer Dump Truck Company, commanded by Capt. Clyde L. Koontz arrived in July 1942. By 1945 there would be dozens of U.S. Army Engineer units contributing to the reconquest of Burma, including some who fought alongside the infantry.

The American army engineers were concerned primarily with building the Ledo Road and supporting the American and British air and ground forces in the CBI theater of operations. This task required them to plan, create, and maintain the numerous lines of communications in the theater. All types of units were needed. General engineer service regiments had to maintain the roads and ports, and about eighteen engineer combat battalions were scheduled to work on the advance of the Ledo Road, while aviation engineer battalions were needed to construct and maintain the air bases from which both the Tenth and Fourteenth Air Forces would fly.

Airborne engineer battalions also planned to accompany the British behind-the-lines offensive planned for 1944. These men suffered casualties as real as those of the combat troops and air crews they supported. In one instance a company of the 45th Engineers had to be relieved from working on the Ledo Road when only a handful of its men could still report for duty, the rest having succumbed to malaria and dysentery. Colonel Lewis A. Pick arrived on 17 October 1943 and was given command of construction on the Ledo Road. By shifting units from less important assignments, creating around-the-clock schedules, using lights at night despite the possibility of enemy attack, and rotating his units as they became worn out, he managed to keep the road advancing close behind the ground troops. As more units arrived they were immediately put to work on the road, despite their supposed specialty. For example, the 849th and 1883rd Aviation Engineer Battalions (Colored), normally charged with building and maintaining airfields, were put to work at grading and graveling the road from Pangsau Pass southward. The 209th Engineer Combat Battalion operated a sawmill, did road maintenance at the same pass, and built a 157-foot-long girder bridge over the Nawngyang River. The engineers, who called the road Pick's Pike, worked at whatever assignment needed their attention.

Construction was not limited to roadwork. China needed fuel to run its war machinery, and that fuel, like all other supplies, had to be piped from India. A pipeline was built alongside the Ledo Road. Engineers from the 330th Engineer General Service Regiment, the 209th Engineer Combat Battalion, and the 382d Construction Battalion worked on the project. A four-inch pipeline was laid from the refinery at Digboi toward Ledo, a distance of fourteen miles. As the road progressed forward from Ledo, so did the pipeline, advancing at an average of more than a mile a day. Moving closer to the front, the engineers often did not know where the Japanese troops were emplaced. Liaison with the leading Chinese troops was practically nonexistent. Often the engineers did not know if they were behind or in front of the forward Chinese positions.

Master Sergeant Stanley Silver remembers working on the Ledo Road and converting dump trucks to cargo trucks when there were shortages. The heavy rains and constant flooding during the rainy season were more feared than enemy shelling, because the rush of water could easily sweep a soldier away to his death. Sergeant Silver's 898th Heavy Ordnance Company was always protected by a

British antiaircraft unit as the men advanced along the road. During the two years that they toiled in the jungles of Burma and India they never received replacements for American soldiers who left the company. Instead they were given Indian civilians "who had been kicked out of India by the British as troublemakers." Sergeant Silver recalls these men as "very productive" and "intelligent," and as a whole the company found these civilian replacements useful. After some time one American soldier could supervise eight work bays by using these civilians. Eventually they could change the entire engine of any truck in three hours.

The civilians were inventive as well, creating many field expedients to improve the conditions of the equipment they repaired. One field expedient enabled a truck radiator to make three or more round trips over the road before needing replacement, instead of the normal one round trip. Sergeant Silver remembers that strong discipline throughout his company kept them productive and efficient.[8]

Engineers also provided combat support for the Chinese. Companies of the 330th Engineer General Service Regiment had to scout and clear sections in advance of the route of the Ledo Road. Others were assigned to the 1st Provisional Chinese-American Tank Group to clear and maintain roads for the heavy combat equipment. Still others, like T5 Joseph Tannenbaum, were assigned as radio men with all-Chinese units and had to learn Chinese just to perform their duties. Sergeant Tannenbaum spent years with the 21st Field Artillery, Chinese army, in place of a commissioned officer and performed all the duties of a liaison team almost single-handed. Along the coast, and not a part of General Stilwell's command, was a group of navy and Marine Corps officers and enlisted men operating as the United States Naval Group, China. Under the orders of the Chief of Naval Operations, they were to report weather conditions for Pacific fleet operations and prepare for a projected assault on the Chinese mainland later in the war. In the interim they conducted guerrilla operations, led by Comdr. Milton E. Miles.

Also present in the theater were American women. Red Cross workers served primarily in various air corps stations in China, although many flew the air route over the hump on occasion. These women often had to dive into slit trenches during Japanese air attacks on their bases. In one case a dance that the women had organized between a group of American fliers and Chinese university women was interrupted by a bombing. Both groups ran for the trenches. Subsequent dances prohibited the attendance of the Chinese women, because nine of them had become pregnant as a result of that bombing.

One young woman, Phyllis Braidwood Dolloff, who served as a recreational director in China and Burma, later remembered observing a distinct difference between the air corps men and the infantry. She noted that with the infantrymen "one could almost reach out and touch their loneliness."[9]

Serving the eventual fifty thousand American soldiers at the height of the CBI theater's operations were several U.S. Army medical units. They soon became the only real cure for the scrub typhus that decimated both American and Chinese units. Their excellent nursing care was the only real cure for the high fevers, internal hemorrhages, skin lesions, and death that marked the disease. The first hospital in the area was built by an aviation battalion of African-American troops, assisted by British engineers on thirty acres of land between Ledo and Margherita. American nurses had first arrived in July 1942, when four nurses of the 159th Station Hospital arrived at Chabua after flying over the air ferry route, or the "hump." Soon followed by the 98th Station Hospital and later the 20th Station Hospital, American nurses were instrumental in saving the lives of countless American and Chinese soldiers.

The arrival of Galahad was clearly not the first appearance of American troops in the CBI. They were, however, the first ground combat troops and for the time being, the only infantry that General Stilwell could reasonably rely on for carrying out his tactical plans. Other American forces were largely under the umbrella organization known as the 5303d Headquarters and Headquarters Company (Provisional) Combat Troops. These men were primarily service troops and training staff assigned to train the incoming Chinese soldiers. American troops, except Galahad, were assigned to the command while they were arriving in the CBI and awaiting assignment.

The SS *Lurline* arrived at Bombay and disembarked its passengers and equipment between 29 and 31 October 1943. To Stilwell's chagrin, they were attached to the Chinese army, not to his direct command. To Colonel Hunter's confusion, the troops were taken over by Col. Francis G. Brink, "officer-in-charge of training, GALAHAD project" and moved to a British training camp at Deolah. Colonel Brink had assisted in training Chinese troops in long-range penetration tactics in India and was thus the American liaison officer for the Galahad force while in British training camps. Colonel Hunter remained in command of the unit in all non training-related matters.

After three weeks of preliminary training, the command was moved to another British camp at Deogarh, where intensified jungle training continued. Although the unit was still very much an orphan and technically not activated as an American army unit, but still designated as a "casual detachment," Colonel Hunter exercised command as well as he could under the circumstances. Colonel Brink, assisted by Lt. Col. Daniel E. Still, supervised training and also handled administrative matters, again under difficult conditions, as well as he could.

Captain George was assigned the duty of an advance party commander and so left the unit ahead of the main body to proceed with equipment and a small guard to the training camp at Deogarh. He first returned to Bombay to pick up the carload of carbines and equipment he was to deliver to the new camp. "The name of the place, Deogarh, served by a railway stop called Jahklann, proved to be unknown to the Bombay station agent with whom I had to clear the shipment. To find either of these names, he had to pull out a dusty magnifying glass."[10] Captain George enjoyed first-class railway accommodations to Deogarh during the four and a half days it took to make the journey. Arriving safely, he joined Colonel Still to await the main body. A week later the three battalions marched into camp.

The Galahad volunteers were to be trained in long-range penetration tactics by the British and as such were placed under the command of the British South East Asia Command, or SEAC. Preliminary training began in October at Deogarh, and it was there that the orphan unit finally got its army name. Theater headquarters had a list of numbers from which it could activate units within the theater. After waiting for a determination without success, Colonel Hunter randomly selected one of the numbers provided and on 1 January 1944 activated the 5307th Composite Unit (Provisional).[11] The 1688th Casual Detachment was no more.

Individual training focused on shooting and marching. The soldiers also practiced techniques in air supply and working without ground lines of communication. The unit was to have no artillery support other than what it could carry, which limited it to mortars. Instead, ground support by the army air forces was practiced as a part of the training routine. Evacuation by air of casualties, messengers, and returnees was also a part of the training cycle. And there were the mules. Experience and common sense had taught that no soldier could carry the loads required for combat, and especially the heavy mortars and machine guns, over the terrain that the unit was scheduled to cover. Nor were there roads or, in many cases, even trails that vehicles could use for carrying the loads. So the only alternative was animal transport. Fortunately, many soldiers in the command came from farm and ranching areas of the United States, and their familiarity with these animals was put to good use. Additionally, the 98th Field Artillery had been a pack artillery unit, which made those volunteers familiar with mule transport.

It was while undergoing training with the British that the combat organization of the unit took form. The unit had been preliminarily formed into three battalions, and this structure was continued. Lieutenant Colonel William Lloyd Osborne commanded the 1st Battalion, Lt. Col. George A. McGee Jr. the 2d Battalion, and Lt. Col. Charles E. Beach the 3d Battalion. Each battalion was then divided into two combat teams of 16 officers and 456 enlisted men. These were not combat teams in the sense normal to the American army of that time. No additional forces were attached to make it a "team" of combined arms. Instead each combat team had a headquarters platoon, a rifle company of three rifle platoons, and a heavy weapons section, a heavy weapons platoon to support the rifle company, a pioneer and demolition platoon, a reconnaissance platoon, and a medical detachment. Each combat team carried 506

M1 rifles, fifty-two submachine guns, eighty-six carbines, four 81-mm mortars, four 60-mm mortars, two heavy machine guns, two light machine guns, and three 2.56-inch rocket launchers. Because all transport was to be by pack animal the 5307th Composite Unit (Provisional) was assigned about seven hundred pack animals. Each battalion commander was allowed discretion in forming the teams, so that in the 1st Battalion, for example, one team consisted of one rifle company and the second team contained two full rifle companies. Finally, because it was intended that all resupply be by air transport, an air supply section under Maj. Edward T. Hancock was organized to preplan air drops, respond to requisitions, package supplies, and ensure the accurate and timely delivery of supplies to the prearranged dropping points.

In late November, training in jungle warfare began in earnest. In addition to the individual training, which stressed marksmanship, scouting, and patrolling, the soldiers practiced map reading and jungle navigation. Physical conditioning, including marching over increasing distances under jungle conditions, was a regular part of the routine. The soldiers wore packs whenever possible to further their conditioning. Training concentrated on platoon tactics, developing slowly into company, combat team, and battalion exercises. Because of time pressure, most training concentrated on small unit activities, mainly at the squad and platoon level. Men selected for the specialized duties such as demolition and reconnaissance were basically familiar with their duties, and so they were also involved in the physical conditioning process. Personnel assigned to duty as parachute packers, riggers, or kick-out crews were trained separately by the unit's supply officer, Major Hancock.

After the soldiers completed individual and unit training, they participated in a ten-day maneuver alongside General Wingate's troops. Some deficiencies in organization and the need for more pack animals were identified and corrected. The 31st and 33d Quartermaster Pack Troops, a detachment of the 835th Signal Service Battalion, and a platoon of the 502d Military Police Battalion were added to the command. The 33d Pack Troop had already suffered losses—all of its mules—when the ship on which they traveled to India was sunk by an enemy submarine. After being issued new clothes and equipment, the 33d was assigned horses instead of mules. This required refitting saddles designed for mules on what Colonel Hunter described as "already emaciated, unconditioned horses."[12] General Wingate observed the training and maneuvers, remaining in constant touch with the progress of the American Long Range Penetration unit.

Meanwhile, General Stilwell continued to argue for command and control of the unit once training was completed. Despite General Wingate's strenuously voiced objections, the 5307th Composite Unit (Provisional) was released from SEAC control and assigned to Stilwell's command on 8 January 1944. General Wingate learned of this from Colonel Brink during a visit to Galahad. Wingate's response was quoted by Colonel Hunter, who was surprised at the British General's adept use of an American expression, as "Brink, you tell General Stilwell he can take his Americans and stick 'em up his ass."[13] Stilwell's first act was to appoint Brig. Gen. Frank D. Merrill as Galahad's new commander.

General Frank Dow Merrill was born 3 December 1903 in Woodville, Massachusetts, and traced family roots there back to the 1600s. As a teenager he had served as a wireless operator aboard a United Fruit Company freighter and while still underage enlisted in the U.S. Army. He served in Haiti and Panama while trying for several years to gain entry to West Point. Refused because of problems with his eyesight and flat feet, he nevertheless held every enlisted rank and was specially appointed as a lieutenant before finally gaining acceptance to West Point by means of a presidential appointment. A classmate of Colonel Hunter, Merrill graduated in 1929 and then served in Vermont and Virginia to qualify as a cavalry officer. In 1931 he went to the Massachusetts Institute of Technology, earning a bachelor's degree. He attended the Cavalry School at Fort Riley, Kansas, and then taught a course in small arms.

In 1938 Merrill went to Tokyo for four years but stayed for only three years because of increased tensions between Japan and the United States. He then served as a Japanese-language officer. In 1941 he spent several months with a Japanese infantry regiment in China before moving on to the Philippines, where he was stationed when the Japanese attacked.[14] His official military specialty was as a cavalry officer, with a second specialty in signal communications. Assigned as a liaison officer with the British forces in Burma immediately after Pearl Harbor, Merrill has been described as "a shrewd and genial soldier, tall, heavyset and shortsighted, with glasses perched on a sunburned peeling nose."[15] Colonel Hunter described him as "rather tall, he was by no means a rugged individual, being narrow of chest and rather thin. His features were sharp but his nature ebullient, affable and confident."[16] It was Merrill who first briefed General Stilwell upon his arrival in Burma. Merrill was also one of the eighteen American officers who, together with six enlisted men and about one hundred civilians, had made the famous walkout march from Burma with Stilwell in 1942. It was there that his hidden illness first became evident, when at one river crossing he fainted from exhaustion combined with a weak heart. Later he served as Stilwell's operations officer and as a colonel became Stilwell's aide at the Cairo conference of November 1943. Appointed to command the 5307th Composite Unit (Provisional) in January 1944, the newly promoted Brigadier General Merrill assumed overall command of forward and rear echelon elements and retained Colonel Hunter as commander of the infantry forces. Merrill appointed Maj. Louis J. Williams as his executive officer in charge of the command post group.

Captain George recalls:

By the time General Merrill arrived to take command, we were already used to a familiar Marauder scene—the drop field at dawn with the last of the DC-3s passing over, and men and mules hurriedly picking up their litter of parachuted and free-dropped ammo and food in the morning mists, to clear the area re-victualled and re-armed before the still hypothetical enemy could catch us there like sitting ducks.

By agreement among the battalion commanders and Colonel Hunter, several men were transferred from the third battalion to the other two, exchanging places so that each battalion's strength remained as intended. This move was designed to spread the combat veterans among all three battalions in the expectation that the veterans would impart at least some knowledge of jungle combat to the novices from the United States.

General Stilwell's victory in obtaining Galahad for his direct control was quickly followed by orders to move to the front. Immediate movement was necessary for the Americans to meet General Stilwell's deadline of an arrival at Ledo by 7 February. That was the first indication of the demanding nature of the American general on the only American combat unit he had, which he expected to set an example for the Chinese. Even as the unit marched forward, General Stilwell noted in his diary, "The Long Range Penetration Group is arriving at Ledo January 20, and expects to jump off February 15. My God what speed. Snorted at him and he allowed they might better the time. Expect to ride in trucks to the river!"[17] Stilwell's criticism of the speed and method was in direct contrast to the advice of the British instructors, who stressed that the men would need every ounce of their endurance to survive in the Burma jungles and that every opportunity to conserve their strength should be seized. As it happened, Colonel Hunter had recommended to General Merrill that the unit march into Burma as a conditioning exercise. Hunter believed that the march would condition the animals as well as the soldiers.

And so the 5307th Composite Unit (Provisional) marched the last one hundred miles to Ledo. During that march they crossed the comparatively low Parkai Range and covered tropical forests. One other important occurrence happened along the march. One of the newspaper correspondents accompanying the troops for part of the march was James Shepley of *Time* and *Life*. After watching the unit practice a river crossing he remarked to General Merrill on the name of the unit. "It has no appeal. I'm going to call your outfit 'Merrill's Marauders.'"[18] By the end of that march they were known far and wide as Merrill's Marauders." From the nondescriptive 1688th Casual Detachment to the unintelligible 5307th Composite Unit (Provisional) they had at last a name with which they could be known. And they had yet to enter combat.

General Stilwell's rush to get Galahad into action ignored certain facts that were already beginning to emerge about this new American combat force. There were several discipline problems, most likely from the same group who had been coerced into volunteering. More ominous, however, were the reports from the medical officers that many of the men, particularly in the 3d Battalion, were suffering from recurring bouts of malaria. In one case a medical officer suggested that no less than 12 percent of the 3d battalion was unfit to participate in the coming campaign. These reports were ignored, but they would resurface later.[19]

General Stilwell wanted the American force to work in conjunction with his Chinese forces, then about to launch the second Burma campaign. The immediate objective was to clear northern Burma of the enemy and to seize the Myitkyina airstrip. The Ledo Road would continue to be built by engineering units following behind the advancing Allied troops. Eventually this would reopen a direct land line of communications with the Chinese mainland.

To accomplish this, the American Long Range Penetration Unit assembled at Ningbyen, close to the front lines. Together with the Chinese 113th Regiment of the 38th Division they were to envelop the east flank of the Japanese 18th Infantry Division and block the Kamaing Road near the village of Shaduzup. Both General Merrill and Gen. Sun Li-jen, commanding the 38th Division, would have preferred a common command, but General Stilwell's headquarters, about to be formally christened the Northern Combat Area Command (NCAC), ordered them only to cooperate with each other. While the two units outflanked the Japanese, the rest of the NCAC's forces, the balance of the 38th Division, the 22d Division, and the 1st Chinese-American Provisional Tank Group, were to seize Maingkwan in a combination frontal and flanking attack. This, it was surmised, would force the Japanese to fight for Maingkwan or to fight their way past the Marauders and the 113th Regiment. In either case it was hoped that the 18th Japanese Infantry Division would be seriously hurt, if not destroyed.

Colonel Rothwell H. Brown commanded the 1st Provisional Tank Group. A predominantly Chinese force, it consisted of ninety medium and light tanks manned by Chinese crews and led by American officers and noncommissioned officers. It was the only Chinese army unit in the theater commanded by an American officer. The executive officer was Col. Chao Chen-yu. At its peak, American strength in the unit was 29 officers and 222 enlisted men, including an all-American–staffed medium tank platoon.

Some months later *Yank* correspondent Sgt. Dave Richardson left the Marauders and joined the 1st Provisional Tank Group. He later described his impressions:

> My next exercise in armed journalism was in the first American tank action on the Asian continent—a particularly good story because this tank outfit came not from the armored training at Fort Knox but from mess halls and orderly rooms of Army units in India and Burma, where it was recruited and trained by a colorful old tanker named Colonel Rothwell Brown.[20]

Like the Marauders, the tank unit was a collection of untrained volunteers who learned as they fought.

Lieutenant Colonel Joseph W. Stilwell Jr., the general's son and now his intelligence officer, reported that the Japanese had a total of six divisions in Burma. Two of these, the 55th and 56th, were believed tied down in southern Burma and the Arakan, facing the British. Two others, the 31st and 33d, were fighting against the British IV Corps at Imphal. The 54th Infantry Division was believed to be protecting Rangoon and the Irrawaddy delta against a possible amphibious attack. That would leave only the 18th Infantry Division to face the NCAC's attack in northern Burma. Intelligence also believed that the 55th Regiment of the 18th Division had been seriously hurt in previous operations and therefore the enemy facing the NCAC could field only two regiments, perhaps a total of five infantry battalions.

The Japanese forces facing General Stilwell's forces were under the control of Southern Army Headquarters, commanded by Gen. Count Hisaichi Terauchi, who was based in Singapore. The next step in the chain of command was the Burma area army of Lt. Gen. Masakazu (Shozo) Kawabe. Born in 1886 and commissioned a second lieutenant of infantry in the 35th Infantry Regiment in December 1907, he commanded all Japanese ground forces facing the British, Chinese, and Americans in Burma and India. His force included the 15th Army, the 28th Army, and the recently formed 33d Army.

The 33d Army was directly facing the planned Chinese-American assault forces. It was commanded by Lt. Gen. Masaki (Seizai) Honda. Born in 1889 in Nagano, he was commissioned as a second lieutenant of infantry after graduating from the military academy. He served in the 4th Infantry Regiment of the Imperial Guards Division before assuming staff positions. Later he served as an attaché in Paris for three years and lectured at the infantry school. He commanded an infantry regiment and was chief of staff to the China Expeditionary Army before taking command of the 33d Army.

The 33d Army had direct command of the 18th, 55th, and 56th Infantry Divisions. Later it would add to its troop list the 49th Infantry Division and the 24th Independent Mixed Brigade. It was the 18th Infantry Division that directly faced the planned attack. This division was considered an elite force, having captured Singapore and participated in the first Burma campaign. It was one of the best-trained units in the Japanese army and had one of the most respected commanders in the Japanese officer corps.

Lieutenant General Shinichi (Sumichi) Tanaka was born in Hokkaido in 1893 and graduated from the military academy in July 1913. Commissioned as a second lieutenant of infantry, he served with the 52d Infantry Regiment before graduating from the War College in December 1923. He commanded a section of the Inspectorate General of Military Training and then served as a staff officer for the Kwantung army. After holding a number of prestigious staff and command assignments he was promoted to lieutenant general in October 1941. In March 1943 he was given command of the 18th Infantry Division as a punishment for disagreeing with Japanese Premier Tojo on the conduct of the Guadalcanal campaign. General Tanaka, then chief of the Operations Bureau, had argued strongly for continuing the campaign and increasing the amount of men, equipment, shipping, and supplies sent to the island despite Premier Tojo's already announced intention to withdraw.

General Stilwell first had determined to send an armored spearhead down the Kamaing Road with a strong infantry force behind it. Only a few days after the plan was prepared it needed to be changed. Weather conditions would prevent the ground from staying dry enough for armored operations. General Sun, commanding the 38th Chinese Division, appeared reluctant to cooperate. Born in 1900 and graduating from Purdue University with a civil engineering degree, Gen. Sun Li-jen went on to the Virginia Military Institute, graduating in 1927. Returning to China, he was commissioned and as a general fought at Shanghai, where he was seriously wounded. After recovering he organized and trained the new 38th Division, which he was now about to lead into Burma.

Changing plans, General Stilwell ordered Gen. Liao Yao-tsiang's 22d Division to replace the 38th Division in the attack. Instead of a direct attack by the armor, two Long Range Penetration Groups, the Marauders and Wingate's 16th Infantry Brigade (Brigadier B. E. Fergusson), would strike for the Japanese rear at Shadazup and Nsopzup, respectively. The 22d Division would attack frontally to push the Japanese back and keep them occupied while encircling them. Because the weather also slowed progress on the Ledo Road, this method would allow for the road to catch up with the front while giving the Allies a chance to severely damage the principal Japanese force in northern Burma. It was known that several jungle-covered defensive positions protected the Kamaing Road, each manned by a platoon or a company of Japanese infantry.

Things started badly. Stilwell counted on the Chinese 65th Infantry Regiment to join with its sister 66th Regiment in time to push down the road. After several agonizing days of contradictory reports it became clear that the 65th Regiment was lost in the jungles. Stilwell and the division commander, General Liao, went forward to the regimental headquarters. Here they found the entire regiment grouped around the headquarters. Sending out scouts, the generals determined that the road was clear and that the Japanese had retreated.

Finally, on 23 February, the Chinese 65th and 66th Regiments seized the initial objective of Yawngbang Ga unopposed. Stilwell reported that a combination of adverse weather conditions and a lost regiment had cost him an opportunity to seriously damage the main Japanese force in northern Burma. Still looking along the Kamaing Road, the NCAC noted that after running fairly straight for some ten thousand yards to the west the road makes a sharp ninety-degree turn to the east. It continues until, at the village of Walawbum, the road makes another ninety-degree turn, this time to the south. A force in position just to the east of Walawbum on the high ground would have that advantage plus a river moat facing an enemy coming from the west, the direction from which any retreating Japanese would have to approach.

Orders were soon issued to General Merrill to establish a trail block in the vicinity of Walawbum, while the 1st Provisional Tank Group followed along any passable trails to link up with the Marauders at Walawbum. On 24 February 1944 the Marauders moved forward on their first combat mission in Burma.

3. First Mission: Walabum

On February 24 we rolled out of our ponchos in the black dark, wondering why we had ever been born."[1] The Marauders were on their first mission. Leaving behind a small detachment to occupy the bivouac area and light fires each night, assuming enemy observation, the main force moved forward over the trail from Ningbyen. A five-day march would take them to the intermediate objective of Tanja Ga. Each battalion moved out in identical order. The 1st Battalion led off, departing at 0600 hours. It followed its intelligence and reconnaissance platoon, commanded by 1st Lt. Samuel V. Wilson, which had departed at 0100 hours. A rifle platoon led the march, and then a rifle company with half the heavy weapons platoon. Combat team headquarters and the medical detachment came next, followed by another rifle platoon and the rest of the heavy weapons. Each battalion's I&R (intelligence and reconnaissance) platoon scouted the trails in advance of the main force, to avoid ambush or surprise.

After covering about eighteen miles, the 2d Battalion's I&R platoon, under 1st Lt. Logan F. Weston, turned off the trail to determine if they had yet passed the enemy flank. Farther along the trail the 3d Battalion's I&R platoon, led by 1st Lt. William C. Grissom, did likewise. The men soon learned that things were different in the jungle, that there the trail was the dangerous point. Any threat would have to be either waiting on the trail or moving along it. The jungle, too thick for organized forces to move threateningly, provided concealment and safety. Yet despite the proximity of enemy forces, the first day passed uneventfully.

The methods of the I&R platoons of Galahad impressed the more experienced Chinese. General Sun Li-jen, commanding the

38th Chinese Division, with which Galahad was operating, had assigned Col. Chun Lee of his staff to act as liaison officer with Galahad. As Colonel Hunter recalled, "Colonel Lee, to the day he left us at Myitkyina, continued to express amazement and concern over the distances at which the I&R platoons habitually operated away from the main body of Galahad or its separated battalions."[2] The platoons carried with them the Signal Corps 284 radio and contacted at prearranged times the parent battalion. Although the SCR-284 was a larger and more cumbersome radio, which required a hand-cranked generator, the distances covered by the scout platoons made it necessary. The smaller and more compact SCR-300 radio was used within the Galahad columns for messages, column control, and directions.

After resting in jungle hideouts and observing the trail, the scout platoons moved out again at first light on 25 February. The morning passed quietly with steady progress forward. Then, at about 1330 hours, the reconnaissance platoon of Maj. Lawrence L. Lew's Orange Combat Team, 3d Battalion, ran into an unidentified group near Nzang Ga. Lieutenant Weston moved forward when his lead scout halted the column. Passing the three-man "shock group," then the second scout, he moved to the lead scout, Cpl. Werner Katz. A German-born veteran of the Spanish Civil War and Guadalcanal, Corporal Katz told his lieutenant that he had heard voices just ahead. Thinking it might be a Chinese unit, Lieutenant Weston and the second scout covered Corporal Katz as he slowly moved forward. Seeing troops in the trail ahead, he turned to Lieutenant Weston and shouted "They're Chinese. They're waving us to come on." Corporal Katz began to walk forward. An immediate outbreak of firing resulted. The Americans dived for cover. The Japanese machine gun swept the road in fixed traverse, allowing Lieutenant Weston and the second scout to escape unscathed. Corporal Katz, sheltered in a ditch, fired his M1 rifle before a ricochet caused a slight wound across his nose, but he accounted for one enemy soldier before crawling back to the platoon.[3]

"My patrol moved about 6 hours marching time ahead of the parent 3rd Battalion," remembered Lieutenant Weston. They discovered and marked an enemy mine field along the trail. After the ambush fight they continually engaged an enemy force that used delaying tactics to slow the Americans. Lieutenant Weston extricated his platoon and reported to headquarters on his encounter with the enemy. Having determined that the vicinity was defended, he received orders to return to the main column.[4] Shortly afterward Maj. Richard W. Healy's Blue Combat Team of the 2d Battalion suffered the same fate, and Pvt. Robert W. Landis became the first Marauder fatality when enemy machine-gun fire opened up on his platoon approaching Lanem Ga. The village was so strongly held that the platoon could not recover Private Landis's body until the following day.

Meanwhile, Lieutenant Wilson's platoon continued on its mission. Early on the second afternoon the platoon froze in its tracks upon hearing firing behind it. Immediately the men dove off the trail and into the jungle. It was only then that they realized that the machine gun they heard was well behind them. Lieutenant Wilson ordered his men to continue forward, knowing as they all did that the enemy was now between them and the rest of their force. A second occurrence a few hours later confirmed their worst fears. They were alone in the jungle, surrounded by a merciless enemy. Lieutenant Wilson now knew that both of his fellow reconnaissance platoons had bumped into enemy forces. The only option remaining was for his platoon to find a way around the main enemy forces.

They continued on, more cautious than ever. Firing of all types, including artillery, could be heard no more than five miles away. Clearly the main battle lines were close. Each bend in the trail brought danger. Yet they continued on, knowing that their route was now the only possibility. Finally they came to the objective, the village of Tanja Ga. Carefully the platoon entered the deserted village. Although signs of enemy presence were all around, no one was there. Quickly the Americans set up defensive positions to wait for the enemy to return. They had to hold the position until joined by the main force, now no longer a certainty because of enemy forces all around them.

They swiftly made a local reconnaissance. They were in the correct position, they had located a ford over a nearby stream, and they had turned the enemy's flank. Now word had to be transmitted to General Merrill. The SCR-284 radio was set up, and contact was attempted just as darkness fell and the time arrived for the regimental net to receive and send messages. Contact was made but soon broken; the complete message did not get through. Atmospheric conditions prevented reestablishing contact. The SCR-284 pack-transportable one-hundred-pound radio had a range of five to twenty miles but was often inadequate to overcome the conditions encountered in the Burmese jungles.

Lieutenant Wilson now had no choice. Taking his favorite horse and one other mounted soldier, he started out at about 2200 hours, in full darkness, back along the dangerous trail that his platoon had taken two days to cover. Riding several yards apart the two Americans retraced the twenty-two miles they had come, until they arrived at a stream. While crossing this stream Lieutenant Wilson's saddle turned sideways and two wildcats suddenly roared close by. Yelling and firing his carbine to scare off the cats, he managed to recover, and the two swiftly left the area, with any enemy within miles alerted to their presence.

As dawn broke they came to a village. Straining to see what was ahead, Lieutenant Wilson lost his helmet. After dismounting to retrieve it he continued across a clearing on foot. An early-morning fog covered the area, and suddenly there appeared an American officer pointing a .45 pistol at Lieutenant Wilson. Fortunately, the officer recognized Wilson, who learned that he had walked into Lieutenant Grissom's platoon bivouac. The news was passed quickly back to headquarters, and Wilson advised General Merrill and Colonel Hunter, who had trained Lieutenant Wilson at Fort Benning, that his route was clear. Immediately General Merrill issued orders for the three battalions to march to Tanja Ga over the route scouted by Lieutenant Wilson's platoon. General Merrill then released Lieutenant Wilson to return to his platoon. Concerned that it was asking too much of his good fortune to travel that route three times, Wilson nevertheless arrived safely back at Tanja Ga. He was later decorated for his activities during this mission.

The American officer who nearly shot Lieutenant Wilson was not a Marauder officer. He was a member of the highly secretive intelligence organization known as the Office of Strategic Services, or OSS. Colonel William J. Donovan was one of America's most decorated heroes of World War I, having earned our three highest decorations, including the Medal of Honor. A close friend of President Roosevelt, Donovan had often acted for the president while conducting his law practice in New York City. At the outbreak of the war he was summoned to the president's side and given permission to create an intelligence organization designed to operate behind enemy lines. The objective was to disrupt enemy lines of communication, encourage guerrilla warfare behind enemy lines, and gather intelligence. The organization would range all over the world, wherever America's enemies were located. Originally known as the Office of the Coordinator of Information, it soon evolved into the OSS. Recruits had to volunteer and were selected for intelligence and language capabilities. Training was intense and secret. Within months OSS operatives were spread across the world at war.

In Burma the OSS organization was known as Detachment 101. Commanded by Capt. William R. Peers, who later became a colonel, its primary concern was the organization and direction of the major native population in northern Burma, the Kachins. A people known for their fighting qualities, they had fought their way into northern Burma from the mountains to the north. Known as expert woodsmen and uncannily adept at invoking the *nats*, or minor deities, of the surrounding hills, the Kachins reminded some of the OSS Americans who lived and worked with them of American Indians in their greatest days on the plains. One of the most notable traits of the Kachins greatly pleased the Americans assigned to them: they could not deceive another person. In one case a Kachin appeared in an American camp and announced, "The Japanese have sent me to spy on you. Please, how do I begin?" The Kachins worked with Americans to gather intelligence for Tenth Air Force targeting, attacked small Japanese working parties or patrols, and cut Japanese lines of communication. When British and American ground combat forces advanced into the area they served as scouts and as advance and flank guards and were considered invaluable by the American commanders.[5] Known as Kachin Rangers, they were attached to all Marauder battalions.

Detachment 101 also provided an experienced British guide for the Marauders. Jack Girsham was already a legend in Burma when the war came. Born to an English father and a Burmese mother, he had already enjoyed a long career as a game ranger and big-game hunter. He had been fighting the Japanese since they invaded Burma and had had several close calls. In his latest sojourn against them he had led a patrol that had fallen into a field of "pungees." These sharpened sticks were set to penetrate into any passing man or animal and would later be used by other American enemies in Vietnam. Badly injured by a pungee that had penetrated his leg, he was recovering at a Detachment 101 camp when he was approached by Col. Carl F. Eifler, another OSS commander. Asked to join Merrill's Marauders upon his recovery, he agreed and was able to join as the 5307th marched down the Ledo Road.

Another feature of long-range penetration operations came into effect in this first mission: the unique nature and type of supply operations required by such tactics. Normal methods of supply were impractical for a highly mobile force operating behind the enemy's main line of resistance. Any attempt to maintain a regular supply route on land, even if the terrain and climate allowed it, would have been impossible. The lack of any adequate roads in the combat zone further prohibited supply by land. As a result, planners from the very first had insisted that air supply was the only way to ensure that the needs of a long-range penetration group could be met once it was committed behind enemy lines.

The combatants in the CBI theater were pioneers in the development and use of air supply methods. The first experiments with air supply were in May, June, and July 1942, when this method was used to aid the refugees fleeing from Burma because of the Japanese advance. General Wingate had noted this and had trained his first expedition to rely solely on air supply. At about the same time, in New Guinea, a small group of Australian soldiers, retreating across the forbidding Owen Stanley Mountains, were likewise supplied by air. During the retreat from Burma several isolated groups of Chinese and native Burmese had remained behind to set up advance outposts or early air-warning stations. They also had begun to depend on air supply for survival.

Indeed, by the time the Marauders entered their training in October 1943, air supply in the CBI was taken as a matter of course. As

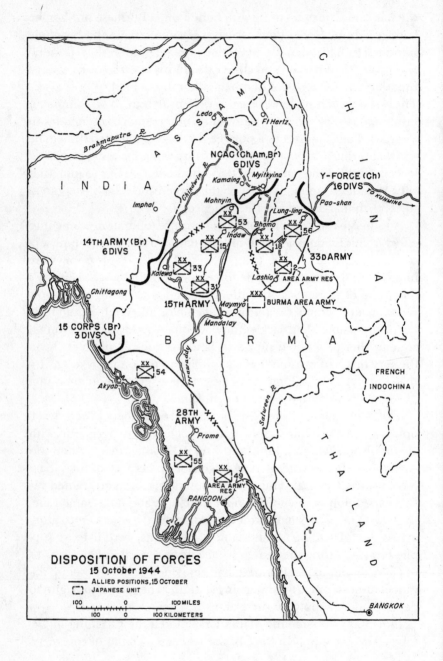

DISPOSITION OF FORCES
15 October 1944

the Marauders entered Burma, air supply resources committed to the campaign included the 1st and 2d Troop Carrier Squadrons, the 518th Quartermaster Battalion (Mobile), the 3841st Quartermaster Truck Company, and the 3304th Quartermaster Truck Company. The ground units, except for the 3841st Truck Company, were responsible for preparing and shipping the needed supplies. The 1st and 2d Troop Carrier Squadrons carried and dropped the supplies while the 3841st Quartermaster Truck Company rode along to perform the dangerous task of kicking out the supplies, without wearing parachutes, from a moving plane with its cargo doors wide open. On drops for Galahad, Marauders assigned to Major Hancock's supply section acted as kickers. As more and more Allied troops were committed to the campaign, additional aircraft—including the 27th and 315th Troop Carrier Squadrons and the 31st, 62d, 117th, and 194th Squadrons of the Royal Air Force—were added to the lift. By mid-1944 more than four hundred allied aircraft were engaged in keeping the ground troops adequately supplied.

The techniques of total supply by air were complex. Adequate air and radio equipment was essential, for without communication neither supply lists nor dropping points could be established. Planning had to be done with extreme care, because the slightest error in map coordinates could send a supply drop well out of reach of those who needed it. Adequate supplies had to be stored for immediate availability in the event of a sudden crisis. An unexpected intense battle, for example, could rapidly deplete a unit's ammunition stock, leaving it nearly defenseless without immediate and accurate resupply. Packaging methods had to be developed and followed closely. Some supplies could be dropped without a parachute, such as feed for the pack animals, while others required parachute delivery.

Dropping supplies accurately called for skilled pilots and crews who could approximate low-level bombing techniques with only small jungle clearings as their targets. Because many squadrons were flying the C-47 transport aircraft, which had no drop port in the floor, pilots had to make sure they were in level flight during the drop or the supplies kicked out the side door could catch on or damage the left horizontal stabilizer. One plane was lost and two damaged by parachutes catching on that stabilizer. Fighter protection and coordination were required to ensure the safe arrival of the cargo planes over the target. Many deliveries were made without fighter protection, but only two aircraft were lost to enemy action during Marauder operations. Supply deliveries were often made in poor flying conditions because the troops needed immediate supplies.

There were generally three standard methods of delivery during the campaign. The first was to land the cargo aircraft at a forward airstrip protected by the long-range penetration group. This method was used predominantly by the British as they established several patrol bases behind the enemy lines and prepared rough airstrips for supply and evacuation purposes. The Marauders used this method occasionally, and when they did it was usually for a small, light observation plane to evacuate the wounded. The second method was to parachute supplies into a predetermined drop zone, usually a clearing in the jungle. The final method was called free-dropping, in which supplies packed in sacks were simply kicked out of the plane at a drop zone. Parachutes and specially constructed "country baskets" were locally made in India. These country baskets were woven bamboo frames covered tightly by hessian cloth, with a cradle of heavy three-quarter-inch ropes fastened to the parachute. The baskets proved so sturdy that there was no need to protect the loads with rice husks or sawdust around the contents, as had been done earlier. Some theater-level supply officer later determined that it cost $1,909.65 per ton of supplies parachuted, $94.07 per ton of supplies free-dropped, and $49.61 per ton of supplies air landed.[6]

Major Hancock, using bamboo warehouses at Dinjan, thirty-two miles west of Ledo, had ready access to airstrips at Chabua, Tinsukia, and Sookerating. Procedures quickly developed for the supply section to monitor all radio communications between Marauder units, and especially those directed to General Merrill's headquarters, so that they could speed up preparation and delivery time. Standard units of each category of supplies, based upon estimated requirements for one day, were packaged and ready for delivery. During March alone, in seventeen missions averaging six to seven planes, 376 tons of supplies were delivered to the Marauder units.

Eighty percent of the rations delivered to the Marauder battalions
were K rations, 5 percent were C, 5 percent "10-in-1," and 10 percent B. The only variety came during the second mission, when the
2d Battalion received fried chicken and apple turnovers during the
siege at Nhpum Ga.

By the time the mission was well under way the supply group had
prepackaged supplies waiting for any unexpected call. A situation
map, kept up-to-date in Major Hancock's office, was followed
closely in an effort to anticipate the supply needs of the battalions.
Assisted by about 250 enlisted members of the 5307th, including
packers, riggers, drivers, and droppers, the supply staff was always
prepared to act on behalf of their comrades in the jungles. Major
Hancock and his executive officer, Capt. Willard C. Nelson, never
allowed any obstacle to interfere with supply delivery. Aided by 1st
Lt. Robert O. Gardiner, who supervised the packing of parachutes,
and by 1st Lt. Marlan E. Lowell, who handled air liaison, the supply
section ably supported their men in the field, allowing them the essential mobility and secrecy necessary for them to succeed.

The first contact with the enemy on the route to Walawbum also
brought the first casualties. The 71st Liaison Squadron, using L-4s
and L-5's flying from airfields at Ledo, evacuated most of the Marauder casualties during the campaign. After medical corpsmen
treated the wounded on the scene, the light liaison planes would be
called upon to land on drop zones, rice paddies, or gravel bars
along the rivers. The wounded would be loaded aboard, and often
within a few hours would be at a rear-area collecting station. From
there C-47 transport planes converted to ambulance planes would
carry the wounded to the 20th General Hospital, the 14th Evacuation Hospital, or the 111th Station Hospital, all in the Ledo area.
Many Marauders owed their lives to the speed of air evacuation,
later developed into the fine art of medevac helicopters in Korea
and Vietnam.

Behind the enemy lines, the three Marauder battalions moved
forward to Tanja Ga, arriving on 28 February after two days of
marching. Upon arrival they received orders from the NCAC to proceed as quickly as possible to Walawbum. The Chinese forces were
also moving in that direction. Their objective was Maingkwan.

Both forces faced elements of the 18th Japanese Infantry Division, commanded by Lt. Gen. Shinichi Tanaka. A combat experienced unit that was rated highly by both American and Japanese officers, it was strung out to protect northern Burma. General Tanaka had been observing the advance of the Chinese forces facing him and noted the improvement in both their equipment and tactics, the result of American supply and training. He noted also, however, that the Chinese consistently moved slowly and cautiously, while always going for the outflanking maneuver, the result of Stilwell's determination to trap the division and destroy it. Thus he was free to operate on interior lines, moving his reserves to threatened points faster than the Allies could marshall theirs against his weak points. He was determined "to defeat in detail the slow-moving Chinese forces [acting] without coordination on the exterior lines."[7]

Walawbum is in the southern end of the Hukawng Valley, on the road running south to Kamaing. About ten miles south of Walawbum the ground rises as the road approaches the Jambu Bum, the ridge line forming the southern end of the Hukawng Valley. The village's location on the Kamaing Road at a critical turn in the road made it a military objective. Indeed, described as "a pathetic cluster of sagging uprights and fire scars where once a few Kachin families had pursued their simple, inoffensive lives,"[8] it had no other importance except its location.

Walawbum was a forty-mile march from Tanja Ga. Using the intelligence and reconnaissance platoons as screening forces, the Marauders moved out toward Walawbum. Three days of marching put them within striking distance. During a break taken after crossing the Tanai River on 2 March, General Merrill issued his attack orders for the assault on Walawbum. Colonel Beach's Khaki and Orange Combat Teams of the 3d Battalion were to advance at 1600 hours and pass through Sabaw Ga and Lagang Ga to secure control of the Kamaing Road at Walawbum by occupying the high ground along the Numpyek River east of the road. Colonel McGee's 2d Battalion was to move to Wesu Ga, cut a trail through the jungle in a westerly direction, and strike the Kamaing Road east of the Mambyu River about two and a half miles west of Walawbum. Its Blue and Green Combat Teams were to build and hold a roadblock at that location.

Colonel Osborne's Red and White Combat Teams of the 1st Battalion were to block the trails at Sana Ga and Nchet Ga, establishing at least one platoon at each point. Combat patrols were also to monitor the area along the Nambyu River between Shimak Ga and Uga Ga. The balance of the 1st Battalion was to be held in reserve at Wesu Ga, an assignment that included protecting the vital light-aircraft landing strip to be established there. The Marauders were to hold their positions until the Chinese came up to relieve them.

General Merrill had been given explicit orders to cut the Kamaing Road south of Walawbum—that order was subsequently changed to those he issued at the Tanai River—and to seek out and attack the headquarters of the 18th Division, believed to be at or near Walawbum. His orders also included instructions to hold down casualties as much as possible, a point whose interpretation would later cause some problems for both the NCAC and the Marauders.

At dawn on 3 March the 5307th Composite Unit (Provisional) moved on Walawbum. About twenty miles behind them Colonel Rothwell Brown's 1st Provisional Tank Group, less its 2d Battalion but reinforced with a battalion of the Chinese 65th Regiment, also moved forward to begin the major portion of the offensive. The tanks encountered enemy forces five thousand yards north of Maingkwan early in the afternoon. They moved east in an attempt to outflank the opposition but encountered even heavier resistance. Estimating that he faced an enemy regiment, Colonel Brown secured his position for the night and advised General Stilwell that there was a strong enemy force on his flank.

The Marauders knew nothing of the events behind them. Nor did they know that radio communications between the 2d Battalion, 56th Japanese Infantry, and the 18th Division Headquarters had broken down, so that General Tanaka was as yet unaware that he had an American long-range penetration group behind him. As the Marauders set out, the 3d Battalion Headquarters walked into the village of Lagang Ga and encountered a party of seven Japanese soldiers carrying one wounded officer on a stretcher. A fire fight resulted in five enemy dead with no American losses.[9] Later that same battalion would fight to establish its drop zone, killing thirty enemy in the defense of the vital supply area. Major Edwin J. Briggs's Khaki

Combat Team remained at Lagang Ga to secure the distribution of supplies while the Orange Combat Team secured the high ground east of Walawbum and dug in for defense. Establishing its heavy weapons on the ground above the Kamaing Road, the Marauder Battalion had established control of the vital road. At the same time, the 1st Battalion had established its reserve positions at Wesu Ga, setting up trail blocks and listening posts, many of which encountered enemy groups. No American casualties were suffered in these actions. The following day, 4 March, the 2d Battalion established its roadblock across the Kamaing Road west of Wesu Ga.

That day also saw the I&R platoon, Company K, Orange Combat Team, ambushed by the enemy. They had been ordered across the Numpyck Hka River to protect the battalion's right flank. They dug in for the night and awoke on 4 March to a heavy ground fog. Ordered to move forward for better observation, the platoon had just begun to dig new positions when Pfc. Pete Leightner moved a short distance forward to gather camouflage material. As he stood forward of the platoon he was shot by an enemy sniper. They soon discovered that they were surrounded by an estimated ninety enemy soldiers. A fight began, lasting about four hours. Armed with three Browning automatic rifles and six Thompson submachine guns, the forty-five men of the platoon fought back against four determined attacks. As noon approached, the platoon withdrew under cover of mortars firing smoke as well as high explosive. Despite an enemy crossfire on the only crossing site, the platoon made its withdrawal, losing two more men, Cpl. Lionel J. Paquette, who was hit in the head by an enemy tree burst while not wearing his helmet, and Pvt. Thomas E. Farren, who was severely wounded in the arm by enemy mortar fire.[10]

General Tanaka now knew for sure that the Americans were behind him at Walawbum. Estimating that the Chinese forces attacking at his front were moving with their usual slowness, he felt he could contain them with a small holding force while he turned his main attention to the Marauders. He began moving his forces into position on 3 March. He directed his 55th Regiment to attack the Americans from the north, while the 56th Regiment attacked to break the enemy hold on the Kamaing Road, where it crossed the

Nanbyu Hka. The first result of General Tanaka's orders was an attack on the Khaki Combat Team at the drop zone near Lagang Ga. The defenders under Major Briggs had constructed a small airstrip for liaison planes and had just sat down to breakfast when elements of the 56th Japanese Infantry Regiment attacked. Concealed by heavy brush and gullies, as well as by a heavy fog that had settled over the area, the Japanese were able to get close to the defenses before they were discovered. A squad of Marauders, reinforced with two light machine guns and some 60mm mortar crews, drove off the attack after ten of its number were killed. Six of the Khaki Combat Team were wounded, of which four had to be evacuated from the landing strip they had just completed.

Less than an hour later another Japanese force, estimated at ninety strong, hit the Orange Combat Team's intelligence and reconnaissance platoon in what turned out to be the heaviest fighting of the day. Lieutenant Weston's platoon had led the way to Lagang Ga, fighting the whole way against an enemy platoon that was moving ahead of it along the trail and was constantly ambushing the American platoon to delay its advance. Now the Americans were entrenched on high ground along the river, about three hundred yards southwest of their earlier night position. From this location, about six hundred yards from Walawbum, they could see into the village. They could also stop any attempted enemy crossing of the river either up- or downstream against the flank of the Orange Combat Team. At about 0720 hours an enemy patrol brushed against the position, and a few moments later a larger enemy group attacked from the north. Three more enemy groups came at the platoon, each from a different direction. The Americans were in effect surrounded except along the river itself. Lieutenant Weston had formed his platoon into a three-pointed star position, and from that formation moved his only reserve, two Thompson submachine gunners, from threat to threat. Sergeant Henry H. Gosho, a nisei interpreter assigned to the platoon, was able to translate the shouted orders of the Japanese officers and allow his lieutenant to shift his meager reserve in time to meet each new attack. After the fourth attack Lieutenant Weston radioed to Major Lew, who was commanding the combat team, for supporting fire from his 81mm mortar section. "The firing and mortar bursts were so intense at this time, that we had difficulty hearing and calling for 81mm mortar support from the battalion," Weston wrote. "By radio we directed high explosive mortar fire completely around our perimeter. We had 3 seriously wounded men and were running low on ammunition."[11]

During the fifth enemy attack on the platoon, 2d Lt. William E. Woomer's men fired 225 rounds of light, heavy, and smoke shells in response to Sgt. Alfred Greer's radioed directions. Under this covering fire, at about noon on 5 March the platoon waded the stream, carrying three litter patients, one of whom was mortally wounded. The Japanese followed the retreating Americans but were turned back by a squad that Lieutenant Weston had formed as his rear guard. He wrote:

> The men most heavily engaged against the enemy were evacuated last. When they had crossed through the platoon HQ position, along with three riflemen, I slipped down over the river bank and continued firing overhead fire while they withdrew through us to the south. After the entire platoon was evacuated and safely on the south shore these 3 men and I then withdrew to the skirmish line.[12]

The platoon safely reached the Orange Combat Team and joined the defense. An estimated ninety enemy soldiers had fallen to the combined fire of Lieutenants Weston and Woomer's commands. Colonel Hunter later recorded:

> Weston's platoon had to fight for its life. One of his men had been killed.and several wounded. He was in the dumps when I arrived and blaming himself for losing one of his men. I assured him that he was in no way at fault, and I intended to recommend to General Merrill that he be given the Silver Star for his conduct during that hectic morning.[13]

The Orange Combat Team meanwhile had established itself in a perimeter along the Numpyek River, on the high ground facing Walawbum, thereby blocking the Kamaing Road with mortars and machine guns. That afternoon Major Lew had about one hundred mortar rounds fired on the village and the road, to impress upon the enemy the cutting of their main supply and withdrawal route. The Japanese immediately replied with their own mortar fire, adding some artillery as well. The enemy artillery crews soon concerned themselves with the air activity at Lagang Ga, leaving their mortars to punish the Orange Combat Team. As it turned out, neither the Khaki nor the Orange Combat Teams suffered losses from this fire.

The men of the 3d Battalion had always considered themselves somewhat superior to the rest of the unit. Veterans of several South Pacific campaigns, they had come to call themselves the "Dead End Kids" and frowned upon the other battalions as novices to combat. Several had volunteered because they believed that they would return to the United States for training. Instead they found themselves in India. During the recent Christmas holidays many had gone absent without leave and roamed the cities of India until recalled. Some had spent all their pay, accrued after months in the South Pacific, and then were reduced in rank to privates. But few cared. They had enjoyed themselves for the first time in many months, and to them it was worthwhile.

Now an Orange Combat Team's platoon, led by 1st Lt. Victor J. (Abie) Weingartner, was dug in above the forty-foot-wide muddy Numpyek River two hundred yards above Walawbum. They could hear Japanese trucks pulling up in the jungle across the river and occasionally would spot one through a break in the foliage. They knew they were facing the Japanese 18th Division, and they knew that unit's reputation. They also knew that the quiet of that Sunday morning would not last much longer. To prepare for what was coming, patrols had been sent across the river to observe the enemy. They returned to report that the trucks were bringing in artillery, mortars, and loads of ammunition. An attack was obviously being prepared. Yet the Sunday had passed quietly.

At 0930 hours the next morning, Sgt. Andrew B. Pung, a mortar observer, climbed a forty-foot tree to look across the river. He could see a grassy clearing and had begun reporting positions and communications wire when suddenly he shouted into his radio, "Listen, there's a bunch of Japs coming out of the jungle and into this grass across the river. A big bunch. Get ready for an attack. I'll tell you when they're near enough to open fire."[14] While Sergeant Pung directed his mortars the men of Lieutenant Weingartner's platoon set up their weapons to receive the coming attack.

When the enemy closed to within thirty-five yards of the opposite river bank, still out of sight of the men in the foxholes, Sergeant Pung gave the command to fire. Immediately, machine guns, Browning automatic rifles, rifles, and mortars opened up a deluge of fire. Screams and yelling answered from the opposite bank. Swiftly the Japanese returned fire. Their 90mm mortar shells began crashing around the platoon. Having lost his canteen to shrapnel, Sergeant Pung dropped out of his observation post and took up a position with the platoon. He was later credited with dropping a mortar round into a truck filled with enemy troops during that action. Firing from the high ground, the Americans had an advantage that they used to the fullest.

Repeated Japanese skirmish lines attempted to cross the river. Yelling "Susume!" ("Advance!") and "Banzai!" they kept coming in waves across the grassy space observed by Sergeant Pung. An estimated two enemy companies were attacking. Relying chiefly on the machine guns and automatic weapons, the Marauders cut down wave after, wave. Private First Class George Fisher used his M-1 rifle to pick off stragglers or single targets ignored by the machine guns. Lieutenant Weingartner later remarked, "Those little bastards must think we're amateurs at this jungle fighting stuff. Banzai charges might have terrified the civilians in Singapore, but they're nothing but good, moving target practice for us."[15] Lieutenant Weingartner, who insisted on wearing his lucky nonissue mechanic's cap despite being fined for wearing it at inspections, led his platoon from the front. His cap had gotten him through the fierce New Georgia campaign, and he felt confident that Burma would be no different.

After half an hour of attack, the Japanese became quiet. Enemy artillery opened up on the Americans while the Japanese decided what to do next. The enemy artillery overshot the river positions and instead landed on the dropping field protected by the Khaki Combat Team. The Dead End Kids, as they were called after the popular movie series, cleaned their weapons and waited for the next move by the Japanese. They could hear the enemy digging positions and more trucks arriving. Just as the sun set, shining into the Marauders' faces, the enemy came again. Two heavy machine guns opened a suppressing fire, supported by artillery and mortars. The infamous Japanese knee mortars also chimed in with support. In larger and wider waves the Japanese came again. Two-man teams carried heavy machine guns forward, trying to support the attack. As each team was downed by the Americans' fire, another team rushed forward and again advanced the gun. This time a few reached the American side of the river but were cut down before they could cross the bank. At least a battalion of the enemy was believed to be in the attack. Technician Fifth Class Bernard Strasbaugh was manning a BAR when enemy fire smashed two of his ammunition magazines. Another bullet nicked his helmet. Once, spotting a small group of enemy running to recover a machine gun, he rose suddenly and fired into the group, dropping down just in time to miss the return fire. He was heard to say, "All a guy has to do to get a Purple Heart here is stand up for ten seconds."

Private First Class Clayton E. Hall was manning a machine gun on the right flank. A knee mortar shell burst within three yards of him. Then two bullets pierced the water jacket on his gun. Aided by Cpl. Joseph Diorio, Private First Class Hall managed to keep the gun in action by pouring water into the jacket from every available canteen. He burned his hands on the red-hot jacket while doing it, but his gun fired four thousand rounds in forty-five minutes.

Meanwhile, Major Lew was checking to see what help was available. His men were holding and not asking for assistance, but ammunition was running low, as was water. He was told to hold his position until 1730 hours, when Chinese units would relieve him. With ammunition still at dangerous levels, the Japanese continued to attack. Suddenly, just as the sun went down, the enemy attack ceased as suddenly as it had begun.

Not content to leave well enough alone, one Marauder rose to his feet and shouted across the river, "Come on, you little bastards. Come and get your lead." Fortunately for the Orange Combat Team, the enemy chose to ignore this bit of bravado. There was some question as to just how much lead was left. Instead, the Marauders and the surviving Japanese began shouting insults to each other. Clearly, the crisis was over for the moment.

As full darkness took hold of the battlefield the Americans could hear the enemy removing their dead. As for the Americans, they had suffered only three casualties during the day. Several pack mules had been killed or wounded by enemy artillery and mortar fire. The remaining ammunition was distributed evenly among the combat team, and shortly afterward a resupply was received with the arrival of Major Briggs's Khaki Combat Team. During the battle TSgt. Jim Ballard, chief of the unit's radio section, had tried to contact General Merrill's headquarters for additional ammunition. Unable to get through on the radio, he had run back four miles over trails known to be used by enemy patrols, with a message from Major Lew asking for ammunition. Running through enemy shellfire, he managed to bring back a mule carrying ammunition just as the last enemy attack died away. With signs still clearly indicating that the enemy planned to renew the attack, Sergeant Ballard's efforts were appreciated.

By this time the men were exhausted, all the previous cockiness having left them. Straining in the darkness, they could hear enemy infiltrators coming across the river to booby-trap the trails around them. More enemy could be heard coming up on the other side of the river. Then at 0200 hours came the message to withdraw. Chinese units were coming up to relieve them. As they moved back along the trail, they passed the Chinese coming forward. One formerly cocky Dead End Kid turned to his friend and remarked, "You know, I could almost kiss those guys, they look so good to me now."[16]

While the Orange Combat Team was holding its river bank, north of Walawbum two Japanese soldiers managed to infiltrate the American perimeter at Wesu Ga. They were first seen as they were setting up a machine gun to wipe out the command group of General Merrill near the village. Both were chased off, with indications that one had been seriously wounded. Colonel Hunter led a small group consisting of himself, Colonel Lee, and six 1st Battalion riflemen, to a village a few miles north to meet with Colonel Brown. Instead they found enemy soldiers and immediately became involved in a fire fight. After dispersing the enemy garrison they were attacked by a larger force, estimated at fifty enemy soldiers, and had to take to the woods to escape. Colonel Beach was walking along one trail when an enemy soldier popped out of the jungle, taking aim. Before he could fire, the Colonel's orderly, Pfc. Joseph F. Sweeney, killed the soldier with a shot to the head. Later the same two Marauders—the Colonel—and the private—had another close call, when making a personal reconnaissance of Walawbum. They were within ten yards of an enemy position when they discoverd it, and they retreated before the enemy could react.

Colonel Beach was not the only Marauder field grade officer to have a close call. Major Briggs was leading the Khaki Combat Team forward along trails booby-trapped by the enemy. One booby trap exploded five feet from him and killed Sgt. William F. Hoffman, his radio man. Sergeant Hoffman was blown into the jungle, and his body was not found until the following day.[17]

While the 3d Battalion was occupying the Japanese, the 2d Battalion was chopping its way through the jungle to the Kamaing Road. Without meeting any serious resistance the men reached the road and dug in, throwing up a roadblock as ordered. Along the road they discovered the communications wires of the 18th Division. Technician Fourth Class Roy H. Matsumoto, another nisei member of the Marauders, tapped the telephone line and began to listen to enemy communications. In one instance he overheard an enemy sergeant who was guarding an ammunition dump report that he had only three men armed with rifles to protect the ammunition. He begged for help and advice from his officer, because he knew the 2d Battalion was in his vicinity. By reporting the location of the 2d Battalion in relation to his own position, he gave away his location to Sergeant Matsumoto. With the next supply drop the 2d Battalion requested fighters to terminate the enemy sergeant's problems.

The Japanese also tapped American communications. General Merrill was on the radio when he suddenly heard Japanese voices. Instantly recovering his composure, he began reciting over the radio a Japanese fairy story he had been required to memorize when studying the language a couple of years earlier.[18]

It was on 5 March that the enemy made its major effort to destroy the Americans. Although the Marauders believed that the enemy was attacking only to cover its withdrawal, in reality the 18th Division was following its commander's orders and trying to destroy the American force before turning to face the oncoming Chinese. It was the 2d Battalion that suffered the brunt of the enemy effort. On 5 March it received considerable shelling and six infantry attacks, all of which were turned back with losses to the Americans of one man killed and five wounded. Major Lew, of the Orange Combat Team, had set out ambush positions and placed numerous booby traps along the approach routes to his original position. Seventy-five Japanese fell prey to these prepared positions against a loss to the Americans of one man killed and seven wounded. As evening approached, the attacks slackened, but word came from fighter aircraft that they had strafed and bombed enemy reinforcements moving forward from Kamaing.

General Tanaka had been frustrated by several unanticipated events on 5 March. First, his plan of attack had gone awry when the 55th Regiment had been unable to use its planned line of attack because that trail was being used by Colonel Brown's tanks. As a result, it had to sideslip and found itself following the 56th Regiment, thus cutting the attacking force in half. The 56th Regiment had made little headway against the Marauders without the support of its sister regiment. To further disrupt matters, Colonel Brown's 1st Provisional Tank Group continued to pressure the division's front lines, pushing them back much faster than had been anticipated. Colonel Brown's reconnaissance had located a good trail running south from Tsamat Ga, and the tanks were coming on through the jungle. After the group's engineers had prepared a small stream for crossing, the tanks broke into a freshly evacuated Japanese bivouac area. Slowed by jungle conditions, the tanks nevertheless moved forward. Late in the afternoon of 5 March, the armor broke out on the trail running east and west between Maingkwan and Wesu Ga. The tanks immediately encountered what seemed to be a company of enemy infantry defending a small marshy stream. Colonel Brown did not think his tanks could safely ford the stream and so ordered that they attack by weapons fire only. This they did, scattering the enemy force. Unknown to the Americans, they had fired on and dispersed General Tanaka's divisional headquarters. Not only that, but they had separated the general from his 56th Infantry Regiment.

All these factors combined to convince General Tanaka that he could not continue with his plans to destroy the 5307th Composite Unit (Provisional). Instead he ordered his command to withdraw by swinging around the American flank, avoiding the roadblock by using two Japanese-built roads of which the Americans as yet knew nothing. These roads had been built with the foresight of the division's engineering officer, Colonel Fukayama,[19] who anticipated a withdrawal. One road led west, back to the main road, while the other ran south and then west, back to the main road. In some places the width of these roads allowed up to six files of soldiers to march abreast. Once disengaged, the 18th Division would reestablish its front line across the Kamaing Road. General Tanaka sent his new orders to all his units. Unknowingly, he also sent them to Sergeant Matsumoto. Almost as soon as the Japanese unit commanders received their new orders, so did General Merrill and Colonel Hunter. They also learned that to cover the withdrawal the enemy planned to attack the 2d Battalion at 2300 hours the night of 5 March. Artillery support for that attack was also indicated in the orders.

This presented a problem for the Marauders. The 2d Battalion had used up most of its mortar and machine gun ammunition during the day's battle and had been unable to obtain sufficient resupply. In addition, they had been without food or water for the past thirty-six hours. Colonel McGee discussed the situation with General Merrill by phone. General Merrill, mindful of his admonition from General Stilwell to avoid heavy casualties, ordered Colonel McGee to withdraw his battalion after dark in the direction of Wesu Ga. He was to join Colonel Beach's 3d Battalion east of the Numpyek River. After blocking the road with felled trees and placing booby traps throughout the area, the 2d Battalion withdrew along the trail they had cut two days earlier. Alert to the possibility of enemy booby traps, they placed a mule in advance of their scouts, which saved further losses when the animal was destroyed by explosive traps along the trail. The battalion joined with the 3d Battalion without further incident at noon of 6 March. The very first order of business was an air drop of rations and ammunition.

The withdrawal of the 2d Battalion left the Orange Combat Team the only force commanding the Kamaing Road. The Khaki Combat

Team was withdrawn from its mission of protecting the field at Lagang Ga air strip on the morning of 6 March and was ordered to
join Major Lew. Major Briggs, retaining command despite his
wound, led his men to extend the left flank of the Orange Combat
Team, while General Merrill advanced his headquarters from Wesu
Ga to Lagang Ga to be closer to the scene of the anticipated action.
Japanese artillery and mortar fire fell with regularity on the Orange
Combat Team, presumably as a cover for the withdrawal. Infantry
reinforcements were also observed coming up from Kamaing.
These were taken under fire by the 81mm mortar section.

Shortly before the last attack on the Orange Combat Team, General Merrill had gone to Kasan Ga, where he was pleased to meet
with a Chinese battalion commander, coming in advance of his regiment to relieve the Marauders. Officially the meeting took place at
1600 hours on 6 March between General Merrill and the 113th Regiment, 38th Chinese Division. Merrill now ordered his battalions to
disengage and pull back in preparation for another flanking maneuver. Over the protests of his battalion commanders, who may
not have known of Stilwell's order to conserve manpower, Merrill
formed the battalions for the next assignment.

As the Marauder battalions moved to the assembly area they encountered the relieving Chinese forces. On 7 March units of the
38th Chinese Division unexpectedly came upon unidentified soldiers wearing a strange type of helmet and opened fire. The fire was
immediately returned, and it was not until one of the Chinese in-
terpreters identified the opposing force as American that the battle
ceased. The Chinese had attacked the Red Combat Team. The two
forces joined, and the Americans found that they had wounded a
Chinese major and three enlisted men. Marauder medical personnel treated the wounded, and soldiers from the Red Combat Team
carried them to the air strip for evacuation. There were no American casualties.

Marauder Al Fedder, a member of the Red Combat Team's I&R
platoon, had volunteered to lead the Chinese to the battalion's positions. He had gone ahead to report "to HQ that the Chinese unit
I was sent back to bring forward was approximately one-quarter
mile back with the lead elements crossing the river,"[20] when firing

broke out, announcing the battle between the Chinese and the Marauders. This was one of several instances that would occur during the campaign where friendly forces would fire upon each other.

General Merrill wanted to assemble his forces and circle south to cut the Kamaing Road again farther to the south. He didn't want to waste his men in pitched battles for which the Chinese forces were better suited and equipped. This rapid withdrawal was later interpreted by some Chinese historians as "fleeing" the enemy despite the fact that Merrill had officially been relieved by General Sun. Apparently, some Chinese commanders denigrated the Marauders' performance until they actually arrived at the battlefield and counted over eight hundred enemy dead. General Merrill also released Colonel Brown from attachment and told him to find his own assignment. Brown radioed the NCAC for new orders and while waiting for a response on 7 March tried to get the Chinese 113th Regiment to join him in an attack directly at Walawbum. The Chinese refused, citing orders to secure Wesu Ga. Encountering another Chinese officer, a battalion commander of the 64th Regiment, 22d Division, Brown found a kindred spirit. Having no orders to the contrary, this officer agreed to join Brown in his planned attack. They decided to move down the Kamaing Road and establish a roadblock east of Walawbum.

The attack began at about 1500 hours on 7 March and moved out along the Kamaing Road. Blocks were established at one and two miles, respectively, west of the Nambyu Hka. The infantry set up the roadblocks while the tanks ranged outward from the blocks to the east and west. One tank company moved west along the Kamaing Road and had no luck, encountering a stream that they could not cross. A second company went east until it came to a small bridge covered by Japanese antitank guns. The first tank attempted to force the bridge and was nearly across when the bridge collapsed under it, throwing the vehicle and crew into the stream under enemy fire. Only one crew member survived. A third tank company was more successful. Its commander decided to turn off the road and onto a trail that showed signs of recent heavy traffic. This may have been one of the secret Japanese roads that was used for their withdrawal. The tanks encountered a large group of Japanese infantry and opened fire. Two weeks later, Allied troops discovered a mass grave of some two hundred Japanese soldiers in the area.

At 1845 on the evening of 7 March General Merrill held a staff meeting to advise the officers that the first phase of the Marauder operation had ended. He conveyed to the group General Stilwell's congratulations for a job well done and requested the officers to relay the message to their men. A three-day rest period was now in order.

During the rest period the men of the 5307th Composite Unit (Provisional) cleaned and overhauled their equipment, made out the usual reports, repaired or replaced damaged equipment, exchanged rations and souvenirs with nearby Chinese troops, and generally rested. In the five days of battle between 3 March and 7 March they had killed 800 of the enemy against a loss of 8 of their own killed and 37 wounded. In addition, they had lost 19 men evacuated with malaria, 8 with various fevers, mostly dengue, 10 with psychoneurosis, and 33 with injuries. Miscellaneous sickness losses added another 109 to the total men lost to the unit. Of the 2,750 men who had started out for Walawbum, some 2,500 remained to carry on. Against this they had cooperated with Chinese forces to advance the Allied lines by dozens of miles and had forced a major Japanese withdrawal.

Although the men were out of contact with the enemy, casualties continued to occur. Private First Class Carter Pietsch was resting at the edge of a drop field when a box of mortar ammunition separated from its parachute and killed him instantly. Staff Sergeant John Zokosky of the Orange Combat Team was cleaning his rifle when another soldier across from him, also cleaning his rifle, accidently fired, hitting him. Sergeant Murray P. Clayton of the headquarters company, Khaki Combat Team, was loading a 60mm mortar when the explosive charge exploded prematurely, killing him. There were also cases of friendly fire, as when Pfc. Raymond L. Braaten led his patrol of the Khaki Combat Team's I&R platoon out of thick jungle and into a clearing. Another nearby American patrol fired, hitting Private First Class Braaten.

Medical arrangements had developed in accordance with needs and conditions encountered in the battle. Casualties were evacuated from the emergency field at Taipha Ga by the 803d Medical Air Evacuation Squadron. About 135 evacuees were delivered by this method to either the 20th General or the 73d Evacuation Hospital near Ledo. The 13th Mountain Medical Battalion relieved the Marauder medical detachments at the forward sites as early as possible, and one of its surgical teams had accompanied the 1st Battalion. In the larger rear-area fields the 151st Medical Battalion assumed responsibility for processing the evacuees. The battalion had a ward tent and facilities for an average patient census of 30, first-aid supplies for a divisional emergency, trucks and ambulances for transport, and related housekeeping equipment.[21] It was not unusual for Col. Vernon W. Peterson, the northern combat area command surgeon, to drop in at a clearing company installation and ask for a medical team to accompany a specific unit about to embark on a combat operation. So detachments from both the 13th and 151st Medical Battalions often accompanied Marauder battalions without formally being attached to them.

Not all evacuations were successful. Lieutenant Weston recalls the story of one of his wounded from the Walawbum fight, described earlier.

Pete Leitner, an Indian from Florida and one of my scouts, had only partially completed his slit trench and was out in front of his position, gathering camouflage material. It was very early in the morning, and the very first shot that was fired by an enemy sniper hit him in the abdomen. Pete slumped helplessly about 35 ft. in front of his slit trench position. I think it was Sgt Mathis, crawled out and helped me drag Pete back inside the platoon position where he could be placed undercover in a safe position. Gomez, the aid man, then rendered first aid. We did lose Pete, however, during the evacuation process at Lagang Ga when the plane that came in to evacuate him crashed.[22]

Here also occurred the first evidence of the earlier fears of the medical staff of the Marauders concerning the men of the 3d Battalion. Sergeant Ed King was the platoon sergeant of the I&R pla-

toon of the Khaki Combat Team. He had volunteered from the 43d
Infantry Division, which had just fought in the New Georgia campaign. By the end of the Walawbum fight King weighed only 118
pounds. He was declared unfit for combat and sent off to the hospital, never to return.[23]

General Merrill planned his next operation during the rest period. On 9 March he sent Colonel Hunter by L-4 liaison plane to
General Stilwell's headquarters to confer with Col. Joseph Cannon,
acting chief of staff during General Boatner's absence. Merrill's
plans received criticism regarding the proposed routes of advance,
with the objection being made that there were no known areas to
receive an air drop. Colonel Hunter replied that his own intelligence officers had located suitable areas along the route. General
Stilwell appeared to be unconvinced, remarking that he knew of no
such areas. Colonel Hunter was left alone to eat a K ration he had
brought along, after which the conference reconvened. Grudging
approval was given to the plan, with General Stilwell commenting
that he had confidence in Merrill. Colonel Hunter also left with the
impression that Stilwell felt that Merrill had misunderstood his orders to conserve manpower when he pulled out of Walawbum. Apparently he had planned to use Galahad, the Chinese, and Colonel
Rothwell's tanks for a direct assault on General Tanaka.[24]

One of the reasons that General Merrill had withdrawn upon the
arrival of the Chinese was the alarming rise in illness among the Marauders. Colonel Hunter and many others blamed this directly on
close association with Chinese military units. Although the Chinese
themselves were strict about boiling all their drinking water and eat-
ing only cooked food, their sanitation was not even close to American standards, despite American training. They ignored the rudi-
ments of field sanitation and caused the Americans, who relied on
halazone tablets to purify their drinking and cooking water, to become susceptible to various illnesses, particularly amebic dysentery.
Only those few Americans, like Colonel Hunter, who boiled all the
water they drank, avoided this illness. For the average American rifleman, boiling drinking water was a luxury he could not find the
time to enjoy. The initial effects of this problem were first felt at
Walawbum.

Another factor was the American diet. Jack Girsham, a native of
the area, soon fell sick along with his American comrades. He
recorded later, "I was quite sick by then, not being used to a diet of
K rations." General Merrill was concerned as he relied heavily on
Girsham's knowledge of the terrain, and so he ordered a special
food drop for the Britisher and his four native Kachin guides. Girsham noted:

> Food is all important in the Jungle. The American soldiers
> didn't understand it at first. They watched the Kachin scouts
> and me picking mushrooms or tender bamboo shoots and
> catching the fish we poisoned in the streams with roots and
> bark, and remained puzzled until they tried our diet. Then the
> Americans would eat rice and the stuff we ate whenever they
> could. They agreed with us that K rations were too light for the
> rigors of jungle warfare.[25]

For all his earlier optimism, General Tanaka had been forced to
withdraw earlier than anticipated. His division, code-named Kiku
"chrysanthemum" had been ordered to send one of its regiments,
the 114th Infantry, north to aid a sister division facing the Chinese,
and originally only Colonel Nagahisa's 56th Infantry Regiment was
to defend the Hukawng Valley (known as the Valley of Death). Now,
although he had sent another regiment to support Colonel Nagahisa, the division's flank had been turned. Enraged by the defeat,
General Tanaka requested permission to attack directly at General
Stilwell's headquarters, known to be at Shingbwiyang, to inflict a
telling defeat and regain the entire area of North Burma. Permission was denied. The Japanese command was more concerned with
the British Chindit offensive and events at Imphal and Kohima.
There the bulk of the Japanese forces were engaged against General Slim's British XIV Army, and things were not going well. Instead, General Tanaka was ordered to defend the area around Kamaing, a major supply and communications center supporting the
main attack against the British. He was about to find even that task
more difficult than expected.

4. Second Mission: Shaduzup

The Pacific war was characterized by a lull in operations on both sides in 1943. This lull was the result of the Japanese forces needing time to assess their goals while restructuring their resources. The Americans and their allies also needed to reorganize their forces and move them to the decisive areas of future combat. As 1944 dawned, that hiatus ended abruptly with the American navy's seizure of the Marshall Islands, the southwest Pacific theaters attack at Saidor, and the renewal of the campaign in Burma.

The Japanese had planned to create an "absolute national defense sphere," which, after being seized from the Allies, would be held to protect the homeland from attack while providing the vital raw materials necessary for continuing the war. Burma, with its oil, tungsten, and large annual rice harvest was included within this original vital sphere. India had never been mentioned as being vital to the defensive scheme contemplated by Japan. Once Japan had successfully seized Burma, however, the problem of its defense arose. Clearly the main attack would come from India, the British stronghold on the continent. Even acknowledging this inevitability, the Japanese commanders never envisioned an invasion. Rather, they saw an active defense that would include seizures of border areas of India as room for maneuvers and for keeping attackers out of Burma itself. The Japanese felt that rather than defending the long line of the India-Burma border along the Chindwin River, it would be more advantageous to them to seize the key mountains of Assam in and around the towns of Kohima to the north and Imphal to the west. By taking and holding those areas the Japanese could channel any counterattack along mountain passes, which they could easily control with a minimum of forces committed to the defense. The capture of Imphal would also provide them with all-weather airfields and supplies hoarded there by the British. It would further cut General Stilwell's supply lines and, they hoped, render powerless his Chinese-American counterattack from the north. General Mutaguchi, commanding the 15th Army, was particularly interested in the campaign, seeking more glory for his name, which had first become known at the Marco Polo Bridge incident, where he had been the local Japanese commander on the scene. Supported by Tokyo, which after defeats at Midway, Guadalcanal, and New Guinea sought a victory to restore its prestige and the people's morale, the plan to seize the two localities was approved.

The Japanese were taking great risks with this attack. The Japanese army was well known for its ability to operate on a logistics scale that other armies would consider unacceptable for their own operations. In the case of the Imphal-Kohima attack, those risks were taken to the extreme. Japanese supply lines in Burma were already stretched to the limits by even Japanese standards. They were attacking in an area that General Slim, commanding the British XIV Army, on which the attack would fall, described as "some of the world's worst country, breeding the world's worst diseases, and having for half the year at least the world's worst climate." In addition, the British intelligence service, led in India by future noted spy-novel author Maj. Ian Fleming, was planting misinformation with Japanese intelligence-gathering sources.[1] Ignoring the risks, the Japanese attacked into India, a land covered, like Burma, with snakes, leeches, mosquitoes, malaria, scrub typhus, and amebic dysentery. They had conquered these things in Burma and saw no reason why they could not do so in India. This time, however, the British and Commonwealth forces of the XIV Army were prepared, trained, and equipped to fight the Japanese on their own terms. And behind their own lines, British, American, and Chinese forces were about to wreak havoc on the essential supply lines that the Japanese command acknowledged were already stretched to the limits.

Not all the Japanese officers were confident of the success of the Imphal-Kohima attack. General Mutaguchi fired his own chief of staff for declaring that he could not supply even one division in the attack, much less the four that planned to participate. His replacement trained fifteen thousand cows for use as pack animals and as emergency rations, should the need arise. General Mutaguchi ordered the attack to be launched in March, knowing that the monsoon was only weeks away. He intended to present Imphal to the emperor for his birthday on 29 April. For his soldiers Mutaguchi issued orders that the army's prostitutes and geishas would fly into Imphal ten days after the attack to reward his successful troops. He would have been pleased to hear General Slim's remark in his memoirs that "when the Japanese struck I am ashamed to say it was a surprise." Yet General Slim had a surprise for General Mutaguchi as well. Although the timing was a surprise, the attack was expected, and General Slim had withdrawn most of his outlying units to the base at Imphal, precisely the enemy objective.[2]

March 1944 was a busy month in the British as well as the Japanese camps. General Wingate had been allocated several long-range penetration brigades for another sortie behind Japanese lines. Despite a few scares about security breaches just prior to the landings, and at the insistence of General Slim, whose XIV Army was already seeing signs of the coming battle at Imphal, the landings went almost as scheduled. More than nine thousand commonwealth soldiers, two troops of artillery, and over fourteen hundred mules had landed behind the enemy at several separate locations. Another three thousand British troops marched in, as did Galahad. Gliders accompanying the landings carried bulldozers, and by nightfall, landings could be made on some of the protected areas. These gliders brought in supplies and artillery pieces, as well as antiaircraft weapons. Wingate himself flew in to one of the landing zones for an inspection. The Japanese, concentrating on their own attack on India, were taken completely by surprise. Although they had known of the possibility of a renewed Wingate operation, they had never considered that its scope, size, and power would be anything like what landed behind their lines in March 1944.

While the British long-range penetration groups, known as Chindits, were setting up bases behind the enemy lines and harassing its communications, Galahad was about to embark on its second mission. Between 7 and 10 March the Marauders rested and replenished their equipment. The advance to Walawbum had given General Stilwell control of the Hukawng Valley. The next mission would seize the next valley, the Moguang. On 10 March General Merrill received approval of the plan from General Stilwell's NCAC headquarters outlining the next phase of operations. Basically, it was an extension of the operation just concluded at Walawbum. Again the Marauders were to move around Japanese defenses along the Kamaing Road and move fifteen to twenty miles behind the main line of enemy resistance. They were to cut supply lines and communications and generally harass enemy rear areas until they reached the next area selected for trail blocks. This time they would be accompanied by two regiments of the Chinese 38th Division. These troops were to follow in the trace of the Americans and to take over the blocks once they had been firmly established.

For the second mission the 5307th would be divided into two groups. Colonel Osborne's 1st Battalion, followed by the 113th Chinese Regiment a day behind, would march the fifty miles to Shaduzup, an original objective. The 2d and 3d Battalions, under Colonel Hunter, were to make a wider movement and strike the road at Inkangahtawng, south of Shaduzup, a march of eighty miles. They would be followed by the 112th Chinese Regiment about one day behind. The march was expected to take about two weeks to complete.

With the Japanese having committed their main effort to the seizure of Imphal and Kohima, General Stilwell hoped that even if a full encirclement of the 18th Japanese Division could not be accomplished, it would be forced to withdraw, thus upsetting enemy rear areas and affecting the main attack on the XIV Army. Generals Merrill and Sun conferred and once again objected to the arrangements that failed to put all units concerned under one commander. Once again American and Chinese units, working and depending on one another for a successful operation, would not be under a single command. General Merrill later recorded that General Sun had offered to place his units under Merrill's command. He sent Colonel Hunter to the NCAC to propose that General Sun's offer be accepted. Colonel Hunter was also to propose that instead of two separate operations, the entire American contingent and the attachments from the Chinese forces be used to set up one trail block at Shaduzup. The proposal also called for a wider movement, to ensure secrecy. As before, the 22d Chinese Division and the 1st Provisional Tank Group would fight along the road, driving the enemy into the trail block.

General Stilwell accepted the wider envelopment but insisted on two trail blocks, which meant that the unit would have to be divided. The American and Chinese forces would continue to "cooperate" with each other, rather than operate under joint command. This latter restriction can only have been the result of the constant reluctance of the Chinese government to give operational command of any of its forces to a foreign officer.

Another problem plagued the second mission, although it was unknown to the soldiers of Galahad. The intelligence about the enemy was extremely limited, and that limited amount was often incorrect. Even General Merrill, who had close ties to the NCAC, was unaware that they were advancing into an area well covered by OSS Detachment 101. This unit could have provided both accurate and timely details of enemy dispositions, thus allowing a more knowledgeable scheme of maneuver to be planned. The lower Hukawng Valley was well covered by a detachment of Kachin Ranger irregulars under the command of 1st Lt. James L. Tilly. Yet there was no coordination between the two forces, both technically under American command, operating in the same area.

Lieutenant Tilly had arrived at Detachment 101 in August 1943. Recruited from ski troops in Colorado, the soon-to-be-famous 10th (Mountain) Infantry Division, he was trained and with typical army logic was sent to an area as far away from ski slopes as possible. At his first interview with Col. Carl W. Eifler, the detachment commander, Tilly was taken aback when Eifler told him to cut out the usual army formal reporting routine and just tell him what he could do. Lieutenant Tilly blurted out that among other things, he could fly. Next thing he knew, he was designated as a pilot of a light observation aircraft that the detachment relied on for all sorts of missions, "notwithstanding the fact I was color-blind and not qualified by the Army to fly."[3] Soon he was assigned to command a detachment of Kachin Rangers in the area around Walawbum. By the time the Marauders arrived, Lieutenant Tilly was an experienced guerrilla leader, wearing wraparound blue Kachin longyi pants and a GI khaki shirt. During the Walawbum campaign he had led his group along the flanks of the Marauders and later claimed that his Kachins had killed an estimated 150 Japanese, blown up several supply dumps, and destroyed several Japanese trucks, all without a single casualty. As the Japanese withdrew after failing to dislodge the Marauders at Walawabum, the Kachins ambushed the columns, destroyed reinforcement attempts, and generally raised havoc along the Japanese lines of communications. Yet as they started out on the second mission, there was no direct communication between Lieutenant Tilly's force and the Marauders.

Yet another problem arose. Generalissimo Chiang Kai-shek was alarmed over the Japanese attack on India. Ever sensitive to his supply lines, he feared that a successful attack could cut off his supplies permanently, leaving China stranded. This in fact was one objective of General Mutaguchi. Messages were sent to General Stilwell, suggesting that the advance be halted, or slowed, or placed in a defensive position to await the outcome of the attack on Imphal. General Stilwell, knowing more of the situation than the generalissimo and in any event not disposed to await another force's success before committing his own, chose to ignore the suggestions, which fortunately were not framed as direct orders. As a precaution, however, General Stilwell advised General Marshall in Washington of the concerns and asked that pressure from Washington be put forward to convince the generalissimo to allow the operation to proceed unhindered. In his messages he also asked for another Chinese division to be sent from China as well as a second American long-range penetration group.

Problems mounted for the Japanese as well. General Tanaka's withdrawal from Walawbum had given him less territory in which to maneuver. He had to prevent, at all costs, the Allied forces attacking him from reaching the Irrawaddy valley. Once there, the superior forces could use the railroad to advance rapidly, pushing his meager forces back without the possibility of holding a position in northern Burma. With his defense centered on Kamaing, he had to hold that position to prevent an Allied victory. Time and space factors were about to cause General Tanaka to stand and fight.

At 0700 hours on 12 March 1944 the 1st Battalion began its march to Shaduzup. Followed by the 113th Chinese Regiment and 6th Pack Artillery Battery at a one-day distance behind, the march covered twenty miles in the first two days. Although the march was uneventful, there was growing concern about the several rainstorms that hit the marching column, forecasting an early monsoon season. Another difficulty was the higher mountains that the troops now had to cross. Whereas paths previously had followed streams that in turn had followed the path of least resistance across the low hills, the tendency now was for the paths to avoid the streams and simply climb one hill after another in a direct line. Soon the 1st Battalion found itself climbing hills two thousand feet and higher.

The hills and rains were not the only difficulties encountered on the second day. Lieutenant Wilson's I&R platoon was leading the advance of Maj. Caifson Johnson's White Combat Team when they came across the tracks of a Japanese reconnaissance party that had reached that point in the trail before turning back. For the next two hours the platoon followed the tracks, which became fresher every moment. Each bend in the trail could be an ambush. Finally, lead scout John Sukup turned out of sight around a bend in the trail and immediately the men heard the sound of a Thompson submachine gun firing full automatic. Lieutenant Wilson crawled forward and found the scout unhurt. He explained that as he turned the corner he noticed an Asian soldier immediately in front of him. Seeing Private First Class Sukup, the soldier reached for his rifle, whereupon the American opened fire. The Asian soldier had dived into the jungle and disappeared.

Lieutenant Wilson could hear the sounds of men farther along the trail. Mindful of the recent incidents of misidentification in which Chinese forces had been mistaken for the enemy, he asked a Chinese soldier attached to his platoon to call out to see if the troops in the distance were friendly. The Chinese soldier called out several times, getting unintelligible shouts back in reply. Convinced that the troops facing him were not Chinese, Lieutenant Wilson gave the order to open fire. Within seconds the platoon was engaged in a fierce fire fight. Finding themselves outgunned and outnumbered, the Americans quickly melted into the jungle alongside the trail and withdrew. They soon encountered Lt. William C. Evans's I&R platoon of Maj. Edward M. Ghiz's Red Combat Team. Lieutenant Evans sent back a report of the situation to the White Combat Team. Major Johnson sent two rifle platoons down the trail to push the enemy forces back. The platoons succeeded in pushing the Japanese across a stream and out of the path of the battalion, but not before the platoon under Lt. John P. McElmurray lost its first man, killed in action. Once across the stream, Lieutenant McElmurray's platoon seized some high ground overlooking the crossing. They held it against an enemy attack so that the rest of the battalion was able to cross in safety.

The Japanese were now alerted to the battalion's presence on the trail. The next day, 15 March, Lieutenant Evans's platoon, now leading the advance, had to fight eight separate skirmishes with enemy parties over the first one and a half miles of trail. As the advance continued, more and more enemy troops joined the defense, bringing heavier weapons with them. The enemy set up leapfrog machine-gun ambush positions. These would pin down the leading squad along the trail with machine guns, and then mortars would pound any attempt at reinforcement. The Marauders countered by getting their mortars in action against the enemy machine guns and sending an enveloping force into the jungle to outflank the position holding up the advance. As soon as the Japanese detected this movement they would withdraw back up the trail for a few hundred yards and start the delaying process all over again. So dense was the jungle that two men ten yards apart often could not see each other.

What the Marauders would not find out until much later was that the Japanese force opposing them was itself fighting its way up the trail. Lieutenant Tilly and his Kachin Rangers, known as the Knothead Group, were behind the Japanese and were using the same tactics against them that the Japanese were using on the Marauders. Unfortunately, there was still no coordination between the two groups, so while the Japanese troops may have been convinced that they were the victims of a carefully staged envelopment, neither of the two American forces were immediately aware of each other. Indeed, so concerned was Colonel Osborne that he ordered the Red Combat Team to keep the Japanese occupied pushing along the enemy-controlled trail while the rest of the battalion would cut its own trail, thus avoiding the delays on the trail controlled by the enemy. Concerned about his timetable, Colonel Osborne decided to risk the fatigue and danger of cutting his own trail rather than be delayed indefinitely by the enemy force holding the trail ahead of his battalion. Major Ghiz was ordered to occupy the enemy on the trail for several hours and then backtrack to rejoin the battalion as soon as possible. The Chinese 113th Regiment had caught up with the battalion because of the delays imposed by the enemy defense of the trail, and it too would follow the battalion into the jungle.

The White Combat Team plunged into the jungle, hacking every inch of the way. Officers took their turns at the head of the column, doing the exhausting work of clearing a path. Hills were now so steep that a climbing soldier could easily lose his footing. Mules had to be unloaded and the loads carried up by hand. When not at the head of the column slashing a path forward, the men waited, trapped in the thick jungle. Dysentery was now prevalent in the column. Uniforms were blotched with dried blood from leech bites. For the next two days the 1st Battalion hacked and chopped its way through the jungle, arriving at the village of Kumshan Ga on the afternoon of 17 March, only four miles from where they had left the trail.

By the time the battalion arrived they were exhausted and starving. A supply drop was quickly called for and a drop zone prepared. Even this practiced procedure had difficulties, for by the time the transport aircraft located the drop zone they had too little fuel to make the necessary runs for the drop. They advised the Marauders that they would return in the morning and make the drop then. During the night and early morning hours the drop zone was widened, and the drop was successfully made on the morning of 18 March. Some of the free-dropped supplies, mostly grain for the animals, was lost because the surrounding mountains forced the transports to drop from a higher altitude than usual. Some parachuted supplies floated wide of the drop zone, but searching Marauders located them all and returned them to the distribution point.

As soon as the supplies were distributed and packed for travel the battalion moved out hurriedly to make up the lost time. By that evening they had reached a point just northwest of Jaiwa Ga. There they made contact with fifty Kachin Rangers under Lieutenant Tilly and learned the story of the other battle of the trail. Lieutenant Ogburn recorded the meeting. "We heard him coming a long way off as a faint voice from down the trail. 'Hey, Yank, don't shoot.'" Repeating this call until recognized, he came into camp with his Kachin Rangers. Lieutenant Ogburn recalled Tilly's appearance as "unexpected," a comment on the lack of coordination between units in the NCAC from a signals officer who saw every transmission, and he noted "his innocent-looking cutthroats under their

Aussie hats with the broad brims turned up rakishly on the side . . ."
Lieutenant Tilly was, as usual, clothed informally in "a nondescript
khaki shirt and a pair of curious, wraparound, blue, calf-length
trousers." Colonel Osborne received the lieutenant with a formal
military welcome and then put him and his detachment to work
scouting for the battalion.

While the White Combat Team struggled to bypass the enemy,
which was holding them up on the trail, the Red Combat Team continued to struggle along the trail to keep the enemy force busy.
They were to hold the enemy's attention until the White Combat
Team had cleared the trail and cut its way behind the enemy. Lieutenant William Lepore's platoon had the lead and was well in advance of the combat team. It was closely engaged and pinned down
as the rest of the command was about to withdraw. Several wounded
had been passed back from Lieutenant Lepore's platoon, and the
sight of these wounded had apparently unnerved the unit's commanding officer, who decided that he could not relieve the platoon
and that they would have to be left behind. He had already given
the command to disengage when Lieutenant Wilson demanded
that they make an attempt to rescue the trapped platoon. After a fu-
tile argument Lieutenant Wilson took matters into his own hands
and together with another officer took a radio and made his way to
the trapped platoon. Together the three officers called in mortars
from the combat team's weapons platoon and placed a high explosive shield between Lieutenant Lepore's platoon and the enemy.
With several volunteers, the officers brought out the dead and
wounded, covered by the mortar barrage and the rest of the platoon. Two men had been killed and several others seriously
wounded. While the rest of the combat team continued to pull
back, the platoon buried its dead in hastily dug graves. The two lieutenants said a brief burial service while behind them the Japanese
mortared the position formerly held by the now departing platoon.
By the time they left they were the only Americans still in the area.
Several days later the combat team commander was relieved of command and replaced by Capt. Tom P. Senff.[4]

The 1st Battalion moved off as soon as possible after being resupplied. As it continued to struggle toward Shaduzup, its objective,
it was often out of communication with General Merrill's head-

quarters. Colonel Osborne was concerned about this, but the mountains and jungles often hindered communications. As the battalion marched along, a light plane suddenly appeared over the area, obviously looking for the column. Lieutenant Ogburn moved out into a nearby clearing and flagged down the passing plane, which dropped a message sleeve. As Lieutenant Ogburn later described the message, "It inquired acidly when we were going to conclude our scenic tour of northern Burma and get to Shaduzup." Colonel Osburne halted the column and composed an immediate reply for transmission to headquarters. "It pointed out that we had fought thirteen actions since jumping off, and in the language was a restrained implication that if the addressees did not like the way we were fighting the war they could come fight it themselves." While the NCAC did not reply, General Merrill quickly sent the battalion a message asking if theirs was a private war or could others join in.

The Americans also learned how to work with the Kachins during that march. As the column neared the village of Mprawa on 20 March the lead American scouts were moving along the trail accompanied by Kachin guides. Suddenly the normally quiet Kachins became talkative, but none of the Americans could understand them. Familiar with the natives of India who often chatted away while begging for food or cigarettes, the Marauder scouts dismissed the jabbering as unimportant. In fact, the Kachins were reporting that an enemy machine-gun position lay just ahead, and the gestures for food and cigarettes were their way of acquiring the normal rewards they were used to receiving for such information. Unfortunately, the scouts walked into an enemy ambush, which resulted in one dead and two wounded. American mortar fire broke up the ambush, and from that point forward every Kachin conversation was interpreted.[5]

The day after the tragic misunderstanding between the scouts and the Kachin Rangers, the 1st Battalion took another resupply drop, which provided them with five days of supplies. The Red Combat Team led the battalion forward from the drop zone and cleared the village of Hpauchye Ga. Leaving the village, the advance platoon, under Lt. Harry B. Coburn, was ambushed along the trail. Failing to push their way along the trail, Lieutenant Coburn's platoon moved off into the jungle to outflank the enemy. While cutting a bypass trail through the jungle the scouts noticed a group of enemy soldiers lounging around well-made foxholes. Crawling up onto the unsuspecting enemy, the Marauders opened fire, killing seven enemy soldiers. They then moved into the enemy positions for a brief rest. While resting in the enemy foxholes a larger enemy force suddenly appeared and attacked, reversing the positions of a few moments ago. So well placed were the enemy positions now used by the Marauder platoon that they were easily able to break up the attack and inflict additional casualties on the enemy.

All this enemy activity again convinced Colonel Osborne that his best course was to once again leave the trail and cut his own trail through the jungle. Selecting a course from Hpauchye Ga toward the Chengun River, the battalion began again the onerous task of cutting a trail through impassable jungle. Again mules and horses had to be unloaded and the supplies hand carried up steep hillsides. For two days, 23 and 24 March, the battalion hacked a trail five miles long through the jungle. Colonel Osborne's decision did ensure that no Japanese were encountered and that the secrecy of the approach was preserved.

Colonel Osborne next prepared to strike at Shaduzup. He consulted with Capt. Charles E. Darlington, of the British army, who had joined from local guerrilla forces, and with Lieutenant Tilly, as to the best approach to the objective. Lieutenant Tilly reported three hundred enemy soldiers at Shaduzup with another five or six hundred in the general area. Discussing terrain advantages with the two guerrilla officers, Colonel Osborne decided to strike at a place where the road and stream were closest, much the same as had been done earlier at Walawbum. Lieutenant McElmurray's platoon was sent off to create a distraction, a mission they accomplished the next day by ambushing an enemy reconnaissance party carrying maps and surveying equipment. In accordance with Colonel Osborne's intentions, Lieutenant McElmurray allowed a few survivors to escape and spread the alarm. Sure enough, a few moments later, enemy mortars began dropping into the area that Lieutenant McElmurray and his platoon were already leaving. Led by Kachin guides, the rest of the battalion had proceeded in a different direction and had soon sighted the Kamaing Road near Shaduzup.

The 1st Battalion established the trail block about four miles south of Shaduzup. There the Mogaung River makes a U-shaped bend at the confluence with the Chengun River. The road there runs parallel to the river, thus giving the Americans the advantage of controlling all access. After resting on the night of 24 March the battalion used the river to approach its objective. Coming within a mile of the planned location, the advance platoon reported that they could see enemy soldiers bathing in the river while others used grenades to catch fish. They also identified an enemy camp between the Mogaung River and the Kamaing Road. Scouts soon reported that there was at least an enemy infantry company at the camp and that they could see what appeared to be a larger camp off to the south. Quantities of food and other supplies were also identified by the scouts.

Convinced that the enemy was unaware of its battalion's presence, Colonel Osborne planned a surprise attack for the early morning of 28 March. He divided his command into six columns that would cross the river at three selected points, after which they would converge upon the northern Japanese camp. The first three columns would directly attack the northern camp, while the three following columns would support that attack if it was necessary, would be kept in reserve to set up a swift defense, or would deter an enemy attack from the southern camp. Major Johnson's White Combat Team would form the leading three columns, while the Red Combat Team provided the follow-up forces. The 113th Chinese Regiment would be held in reserve on the friendly side of the Mogaung River. Until the time for the attack the Marauders tried to get some sleep. During the rest period in the dark hours of the night 2d Lt. Philip S. Weld was awakened by the sound of truck motors. He soon identified them as passing along the Kamaing Road, just across the river. The Marauders got little sleep after that.

At 0300 hours on 28 March the leading columns of the 1st Battalion waded across the Mogaung River. Lieutenant Weld led his platoon into the water, noting as he went that the current pressed his pants against his legs. As the water rose higher it seemed to get colder, and by midstream it had reached the waist of the average soldier. Lieutenant Weld, who was taller than most of the men in his platoon, became concerned about the depth of the water and was about to look for a more shallow passage when the water began to drop and the far bank came into sight. He sent back word that the river was fordable. Seconds later, Major Johnson appeared, leading the rest of the combat team. Major Johnson sent Lieutenant Weld's platoon to cover the right flank while the combat team continued crossing. They found not a single sentry in position. As they crept into position for the attack they could see enemy soldiers starting small campfires for their breakfast. Dawn broke and the order to attack came over the radio. Swiftly the four hundred attackers swept across the camp with fixed bayonets. Enemy troops, many naked or half-dressed, panicked at the completely unexpected attack and scattered in all directions. The few who managed to get their weapons into action fired wildly and were quickly killed.

The leading platoon, under Lt. Meredith Caldwell Jr., reached the Kamaing Road and immediately dug a perimeter to establish the trail block. Lieutenant Caldwell later recalled that when one of his men announced seeing the road, the lieutenant deliberately placed himself on the road south of the soldier so that he could say to himself, "Meredith, you are the furthest man down the Ledo Road."[6]

Having completed their immediate assignment, the Americans placed a minimum guard and proceeded to change into the clean underwear found in a captured enemy truck. Once dressed, they sat down to devour the rice and fish the enemy had left cooking over the abandoned fires. Lieutenant Caldwell noted that some of the rice they salvaged from the truck was purple. One of the battalion's nisei explained that it was in celebration of a Japanese holiday. The Americans swiftly finished their meal. They knew that the enemy would not let the position go without more of a fight.

Lieutenant Weld's platoon had to cross the river twice more before they could reach their assigned position. As they approached it they could see enemy soldiers running toward the sounds of firing that had already broken out from the main camp. Taking position on a small knoll overlooking the road with a few men, Lieutenant Weld soon found himself caught in a crossfire of enemy machine guns. One of his men was wounded. After knocking out several enemy soldiers the group had to race across an open area and back to the river for safety, while Lieutenant Weld carried the wounded man. The enemy fire was too accurate for the lieutenant to race across as

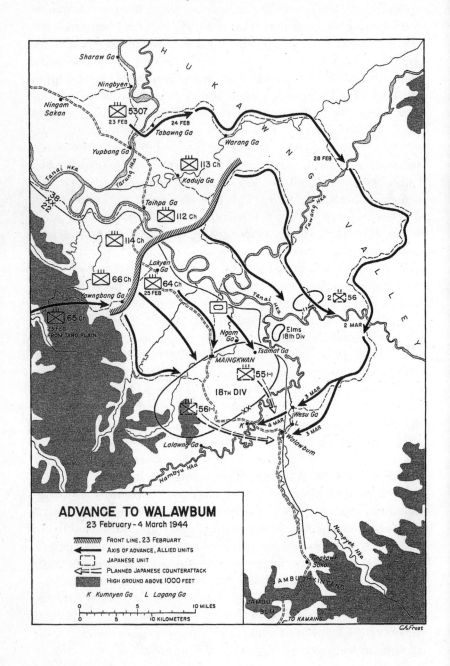

ADVANCE TO WALAWBUM
23 February – 4 March 1944

▨▨▨▨▨	FRONT LINE, 23 FEBRUARY
⬛⬅	AXIS OF ADVANCE, ALLIED UNITS
⬚	JAPANESE UNIT
⬅	PLANNED JAPANESE COUNTERATTACK
⬛	HIGH GROUND ABOVE 1000 FEET

K Kumnyen Ga   L Lagang Ga

0   5   10 MILES
0   5   10 KILOMETERS

C.L.Frost

his men had done, so he crawled, with the wounded man holding on to his legs. His platoon placed mortar and rifle fire on the enemy position, and once the enemy was diverted the lieutenant raised the wounded man to his back and ran the remaining distance to safety. After taking a few breaths he was informed that there were three more wounded out in the field. They had attempted to join the advance force but had been cut down before they could reach the knoll. With two volunteers Lieutenant Weld twice raced out into the field, each time bringing in a wounded man. The third wounded soldier had managed to reach safety on his own.

By 0700 hours signs that the enemy was about to counterattack were plain. Enemy snipers were active and harassed the Americans as they continued to dig defensive positions. Two hours later, Japanese artillery fire hit the Red Combat Team across the river. This came as a surprise to the Marauders, as neither the scouts nor the Kachins had reported the presence of enemy artillery. The White Combat Team's position was masked by a rise in ground, and therefore the enemy artillery did little damage to their positions. The Japanese noted this and placed a second battery in position to reach the combat team, which also came under artillery fire from 77mm and 150mm enemy shells at about 1000 hours. At noon the first enemy ground attack was received and turned back, with heavy losses to the Japanese. At 1300 another attack struck, this time with artillery support, while the Marauders could see enemy reinforcements arriving in trucks behind the attacking forces. Enough time had elapsed, however, to allow the Americans to dig strong defensive positions. The enemy continued to attack from various quarters throughout the day without success.

Enemy tactics mystified the Americans. Lieutenant McElmurray and Lt. Charles R. Scott were sharing a foxhole on the front lines when they both noticed an enemy officer leading an attack and waving a sword. Lieutenant Scott fired first and downed the enemy officer. During the next half hour the two American officers killed twelve enemy soldiers who attempted to recover the body. As darkness fell, the enemy ground attacks ceased but the artillery fire continued against both combat teams. Without artillery of their own, the Marauders could do nothing to stop it. Instead, they concentrated on dealing with enemy infiltration attempts in the darkness, which they handled with mortars or grenades.

Private First Class Herman Manual, a Navajo from Arizona, had also figured out a way to harass the enemy without being discovered. He waited at his mortar tube with a shell poised over the tube. As an enemy shell exploded behind the Americans he would drop the shell into the tube, thus masking the location of his mortar. Finally, a supply drop received on the battlefield also brought a brief respite when the transport's fighter escorts strafed the enemy positions to allow the drop, thus silencing the enemy artillery for a time. It was also during this shelling that one of the enduring legends of the Marauders occurred. According to Lieutenant Ogburn, at a time when the shelling was particularly fierce there was a brief lull during which "a voice of exasperation was heard in the darkness, controlled but distinct. 'Where the hell are the other five thousand, three hundred and six composite units?'"[7]

The second appearance of the American long-range penetration group behind his lines had given General Tanaka serious cause for concern. Pressured by the 22d Chinese Division, he now had a strong enemy force on his essential lines of communication and supply. He immediately directed forces facing the Chinese to withdraw and face the Americans. These were the reinforcements that the Marauders observed arriving by trucks during the counterattacks of 28 March. This diversion of troops in turn permitted the Chinese to advance more rapidly against Tanaka's front. With all other Japanese resources committed to the attack on Imphal-Kohima, there were no other forces he could draw on to assist in what had become a two-front war.

During the night of 28 and 29 March the Chinese 113th Regiment moved into the positions held by the White and Red Combat Teams. The Chinese also brought up their artillery and at dawn began to reply to the Japanese fire. This soon reduced the incoming enemy artillery and allowed the Americans to withdraw at about 1000 hours on 29 March. The battalion withdrew about a mile up the Chengun River to bivouac near a Seagrave Hospital unit established there. This medical unit had accompanied the Chinese regiment on the march and had prepared to receive battle casualties. The thirty-five wounded Marauders were treated there while the eight who were killed were buried. The remaining Marauders rested and listened to the continuing battle between the Chinese and Japanese forces on the battlefield nearby. Later information indicated that the battle had cost the Japanese over three hundred killed, and by the time the Chinese had settled into position, the enemy was preparing to withdraw toward Kamaing. A battalion of the 113th Chinese Regiment followed the enemy withdrawal to Luban, about a mile to the south, where they met the advancing 22d Chinese Division.

The 1st Battalion rested briefly. They were under orders to join the other Marauders at the second part of the mission near Inkangahtawng. Indeed, Colonel Osborne had received a message confirming the earlier instructions and advising him to proceed to Japan in easy march stages as soon as possible after securing Shaduzup. While preparing to move forward, word came of the Japanese attack on Imphal and of the death of British General Wingate, whose Chindits were operating in the same general area as the Americans.

There was yet another ominous sign. As the column set forth to Janpan, retracing much of its earlier path along the river route, three of its horses collapsed from exhaustion and had to be shot. Many of the men were looking forward to relief, believing that once joined with the rest of the unit they would be relieved for rest and recuperation, having completed the assigned missions for this campaigning season. Even their commanders had no inkling of future missions; Colonel Hunter recalled that General Merrill had mentioned before the second mission that "we might hole up on the Jambu Bum."[8]

While the 1st Battalion had been struggling toward Shaduzup the 2d and 3d Battalions had enjoyed a two-day rest before setting out. They were to block the Kamaing Road near Inkangahtawng in the Mogaung Valley. This was at a point about halfway between the enemy 18th Division's front and its major rear base at Kamaing. Timed to coincide with the block at Shaduzup, it would firmly cut the enemy's supply lines to the front by placing two blocks ten miles apart on those lines of communication.

Moving forward on 12 March, the 2d Battalion led off, followed by the command group and the 3d Battalion. After receiving an air

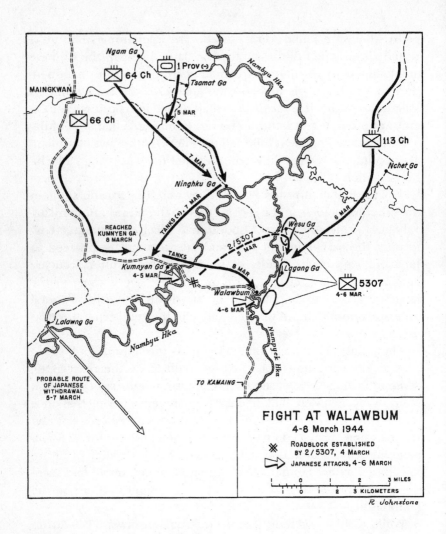

FIGHT AT WALAWBUM
4-8 March 1944

✳ ROADBLOCK ESTABLISHED
BY 2/5307, 4 MARCH

▷ JAPANESE ATTACKS, 4-6 MARCH

R. Johnstone

drop they headed south along the Tanai River and reached
Naubum on 15 March. From that point on they would be in hill
country. It was also at Naubum that they met another member of
OSS Detachment 101. On 17 March, as the lead scout turned a
bend in the trail he saw a caucasian man standing in the middle of
the trail. Dressed in a combination of American, British, and Australian uniforms, the apparition announced to the startled scouts,
"Glad you got here, boys. We've been waiting eighteen months for

you to arrive."[9] This individual was Capt. Vincent L. Curl. Captain Curl had been a noncommissioned officer in the 35th Infantry Regiment before the war, and his commanding officer was then-Capt. Carl Eifler. When now-Colonel Eifler formed Detachment 101, among his earliest recruits was Captain Curl. By the time the Marauders encountered him he had had more than a year's experience in Burma and was the area commander of the Knothead Group, which included Lieutenant Tilly's forces. He was described by Colonel Hunter as a "wiry old soldier [who] sported the finest beard I have ever seen on any human being. Deep auburn in color, it was carefully brushed back, from a precision part in the exact center of his chin, in two luxuriously flowing waves."[10] Captain Curl brought along three hundred Kachin Rangers to join the Marauder column. He also brought along seven elephants, each with her calf. With the continuing loss of pack animals, the elephants were particularly appreciated. Captain Curl did advise, however, that elephants and mules did not get along. Galahad took special pains thereafter to keep the elephants and mules "smelling distance apart."[11]

At that point the battalions proceeded along a fifteen-mile trail of mud to Weilangyang. Warned by the Kachins that the enemy was in the vicinity, they established patrols and trail blocks. Captain Curl used the elephants, which he had captured from the Japanese, who in turn had seized them from local Burmese, to distribute supplies from the latest air drop. General Merrill ordered a two-day halt to receive information and further instructions from the NCAC. During the halt the men enjoyed a brief respite, marred only by the arrival of Lt. James W. Parker, the unit's dental officer. Parker surveyed the dental needs of the troops and also brought to General Merrill the latest intelligence and instructions from the NCAC. The following day, 18 March, a liaison plane dropped a message from General Stilwell to General Merrill, ordering him to use the 2d and 3d Battalions to protect the flank of the Chinese advance by blocking approaches along the Tanai River from the south. General Merrill, expecting the order, had already planned to move his command to the villages of Kaulun Ga and Mupaw Ga, where they could command the trails on both banks of the river. A hill at Mupaw Ga would also provide a unique vantage point of the surrounding area.

At 1300 on 19 March the 2d Battalion, with the command group
and Captain Curl's Kachin Rangers, moved out. Their destination
was the two villages by way of Janpan. The 3d Battalion was to follow after a short delay. The march continued as planned until 1030
the following day. General Merrill then received a message from
General Stilwell that ordered him to accomplish his original mission of blocking the Kamaing Road while also protecting the Chinese flank along the Tanai River. The message stated that an estimated two thousand Japanese troops were believed to be in or
around Kamaing.

The new instructions forced General Merrill to divide his command. He ordered Colonel Hunter to take the 2d Battalion, the
Khaki Combat Team of the 3d Battalion, and Captain Curl's Kachin
Rangers to establish a block on the Kamaing Road between
Warazup and Malakawng. The Orange Combat Team was to be held
at Janpan with the command group as a reserve. The 3d Battalion
Headquarters Group and the Orange Combat Team were to be prepared to move to Colonel Hunter's assistance if needed. They and
some attached Kachins were also to patrol, to protect both the Chinese flank and the Marauders' flank between Shaduzup and Inkangahtawng.

Colonel Hunter moved out on the afternoon of 21 March. "The
plan was to proceed south down the trail which eventually ended at
Kamaing."[12] They headed south from Janpan and arrived the next
day at Auche. The 3d Battalion and the Orange Combat Team followed. While at Auche on the night of 22 March General Merrill received another communication from General Stilwell, which stated,
"Japs withdrawing down the road. Jambu Bum fell today. Come fast
now." Basing his decision on this message, General Merrill ordered
Colonel Hunter to begin his march and establish the block thirty-
six hours before it was originally planned to begin. Colonel Hunter
wrote after the war:

> This was disturbing news. Our air photos had failed to ar-
> rive; there would be no time for reconnaissance and selection
> of a site or to rest the men and animals prior to actual occu-
> pation of the area selected for the roadblock. In addition, the
> Mogaung River lay between us and the road. We did not know

the location of the fords, or even whether or not the river was fordable at this time of the year, although our Kachin scouts stated, on being questioned closely, that normally the river was fordable at this time of the year.[13]

In response to these unexpected orders, Colonel Hunter's force moved swiftly forward beginning 23 March. The new schedule required rapid movement, not easily accomplished over the type of terrain the troops had to cross. Attempting to avoid contact with enemy troops while on the approach march, the force left the trail and used the Nampama River as far as Manpin. The march filled their shoes with sand and further exhausted the pack animals, who had to repeatedly climb the river banks. At Manpin they took the trail leading through Sharaw into the flat Mogaung Valley.

American patrols from the 2d Battalion encountered enemy patrols as they approached Inkangahtawng and reported that they believed a company of Japanese infantry was in position at the village, with reinforcements coming in regularly. The battalion waded across the Mogaung River and began to push the defenders back. Increasing opposition finally halted the attack about one quarter mile north of Inkangahtawng and about three hundred yards east of the Kamaing Road. The Marauders dug defensive positions while the Khaki Combat Team established a position on the east bank of the river to protect the rear of the 2d Battalion, provide mortar fire, and patrol toward the east.

Back along the trail, Colonel Hunter was busy evacuating sick and injured Marauders and trying to establish contact with Colonel Osborne's 1st Battalion, not knowing that he had been delayed. At about the time Colonel Hunter established contact with General Merrill and learned that Colonel Osborne's battalion was behind schedule, he lost contact with Colonel McGee's 2d Battalion. There were now three isolated American infantry battalions in the Burmese jungles, none capable of aiding the other two before the Japanese could act. General Tanaka would not let such an opportunity slip past without reacting fiercely.

5. Siege at Nhpum Ga

The message of 22 March that had prompted General Merrill to accelerate his operations was the result of the ongoing battle along the Kamaing Road. On 15 March the 22d Chinese Division, aided by the 1st Provisional Tank Group, was attacking toward the Jambu Bum. The 64th Chinese Regiment was to the east of the road, the 66th Regiment was to the west, and the 65th Regiment was in reserve. The tank group, under Colonel Brown, attacked along the road itself.

Two battalions of the 64th Regiment attempted to outflank the enemy defenses along the road, but heavy opposition kept the advance to a slow pace. At one point a battalion attempting to outflank the Japanese was itself encircled and had to be extricated by a counterattack from its sister battalion. The two groups, infantry and armor, found it difficult to coordinate their attacks, because the tankers could not tell the difference between their countrymen and the enemy in the heavy jungle conditions. The limited field of view from the tanks further complicated the identification problem. After a few cases of mistaken identity the Chinese infantry refused to work alongside the Chinese tankers. Nevertheless, after two days the enemy roadblock was pushed back.

The attacking force next faced a heavily mined road blocked by felled trees. It took two days to clear the road sufficiently to allow the attack to proceed. A coordinated tank-infantry attack pushed to within four miles of Jambu Bum, but the tanks and infantry became separated under fire and the advance stalled. The attack was renewed on 21 March with the 2d Battalion of the 66th Chinese Regiment leading. Again the tanks and infantry became separated, and a Japanese counterattack cost the Chinese five tanks. The Japanese attack threatened to overrun the battalion command post until two nearby U.S. engineer platoons dropped their road-clearing tools and joined the defense. During that night the 1st Battalion of the 64th Infantry managed to complete its encirclement and cut the road immediately behind the enemy defenders. The 1st Provisional Tank Group attacked at dawn and ran into an ambush consisting of antitank guns, which knocked out another three tanks. Once again the attack stalled.

General Stilwell, unaware of the constant difficulties, believed that the attack was progressing steadily. He also was under the impression that the 1st Battalion of the Marauders was already at Shaduzup. Learning of the successful encirclement by the 64th Chinese Regiment, he believed that the attack was going as planned and would soon reach its next objective. As a result, the message to speed up operations went out to General Merrill.

Unfortunately, General Tanaka had other ideas and continued to defend the Kamaing Road. In an attempt to overcome the identification problem, the tanks and infantry agreed that the friendly infantry would identify themselves with white cloths. As the attack progressed, the Japanese quickly discerned the technique and copied it, causing great confusion and the failure of the attack. This deception by the Japanese cost the tank group several more tanks, which had advanced to meet what they believed were friendly troops, only to fall into an antitank ambush. Heavy and unseasonable rains also made progress difficult.

The 65th Regiment was brought up from reserve, and together the infantry strength of the 22d Chinese Division pushed the Japanese back. They did not go easily, and on 28 March they counterattacked five times. The next day, however, the cutting of the road at Shaduzup by the 1st Marauder Battalion forced the Japanese to withdraw, and later that day elements of the 113th Regiment of the 38th Chinese Division met advance elements of the 2d Battalion, 65th Chinese Regiment, at Shaduzup.

Meanwhile, the 2d and 3d Battalions, 5307th, were implementing Colonel Hunter's scheme to throw up a roadblock at Inkangahtawng. Patrols were to be sent north to contact the Chinese 113th Regiment, then supposed to be moving down from Shaduzup, after which they would cut the road farther south. Colonel Hunter was unaware that the planned attack on Shaduzup, which was scheduled to occur simultaneously with that at Inkangahtawng, had been delayed. When word finally came that the 1st Battalion was delayed, the operation was already in motion and could not be delayed.

Colonel McGee sent two platoons of his 2d Battalion forward on 24 March to envelop the village of Inkangahtawng. They advanced into heavily fortified and prepared positions, which easily repulsed the attack. Rather than get committed prematurely to the attack, Colonel McGee withdrew his attack force. Just as they returned to the perimeter a Japanese counterattack struck the left flank of the 2d Battalion. After a fifteen-minute mortar barrage Japanese soldiers, sheltered by six-to-eight-foot-high *kunai* grass, charged to within twenty yards of the American line before the Marauders opened up with every weapon at their command. The first line of enemy went down, but additional charges went on throughout the day. One Japanese officer managed to breach the perimeter and attempted to skewer a Marauder tommy gunner with his sword. The American was quicker, and both the sword and the officer went down. In another instance, a Japanese soldier and a Marauder struggled hand to hand for a moment, until the American managed to pull away. Nearby Marauders eliminated the intruder. Most of the attacks fell upon Sgt. Norman H. Willey's pioneer and demolition platoon, which managed to hold its position.

As the day wore on, the Japanese moved around the perimeter. Using the river as an avenue of approach, they soon attacked from the south. Mortars, machine guns, and artillery pounded the position. Only when Allied aircraft appeared overhead did the artillery fall silent. Without artillery of their own the Americans could only shelter themselves in their holes and await the next infantry assault. Signs continued to grow ominous. Ammunition was running low, and trucks bringing up additional enemy reinforcements could be heard regularly. Being close to Kamaing, enemy supplies and reinforcements could be easily brought up despite occasional Allied air attacks. The situation was fast becoming desperate. Finally, Colonel McGee learned that the attack at Shaduzup, which had been intended to draw off a part of the enemy's resources, had been delayed, allowing the full weight of the enemy reserves in the area to be brought to bear against his roadblock.

Colonel McGee's original orders had been to hold his roadblock for twenty-four hours but not to delay any longer if he believed his force was in serious danger. He was now faced with a situation in which his ammunition supply was at dangerous levels, the enemy was reinforcing its attacks, and there was no hope of relief within the immediate future. In order to preserve his battalion he decided at 1630 hours to withdraw toward Manpin. The Khaki Combat Team remained behind to cover the withdrawal with mortar fire until the command was well across the Mogaung River. Then both units combined and withdrew to Ngagahtawng, where they bivouacked for the night. Colonel McGee established platoon-sized trail blocks and booby traps on all the trails around the bivouac. Colonel Hunter, who was out of communication, did not yet know of the withdrawal. The 2d Battalion had held the block for the required twenty-four hours at a cost of two men killed and twelve wounded. Some two hundred enemy had been counted as killed. Colonel Hunter, flying low over the withdrawal route, identified the battalion and ordered in litter-bearing liaison planes to evacuate the wounded of the 2d Battalion.

Colonel McGee's withdrawal coincided with intelligence received at General Merrill's headquarters in which a captured Japanese map indicated that at least two Japanese battalions were moving to outflank the American and Chinese attack at Kamaing. The objective of the attack was the Chinese 22d Division at Shaduzup. General Stilwell's reaction was to order General Merrill to block this move and to prevent any Japanese advance beyond the village of Nhpum Ga. That order went out to the units scattered along the various trails between Ngagahtawng and Warong. As Colonel Hunter was still without communications, the battalion commanders received the orders before he did. In accordance with the orders Colonel McGee took his 2d Battalion and Khaki Combat Team east from Inkangahtawng. Plagued by difficult terrain and rains so heavy that holes had to be cut in the bottom of the litters to prevent the wounded from being covered with water, they managed to reach Sharaw by afternoon. There they were able to call in the liaison planes to evacuate the wounded. While conducting the evacuation Colonel McGee received another message from General Merrill, advising him that a strong Japanese force from Kamaing was threatening his rear and flanks.

Colonel Beach and his reduced 3d Battalion had been protecting the rear of the 2d Battalion during the roadblock at Inkangahtawng. He had established a trail block on the Warong-Auche trail with the Orange Combat Team. When he learned on 24 March that the Inkangahtawng block had been established he started forward to join the rest of the force there. As the Orange Combat Team reached Manpin it received word of the enemy advance, and Colonel Beach took steps to block the local trails between Inkangahtawng and Nhpum Ga to protect the American withdrawal to the latter village. Lieutenants Weston and Smith were sent forward with their platoons to block the most likely route of advance for the Japanese. At about that time Colonel Hunter first learned of the change in the situation. Puzzled because the Kachins had reported no enemy movement in his immediate area, he contacted General Merrill and was ordered to assemble his forces at Nhpum Ga.

The following day, 26 March, the two battalions began the march to Nhpum Ga. The 2d Battalion led off and reached Manpin before noon, where they received a much needed supply drop of rations and ammunition. After distribution the battalion moved an additional five miles up the trail. The 3d Battalion arrived in Manpin later in the afternoon and bivouacked for the night. While Colonel Hunter was at Manpin he learned from Kachin spies working in Kamaing that the Japanese were moving north from Kamaing in trucks that could use the trail for some distance. He called for an air strike to delay the enemy advance, but while the strike did delay follow-up forces, the advance force had passed before the Allied aircraft could arrive on the scene. Colonel Hunter believed that Kamaing was now lightly held and could be seized by a reinforced battalion of Marauders.

Now aware of the threat from the flank, General Merrill instead ordered a withdrawal. The two battalions chose the more difficult route along the Nampama River. Although this would make any enemy approach more difficult, it involved about forty river crossings and placed an additional burden on troops and animals who were already exhausted.

The enemy advance took them to the village of Poakum, where Lieutenant Weston's intelligence and reconnaissance platoon had dug in to protect the column's flank. The first enemy thrust was a weak probe by a small force approaching from the Kamaing trail. Having identified the American perimeter, a force of the enemy estimated at company size attacked at 1130 along the trail and from the west. Lieutenant Weston, who had reinforced his defenses with mortars and machine guns from the column, managed to break up this attack with mortar fire. At 1400 a larger force attacked from three sides. Again Lieutenant Weston and his men managed to stand off the attack, but it was now clear that the next attack would either overwhelm or surround the force under his command. Placing a heavy concentration of mortar fire on suspected enemy assembly areas, the reinforced platoon withdrew toward Warong. There they joined with Lieutenant Smith's platoon at about 1800 and prepared for a joint defense of the area as an additional delaying tactic. They had about ninety men available for the defense. They were unable to call for help or instructions, because the only radio available to the force had been destroyed at Poakum.

The enemy allowed them a peaceful night, but morning brought several probing attacks to test their defenses. The morning was spent in repulsing these probes and the first strong attack. As the day wore on, it became clear that the enemy was not only present in great strength but was surrounding the Marauders and was about to close off their only escape route. A messenger was sent back on the only available mule to advise General Merrill of the intent to withdraw. Because of the enemy's increasing threat to the escape route the two platoons didn't wait for approval but took turns delaying the Japanese while withdrawing. This tactic kept the approaching Japanese at bay while allowing a successful withdrawal to the main body.

At one point Lieutenant Smith found himself defending an ambush position with several of his men. The enemy force was much stronger, and he ordered his men to withdraw. Most of his men es-

caped, but five were on the wrong side of a clearing into which the
enemy could fire at will. Lieutenant Smith raced from position to
position firing his Thompson submachine gun to deceive the enemy into thinking his men were still in position, while the trapped
Marauders raced across the dangerous clearing. After his men were
safe, Lieutenant Smith, still firing away, managed to escape to safety.
In the two days of nearly constant fighting, the platoons under Lieutenants Weston and Smith had not suffered a single casualty. They
had also successfully protected the flank of the main force as it withdrew in front of an attacking enemy force of equal size.

While Lieutenants Weston and Smith held off the approaching
enemy, the 2d and 3d Battalions, having resumed their normal
structure with the return of the Khaki Combat Team to its parent
battalion, reached Auche. The 2d Battalion remained there, setting
up a defensive perimeter, while the 3d Battalion moved on to the
north. The following day, 28 March, was remembered as the most
difficult day of the withdrawal. Led by the Khaki Combat Team, with
the Blue Combat Team following, the march began at 0600 hours.
As 2d Battalion headquarters prepared to follow at 0630 hours, enemy shells began to fall around them. The withdrawal now had to
be made under enemy artillery fire. There was no way to avoid the
artillery, because the trail ran along the crest of a narrow ridge. Its
precipitous sides, covered with thick jungle growth, allowed no
room for dispersal, and as the column moved north it became clear
that the enemy was observing its fire from Warong and could correct for accuracy. With the third volley a Marauder was wounded,
and several animals were also hit.

Having found the correct range, the enemy began a constant barrage. The 2d Battalion now had to move uphill over a muddy trail
nearly five miles long under observed enemy fire. Animals fell fre-
quently and had to be unloaded in order to regain their footing.
Repacking took additional time and prolonged the chance the enemy had of scoring a hit. Every attempt to speed the advance met
with difficulties. Medical personnel were ordered to the rear of the
column to deal with the increasing number of casualties.

After ninety minutes under these conditions, the column
reached Nhpum Ga. The toll was beginning to tell on the troops,

however. They had marched some seventy miles under difficult conditions, made about one hundred river crossings, fought a heavy action at Inkangahtawng, and then struggled under impossible conditions to Nhpum Ga. This had come after seven weeks of marching and fighting in the Burmese jungles. The 2d Battalion was now on the verge of exhaustion.

Nhpum Ga was on a sharp, thin ridge at the northern end of a hill mass. Four or five native huts made up the village, which lay on the highest ground, 2,800 feet above sea level, in the area. The elevation continued for half a mile past Nhpum Ga, then sloped downhill over bamboo-covered ground to Hsamshingyang, a clearing in the jungle. To the east the ground dropped off rapidly to the Tanai, falling 1,400 feet in two miles. A mile and a half to the west was the similar valley of the Hkuma Hka, which flowed to the south. Both valleys contained trails by which the Japanese might bypass the Americans at Nhpum Ga. At the northeast quarter of the perimeter established by the 2d Battalion a rocky point overlooked the only waterhole in the area.

General Merrill had ordered the 2d Battalion to Nhpum Ga to block Japanese forces from advancing past that point. Failure would allow them to outflank the advancing Chinese forces and could easily lose all the gains that had been won in recent weeks. The 3d Battalion had been ordered to Hsamshingyang, a point five miles north of the 2d Battalion. There they would establish a supply field for drops and an airstrip to evacuate wounded and ill personnel. The 3d Battalion would also patrol to the north to prevent any enemy attack on the rear of the 2d Battalion or another outflanking maneuver. Colonel Beach's men were also responsible for keeping the trail to the 2d Battalion open for the supply and evacuation of the wounded. Colonel Hunter inspected Colonel McGee's position and felt he had "done an excellent job."[1] Returning to the 3d Battalion with a patrol of military police whose job was to keep open the trail between the two battalions, Colonel Hunter missed the opening phases of the battle.

The Japanese were on the heels of the 2d Battalion as they settled into defensive positions around the village. Major Richard W. Healy's Blue Combat Team held the southern portion of the perimeter, while the Green Combat Team, under Capt. Thomas E. Bogardus, held the northern end. A medical station was set up near the waterhole at the north end of the perimeter. Coming toward them was a strong Japanese force, under the command of Col. Fusayasu Maruyama, drawn from the 18th Japanese Infantry Division. It consisted of the regimental headquarters and one infantry battalion of the 114th Infantry Regiment, the first battalion of the 55th Infantry Regiment, and four field pieces. This was the same force that had pushed the Americans out of Auche and up the trail to Nhpum Ga. Contrary to the beliefs of the Americans, Maruyama's mission was not to outflank the Chinese but to push the Marauders as far away from the right flank of the 18th Infantry Division as possible. That was why the Japanese had followed the Marauders to Nhpum Ga and why they were not attempting to outflank them by taking the trails available to them in the valleys adjoining the ridge on which the village rested. The first notice the Americans had of the arrival of Colonel Maruyama was the pushing in of two platoons that Colonel McGee had placed outside the perimeter to delay the enemy. By 1605 hours on 28 March the first enemy artillery and mortar fire fell within the perimeter. Moments later came the first infantry assault.

The first attack was a probing mission, and the Marauders, familiar with Japanese tactics, withheld their automatic weapons fire to avoid disclosing their positions. Between attacks the men continued to improve the defensive positions as well as they could. Night fell before the Japanese renewed the attack, but the Americans were subjected to an occasional shelling by mortars and artillery designed to keep them awake. This tactic failed, because the Marauders were so exhausted that an occasional shelling did not disturb their sleep. Only those on guard duty managed to stay awake long enough to protect their sleeping comrades. The Marauders feared an infiltration effort during the night, because they were so tired that it had a good chance of success. But the Japanese did not take the opportunity.

The following day General Merrill was ordered to be evacuated. His health, which was never very strong, had deteriorated during the campaign to the point where General Stilwell personally overrode his protests and ordered him evacuated. Merrill did refuse to board a liaison plane until all the wounded had gone ahead of him, and this delayed his departure by one day. But in effect from 29 March Colonel Hunter commanded the 5307th Composite Unit (Provisional). General Merrill never formally relinquished command, and upon arrival at Ledo he ordered two 75mm howitzers sent to Colonel Hunter at the 3d Battalion position. Colonel Hunter had begun to clear the trail, and his two combat teams, Orange and Khaki, needed artillery support to complete the job. Colonel Hunter wrote:

> I had no warning of Merrill's approaching illness. He had not undergone any violent exercise in the last few days to have placed a strain on his heart. I knew he was using some kind of thick purplish medicine taken with water which he told me was for dysentery. He carried it in a small vial with a label, printed in Hindustani possibly. I asked him if our doctors knew what it was, and he said no. I advised him to have Shudmak check the stuff. It must have been potent, for he only used a drop to a pint of water.[2]

At daylight on 29 March, the Japanese again opened with an artillery and mortar attack on Nhpum Ga. A machine-gun attack preceded an infantry attack, which hit the southeast perimeter at 0600 hours. That attack was repulsed without difficulty, as was another attack, from the southwest, at 1000 hours. The Japanese tried again with an attack from the south at 1500 hours, which failed, as had the previous assaults.

Between attacks Colonel McGee radioed to the 3d Battalion, asking if Colonel Beach could send assistance to his command. The 3d Battalion, tied to the vital airstrip, could not send any help. Loss of the airstrip would cause all supply and evacuation efforts to cease and open the rear of the 2d Battalion to encirclement and attack from all sides. Colonel Hunter agreed to have the 3d Battalion keep the trail between Hsamshingyang and Nhpum Ga open by patrols twice daily, but beyond that his resources were stretched to the limit.

As darkness fell, the Americans could hear the Japanese moving around their flanks, and artillery fire began again at 1750 hours. A brief attack on the northwest perimeter supported by machine guns was repulsed. The sounds of the enemy moving on the flanks of the perimeter worried Colonel McGee, and he strengthened the sides of the perimeter with his meager resources. Additional ground was included in the flanks of the perimeter to improve defensive positions. Colonel Hunter called to advise Colonel McGee that at least a battalion of enemy infantry was making the attack on Nhpum Ga. The Americans dug additional defenses, careful to do so in the dark and as quietly as possible to avoid enemy infiltrators attacking under cover of darkness.

The 3d Battalion continued patrolling throughout its assigned area. They encountered one group of Japanese who were attempting to encircle the drop field to the north and repulsed them after a sharp skirmish. Kachin guerrillas, based with the 3d Battalion, conducted several ambushes against small enemy groups attempting to infiltrate into or around the American positions. This activity, particularly that of the Kachin Rangers, created in the mind of Colonel Maruyama the picture of a much stronger American force than actually existed. It also kept unclear to the Japanese exactly which areas were occupied by the Marauders.

Japanese artillery, mortar, and machine-gun fire continued at dawn of 30 March at Nhpum Ga. That day saw the eastern side of the perimeter, neglected the previous day, as the target of the enemy attack. That attack was by far the strongest yet against the defenses and persisted despite intense defensive fires put out by the Marauders. One of the results of that attack was that the Japanese identified the location of the American mortars that shortly after their attack came under artillery attack. Another attack from the north was soon received and repulsed. As each attack resulted in a change in the perimeter, the final defensive line then began to develop. It was in an elongated shape about four hundred yards long and broadening in the northern half to include the high ground on both sides of the trail. The Green Combat Team now held the western and northern side, while the Blue Combat Team held the south and east.

The battalion's aid station had been placed north of the village on a slope protected in part from enemy shelling by a small knoll. Foxholes had been prepared to accommodate the wounded on litters and to provide places for treatment by medical staff. All prior casualties had been carried over the trail to the airstrip at Hsamshingyang. Major Bernard Rogoff, MD, the battalion surgeon and his two assistants, Capts. Henry G. Stelling and Lewis A. Kolodny, prepared to operate in a deserted *basha*, or native hut. Casualties were moved into sheltered positions at the edge of the deserted village. Wounded were carried to Capt. James E. T. Hopkins's 3d Battalion aid station at Hsamshingyang, where they were placed aboard liaison planes for evacuation. A patrol under the command of Sgt. John Keslik had arrived to keep communications open over the trail.

Conditions were becoming difficult within the perimeter. Enemy artillery had caused numerous casualties among the unit's animals, and the carcasses were beginning to rot. Although efforts were made to protect the animals, they could not be dug into the ground, which was the only reasonably safe place from the continuing enemy artillery barrages. Of the two hundred horses and mules that had been brought into the perimeter, seventy-five had been killed so far. In addition to the odors from the dead animals, the Japanese corpses alongside the perimeter added to the stench that now marked the borders of the 2d Battalion's perimeter.

The following day, 31 March, marked the beginning of the siege of Nhpum Ga. Enemy attacks came in from all sides of the perimeter. After a light artillery barrage, enemy attacks came from the south, east, and northwest in a coordinated attack. In the west a machine gun outpost position was overrun, forcing the Green Combat Team to strengthen its defenses on the hill protecting that flank. In the north the enemy attack followed a wide draw in which a sluggish brook led up to the Marauder positions. Every available man including headquarters and mule skinners were put into the defenses.

Even with these reinforcements there were not enough men to cover both sides of the draw, and the Japanese succeeded in reaching the knob above the only waterhole in the perimeter. For an hour the attackers and the pioneer and demolition platoon fought over the knob. Gradually the Marauders were forced off the elevation and away from the vital waterhole. A counterattack failed to dislodge the Japanese from their new positions, and the waterhole was not recovered.

The Japanese attack from the north had also indicated that the 2d Battalion was cut off from the 3d Battalion. This was confirmed at 0800 hours that morning when the normal patrol sent out from Hsamshingyang by the Orange Combat Team under Lieutenant Smith's command found signs that the enemy had been using the trail recently. Approaching within four hundred yards of the 2d Battalion's perimeter, the patrol was fired upon by a strong enemy trail block that had been set up before dawn. Private Robert W. Cole, the lead scout, covered his companion as he moved off the trail to investigate some movement he heard. A sniper twenty yards away wounded Private Cole. Sergeant Aloysius Kazlousky and Pfc. Leroy E. Brown moved to assist him and were cut down by machine-gun fire. Private John P. Carbone was covering the wounded with some brush when he was hit by a sniper from thirty yards away.

Lieutenant Smith prepared to break the block and contacted Major Healy's mortar platoon to have them provide cover fire. The attack failed, despite mortar support. Lieutenant Smith sent runners back to Colonel Hunter asking for reinforcements to help break the enemy hold on the trail. Both messengers were ambushed before they could reach the 3d Battalion. Lieutenant Smith was forced to lead his platoon off into the jungle and back to the 3d Battalion, all the while pursued by enemy forces. At about 1000 hours Colonel McGee was informed that the trail was cut and that his position was now encircled.

After hearing of the failure of the 3d Battalion efforts to break the block, Colonel McGee decided to try it from his end. By carefully thinning out his defensive lines he managed to assemble a reinforced platoon. Providing supporting mortar and machine-gun fire, Colonel McGee sent his attack force against the block. They managed to advance about two hundred yards before running into prepared enemy defenses. The attack caused several casualties and eventually failed.

Colonel McGee contacted Colonel Hunter at 1600 hours and advised him that his rear flank was blocked and that he needed relief from enemy pressure surrounding his force at Nhpum Ga. That day an airdrop provided the surrounded 2d Battalion with sufficient food and ammunition to continue the defense. The main concern was the water supply. The loss of the waterhole had left the men of the 2d Battalion with only the small swampy pools in a draw north of their position, which had been previously used only for the animals. Dead mules lay in the water, increasing the deadly quality of the water supply. A shallow pit was dug to conserve what water could be salvaged from the pools. "We were drinking muddy, and I mean muddy, water," relates the 2d Battalion diary for 1 April. "Nothing else to be had. Even seen fellas taking water from pool where dead mules lie."[3] This water, rationed at half a canteen cup per day, was so foul that even the desperate men of the 2d Battalion could drink it only with great effort. Combined with the stench of the dead animals, which now numbered 112, the uncovered excrement of the soldiers, plus the increasing number of unburied human corpses, the situation had become intolerable.

North of the siege a strong Japanese patrol pressed up from the south to the airstrip at Hsamshingyang. Loss of this position would spell the end of the defenders of both positions. This group ran into one of the covering patrols of the Orange Combat Team, which sent reinforcements to the beleaguered platoon as soon as the sounds of firing were heard. The fight repulsed the enemy at the cost of several Marauders killed and a dozen wounded. During the siege several Marauders reported to Major Rogoff, suffering from battle fatigue, mostly apathy. He put them to work digging foxholes and trenches for the wounded. All but two of the eight men recovered sufficiently to return to the line.[4]

April Fools' Day brought more of the same for the 2d Battalion. The enemy opened the day with the usual artillery barrage, followed by two infantry attacks. Additional enemy artillery revealed itself while supporting these attacks, increasing the pressure on the defenders. The waterhole was still strongly defended, and no progress could be made there. So poor was the water supply that doctors could not make plaster casts and had to give medications without water. Colonel McGee desperately requested that an air drop of five hundred gallons of water in plastic bags be immediately dispatched. Colonel Hunter, learning of the 1st Battalion's success at Shaduzup, radioed Colonel McGee, telling him "Nips running like hell from Shaduzup, too many dead to be counted. Expect your friends to pull out tonight or tomorrow morning. Mortar the hell out of them. Lew will pursue if possible."[5]

Despite his optimism over the success at Shaduzup, Colonel Hunter was still trying to relieve the surrounded Marauders. He decided to try to use the Orange Combat Team, still commanded by Maj. Lawrence L. Lew, to open the trail to Nhpum Ga. Leaving Major Briggs's Khaki Combat Team and headquarters to garrison the airstrip, the Orange Combat Team moved south along the closed trail. The Japanese had moved their defenses closer to Hsamshingyang since the last attempt to open the trail, but the defenses were not strong enough to hold the Orange Combat Team. The attack progressed for two miles under increasing opposition on 1 April before it stopped for the night.

The following day the attack resumed under more difficult conditions. The trail to Nhpum Ga rose a thousand feet over a series of uneven sharp rises. Between each rise the ridge line was comparatively even, providing space for defenses. As the Orange Combat Team began to clear the rises they came to a strong Japanese defensive position. Formed along one of the steepest rises in the trail, it could not be swiftly overcome. The fight opened with the ambush of SSgt. John L. Ploederl's patrol. First scout Cpl. Edgar Robertson and Cpl. Frank L. Graham were in the advance when Corporal Graham saw an enemy heavy machine gun covering the trail. He shouted to Sergeant Ploederl and Corporal Robertson and then dived off the trail to the right. Robertson moved to the left and crawled into the enemy's line of fire, where he was killed. Ploederl was also cut down by the enemy's fire. Another member of the patrol was pulling him to safety when a second burst killed the sergeant. Corporal Graham was severely wounded after killing the crew of one machine gun.

Successive platoon attacks by the Orange Combat Team knocked out several machine-gun positions, but others were always just ahead. In an area where the trail and ridge were only seventy-five yards wide, only one platoon could attack at a time. The terrain also easily allowed the Japanese to site each gun position with the ability to cover all approaches from the American side of the trail. Steep slopes and thick jungle on either side prevented outflanking attacks. About halfway to Nhpum Ga the attack was stopped.

One bright spot on that day was the arrival of artillery support. When General Merrill had been evacuated to Ledo he had ordered that two 75mm howitzers be airdropped to the 3d Battalion at Hsamshingyang. The Marauder rear echelon had swiftly moved to carry out this assignment. At 0930 on 2 April the two field pieces were broken down into bulky segments and attached to double parachutes. They were dropped the same day on Hsamshingyang airstrip, observed by the appreciative 2d Battalion, which was surrounded at Nhpum Ga. Colonel Hunter, knowing that the guns were on the way, had assembled two gun crews from men who had served with the 98th Field Artillery Battalion in New Guinea. Sergeant Major Joe Doyer, a former artilleryman, organized the crews. Staff Sergeant John A. Acker was appointed battery commander. He formed and trained the two crews to prepare them for the coming howitzers. Colonel Hunter contacted Colonel McGee and inquired if any of his officers had artillery experience, so that they could adjust the artillery fire. Colonel McGee responded a few moments later that one of his pack-troop officers had been an artillery ROTC graduate and was ready to observe incoming artillery.

Sergeant Acker had been the noncommissioned officer in charge of the Khaki Combat Team's pack animals. One night earlier in the mission, he had a conversation with Major Briggs. "We men of the 98th Field Artillery had been discussing our need for artillery support. I told Major Briggs that if we had some guns we would fix the Japs up."[6] Assembling thirty volunteers—gun crews, packers, ammunition handlers, and picket guards—Sergeant Acker and his "artillerymen" waited for the drop.

On the 2nd of April we assembled at the drop area as the planes came over for the drop. We had been informed that the gun pieces would be marked by different colored parachutes.

As the drop was made the men began immediately to claim the designated pieces and take them to the designated area. From the time of the drop we had two guns assembled in fifteen minutes. I had been asked by Col. Hunter to come to his quarters as soon as the guns were in place. As I came into his tent, he had on his desk (better described as a card table) all materials spread out as to how to assemble the guns. He was very pleased when I told him the guns were ready to fire. He put his assembly instructions away and spread out a map on the table and began to show me where the Japs' artillery pieces were located and asked me if we could fire in that general area without endangering our own troops at Nhpum Ga.[7]

Sergeant Acker tested the guns with a twenty-five-foot lanyard, to ensure they had been assembled correctly. With the opening salvos the Americans had their own artillery. Within two hours after the guns had been dropped they were firing on Japanese positions surrounding the 2d Battalion. The following day the Americans attempted to use a part of the Khaki Combat Team, supported by the newly arrived artillery, to outflank the enemy defending the trail to Nhpum Ga. The attempt failed, however. A second attack, this time by the 2d Battalion, which had air support, also failed to dislodge the stubborn defenders of the trail. The Marauders who hoped that the new artillery would discourage Japanese resistance were disappointed to learn that the enemy was just as determined as they were.

At the end of 3 April the situation in the 2d Battalion was serious. Wounded men were dying for lack of evacuation, water, and proper medical care. Most of the men now had dysentery and stomach disorders. The airdrop of water requested by Colonel McGee had temporarily relieved the water problem, but not in time to avoid rampant sickness. Reports were coming in of additional Japanese troops marching toward Nhpum Ga. The most reliable source of assistance, the Marauders' 1st Battalion, had only just learned of the situation and could not be expected to arrive for several days. Strong enemy forces were also reported to be moving around the American block, creating the possibility that the entire American force would soon be cut off from Allied lines.

Colonel Hunter called a staff meeting to decide what to do next. Assembling at 1500 hours on 3 April the discussion focused on the fate of the 2d Battalion, which had been surrounded for four days. There were concerns that the Kachins, not prepared for the conventional warfare that was now occurring, might withdraw. The proposal for the battalion to infiltrate through enemy lines was considered. Someone pointed out that Sergeant Keslik's patrol, after spending two days in Nhpum Ga, had successfully rejoined the Orange Combat Team by passing through enemy lines. That idea was discarded, because all the wounded men, the supplies, and the animals would have to be abandoned in order to make the escape possible. Sergeant Keslik's men had split into two small groups and had slid down a steep ravine, an action not possible for the main body. Because the 2d Battalion could receive supplies regularly, the situation was not considered desperate enough that the battalion should go to the extreme of abandoning its wounded in order to escape.[8]

Colonel Hunter was still concerned with his wider mission of protecting the flank of the advancing Allied drive in northern Burma and was wary of Japanese attempts to outflank the block at Nhpum Ga. With enemy forces reported in the Tanai Valley possibly attempting to bypass the block, he had inadequate resources to cover all approaches. Hsamshingyang was only one point at which the enemy could bypass Nhpum Ga. The other, at Weilangyang, was covered only by Chinese patrols. To relieve the 3d Battalion of the responsibility for covering so wide an area, Colonel Hunter dispatched Captain George, TSgt. Lawrence J. Hill, and Sgt. Lum K. Pun, a Chinese interpreter, to Weilangyang to ask that a battalion of the 112th Chinese Regiment be sent forward to assist him. Even if Captain George was successful, the Chinese could not arrive for several days.

Having viewed every possibility and having made every possible arrangement for assistance, Colonel Hunter decided to take every risk to relieve the beleaguered 2d Battalion. He announced to his staff:

Gentlemen, in the morning we start an attack that will drive through to the 2d Battalion. It may take two or three days, but we will get through. All troops except the sick and the mule skinners will be withdrawn from the airstrip. [All] large patrols will be called in, and Kachins substituted wherever possible. Tomorrow, as soon as we can get ready, Orange Combat Team will attack due south along the trail. [The men of] Khaki Combat Team will leave their heavy equipment here, march due south behind Orange Combat Team until they are 400 yards from Jap position, then turn west down the mountain and attack the Japs on their west flank. The artillery will be moved up to where it can fire point blank into the Jap bunkers and pill boxes. Every man of the gun crews volunteered . . . this afternoon.[9]

Colonel Hunter went on to propose that a message be deliberately dropped into Japanese lines that would be addressed to the 2d Battalion. Its intent was to deceive the enemy into believing that a battalion of parachute troops was about to be dropped between Kauri and Auche on 4 April. Colonel Hunter also asked for a dummy drop of supplies into that area to enhance the deception.

The morning of 4 April was devoted to preparation. Colonel Hunter moved his command post back to Mahyetkawang for protection. As the headquarters group arrived they found elements of the Chinese battalion that Captain George had contacted arriving to relieve the Americans. Colonel Hunter remained with the Orange Combat Team to coordinate the attack. Air support was busy overhead, bombing and strafing along the trail. Marauders on the ground also directed the planes over the radio. By 1100 it became clear that because of the problems the Khaki Combat Team was having in cutting its way through the jungle, the attack could not begin on time. Colonel Hunter postponed the attack until 1600. He intended to attack with all the strength at his disposal in one coordinated effort. Another effort was unlikely.

One of Colonel Hunter's deceptions was a fake fight west of the area where the main attack was to begin. At 1530 the pioneer and demolition platoon staged a fake combat off to the west. They used M1 carbines, which in the jungle sounded like Japanese Arisaka rifles, to make the fight sound genuine. The Japanese quickly shifted the fires of their mortars to that area, allowing the Orange Combat Team to attack without that opposition. Supported by aircraft and their new artillery, the Marauders overcame the initial enemy defenses and occupied the steep rise on the ridge that had stopped them the day before. Captain Clarence O. Burch ordered his leading platoons, under Lts. Theodore T. Chamelas and Victor Weingartner, to continue. As the attack approached the next defended rise it was stopped by a new enemy position, and Major Lew, leading his combat team, was seriously wounded by a sniper's bullet.

Although the attack had begun well, it quickly became apparent that it would still be a matter of overcoming one defended position after another. Fighting continued until dusk on 4 April and began again at daylight the next day. There was no gain registered for 5 April. Major Peter A. Petito replaced the wounded Major Lew in command of the Orange Combat Team and continued the attack without success.

Meanwhile, the Khaki Combat Team continued its struggle with the Burmese jungle. On 4 April Major Briggs had equipped two of his platoons with every machine gun and mortar he could find and led them along the trail to Nhpum Ga. As planned by Colonel Hunter, he then veered west, cutting a path along the jungle-covered mountain slopes to a point west of the 2d Battalion's perimeter. The advance was slowed by the need to cross a succession of rough spurs running west toward the Hkuma Valley. As the platoons tried to advance into the perimeter they were met by heavy fire from well prepared enemy positions. Patrols sent forward to find a way through the enemy defenses were turned back at every try. The platoons dug in for the night, prepared to try again the next day. By daylight, however, they discovered that the Japanese were trying to surround them, and they had to cut a new trail to escape back to the airstrip at Hsamshingyang.

The attacks to relieve the garrison of Nhpum Ga worried the Japanese. They renewed the attacks on the surrounded Marauders and on 4 April made the first penetration of the defenses at the western end of the perimeter. Several enemy soldiers reached the Marauders' foxholes after some mule handlers had left their holes under the mistaken impression that the attack had been repulsed.

Two Marauder grenadiers swiftly eliminated the penetration, but the situation had been a close one.

During the night two more assaults came against the perimeter. The Americans had anticipated both of them, thanks to the continuing efforts of Sergeant Matsumoto, who had roamed beyond the edge of the perimeter, listening to enemy conversations and advising his comrades of incoming attacks before they began. Described as a slightly built, quiet man, he went out beyond the lines every night to snipe at the enemy and listen to their conversations. Normally he stayed out until just before dawn, but on this night he came in at 2300 hours and reported to Lieutenant McLogan that the enemy was going to creep up on the Americans and assault without any warning.

Lieutenant McLogan decided to surprise the Japanese. He ordered his men to withdraw from their positions and set up slightly to the rear. Then they waited for the attack. Just before dawn the enemy came, as predicted by Sergeant Matsumoto. They raced for the empty Marauder foxholes. Standing exposed above empty positions, they were suddenly engulfed by the automatic weapons fire of the concealed Marauders, under Lieutenant McLogan. The leading enemy platoon was cut down, and the platoons that followed dived for cover. Then Sergeant Matsumoto took a hand in events. He began yelling "Charge!" in Japanese. Dutifully, the platoons that had taken cover stood up and charged into the prepared American defenses. They too were cut down. Fifty-four dead bodies were later counted, including those of two officers. The 2d Battalion's perimeter remained intact.

Marauder Dale Abbott was with a mortar team of the Green Combat Team. He later recalled Sergeant Matsumoto's actions during the siege:

> He would tap into Japanese phone lines and interrogate prisoners. On the hill he would sneak out every night to listen to the Japanese and find out where they would attack next. If he had ever been caught, I hate to think what they would have done to him. We'd set up our automatic weapons where they would attack. One day they were to attack in two waves. The

first one came but the second was hesitant. Roy jumped up and yelled "attack" in Japanese and on they came. He saved the Battalion.[10]

The following day, 5 April, the Japanese refrained from any attacks, although they continued to shell the perimeter. The pressure from the 3d Battalion's attack had evidently distracted the enemy sufficiently to give some relief to the besieged defenders. Things were still critical in the perimeter, however. Seventeen dead and ninety-seven wounded men needed to be evacuated. Four men were missing. Another water drop had temporarily relieved the water problem, but the trail was still closed behind them.

The Orange Combat Team was only one mile from Nhpum Ga as dawn broke on 6 April. They still faced the single narrow trail, with its steep sides. Only two platoons at most could attack along this narrow channel. Heavy preparatory fires from artillery, mortars, and machine guns paved the way for a spurt in the advance. Lieutenant Boomer, still working miracles with his mortars, crawled to within twenty-five yards of the enemy lines. As the range narrowed he radioed back instructions to his crews: "Deflection correct. Bring it in 25 yards, and if you don't hear from me, you'll know you came this way too far. Then shift it back just a little and you'll be right on it."[11] Fortunately for the lieutenant, the next rounds were right on target.

The preparatory fires had caused the Japanese to vacate their positions until the fires lifted. As they did, both sides raced for the empty positions. In a fight for victory, the Marauders, who had crawled up as close as they dared to the incoming friendly fires, beat the Japanese. The Americans gained five hundred yards. Again they came up against another defended rise. Again the enemy had superior defensive positions prepared. This time there was a sheer cliff off to one side, eliminating any thought of an outflanking maneuver. By this time the Orange Combat Team was exhausted after four days of attacking. Leaving their intelligence and reconnaissance platoon behind, they stood down while the Khaki Combat Team moved up to replace them.

The following day, 7 April, the Khaki Combat Team gained a few yards at the cost of three killed and eight wounded. The meager advance had to be abandoned when it became necessary to consolidate night defense positions. Colonel McGee attempted to help the advance with an attack up the trail, because enemy action on his front was minimal. This effort swiftly failed when it ran into prepared enemy defenses. Indeed, the only good news on 7 April was the arrival of the Marauders' 1st Battalion. Having been alerted to the emergency on 3 April, Colonel Osborne had pushed his battalion for the next four days to arrive at Hsamshingyang. It arrived with 30 percent of its men ineffective because of dysentery. Many others were exhausted beyond the ability to function. Captain Senff, commanding the Red Combat Team, was ordered to assemble as many men as he could find that were fit to fight. He managed to group 250 men out of the entire battalion, of which five would fall out from exhaustion on the way to the front.

While its sister battalions had been fighting for their lives, the 1st Battalion had its own battle in trying to get to them. Sergeant Clarence Branscomb of the I&R platoon of the White Combat Team recalls how it "led off with one of those old British maps that had large areas of uncharted land. It didn't even show mountains or rivers. One time we went clear around a mountain and almost drew down on the tail end of our own main column."[12] Then "we were told to head for Nhpum Ga to help get 2d Battalion out, with no food drop until we got there." The 1st Battalion "traveled by night and day until we arrived in pretty beat condition."

The Japanese were having problems of their own. They were also finding that moving supplies to where they were most needed in the thick, wet, disease-ridden jungles of Burma was no easy task. Supply and reinforcement were constant problems and contributed to the reasons for the slacking in attacks against the Nhpum Ga perimeter. In addition, General Tanaka was becoming more concerned about the security of the base at Myitkyina. He refused to add more troops to the attack, preferring to keep them ready for further Allied efforts to outflank his positions. In fact, he decided that it was time to withdraw and reinforce the garrison of Myitkyina.

Colonel Hunter, now having all the resources he could expect to receive, prepared an all-out attack for 8 April. The Khaki Combat Team would continue its deadly attack along the trail. The Orange

Combat Team would make a flanking effort to the east of Nhpum Ga. Captain Senff's composite force of the 1st Battalion would circle behind Nhpum Ga and cut enemy lines of supply and communication.

The attack went as planned. The Khaki Combat Team battered as before against the prepared enemy positions on the trail, but with limited success. Using the intelligence and reconnaissance platoon and the 3d platoon of Company I, the attack gained little ground. Five times the two platoons attacked, and five times no ground was gained. The casualties continued to mount, with a total of twenty-five men falling, including nine wounded out of the twenty-two in the I&R platoon. The Orange Combat Team tried unsuccessfully to cut a way around the defenses to reach the main enemy forces besieging the 2d Battalion. Captain Senff's force made a wide enveloping movement against little resistance and reached the trail between Kauri and Nhpum Ga. They placed blocks along all paths used by the Japanese to supply their positions. Two enemy supply patrols were caught on those blocks. In the morning of 9 April, Easter Sunday, Captain Senff's force directed mortar fire on a Japanese bivouac they observed near Kauri.

That morning also brought celebration for the 2d Battalion for reasons other than the holiday. Shortly after dawn, patrols from the Khaki Combat Team entered the perimeter. Against no opposition the 3d Battalion joined with the 2d. The enemy had gone.

The Americans concluded that the tough resistance of the defenders of Nhpum Ga, the constant attacks by the 3d Battalion, and the outflanking efforts of the 1st Battalion had convinced the Japanese to give up the siege of Nhpum Ga. All of these had contributed, but the concerns of General Tanaka about Myitkyina, near which British and Commonwealth forces were operating, had added to the cumulative decision to withdraw. The withdrawal was hasty, as evidenced by abandoned equipment and by rice still cooking on campfires. No pursuit was ordered. The Marauders, all three battalions, were in no condition to pursue. General Stilwell agreed and ordered that no pursuit be organized. Limiting their efforts to patrols to ensure security, the Marauders looked to their wounded, buried their dead, and cleaned up one of the worst battlefields of the campaign.

The 2d Battalion moved out of Nhpum Ga and marched to Samlulgahtawng. Prepared to assist if the Chinese forces in the area were attacked, they were soon relieved by a battalion of the 112th Chinese Infantry Regiment.

Nhpum Ga cost the 5307th Composite Unit (Provisional) 57 dead and 302 wounded. All men who earlier had been reported as missing were found and accounted for in that total. An additional 379 men were evacuated due to illnesses that included amebic dysentery and malaria. Enemy dead were reported at 400, not including enemy casualties buried by the Japanese or carried off.

There were other costs as well. Since 9 February the men had marched more than five hundred miles in some of the worst terrain in the world. For more than eighty days they had subsisted on K rations, which had not been designed for the extended nutrition of men engaged in constant strenuous activity. Nearly every man suffered from leech bites, which usually developed into what became known as Naga sores, and from dysentery or fevers, usually both. The unit as a whole had suffered over 700 casualties since entering Burma. The 2d Battalion alone had lost 460 men. So depleted was that battalion, at less than half its original strength, that it had to be reorganized. The survivors of the 2d Battalion were now formed into four companies: two rifle companies, a heavy weapons company, and a battalion headquarters company. The latter included an intelligence and reconnaissance platoon, a pioneer and demolition platoon, and a communications platoon. Three hundred Kachin guerrillas were attached to the battalion, and the new organization, known as M Force, was commanded by Major McGee.

One issue that did not immediately reveal itself was hidden in some statistics that Major Hopkins kept for his own interest. He recorded that at Nhpum Ga more Marauders had been killed or wounded by friendly fire or carelessness than at either of the two previous battles combined. Men were shot in the head because they weren't wearing helmets, others ignored orders to withdraw from exposed positions and were killed, a few wore strange garments such as overalls and were killed by their friends who mistook them for the enemy, and still others were killed while bunching up or walking carelessly into known enemy fire zones. This all pointed to a critical state of fatigue that went beyond the growing numbers of sick and weak Marauders.[13]

While the war went on around them, the Marauders rested as well as they could. Under intermittent enemy fire from long-range guns, they sent out patrols to ensure no enemy surprises. Indeed, patrolling was a mainstay of operations in Burma. British soldiers used to joke of a future military communiqué that said, "Today, the fifth anniversary of the end of World War II was celebrated. On the Arakan front normal patrol activity continued."

Despite the constant danger, the Marauders rested, bathed, ate, and did the necessary military chores to stay prepared for any surprises. Chloride of lime and flame throwers were flown in to dispose of the many animal bodies and to reduce the numbers of flies, which caused serious health problems. Graves were concentrated in the center of the village and carefully marked. Major Rogoff organized a litter train to ensure that the 103 wounded men were gently carried the four miles to the airstrip, where Major Hopkins and his assistant, 1st Lt. Paul E. Armstrong, prepared them for evacuation. Weapons were cleaned and repaired. New ten-in-one rations were received gratefully. New clothing was issued and the old clothing burned. Mail was distributed, the first in two months. Colonel Hunter "initiated a rehabilitation and training program for the units to follow. Close order drill was prescribed, and the sight of the jungle veterans attempting to regain some semblance of spit and polish" caused him to walk around with a sly grin.[14] Mule skinners boasted about the prowess of their individual animals, and eventually a race was held, using the airstrip as a racetrack. A pool was started about the date for the invasion of Europe. Colonel Hunter chose 6 June, the only Marauder to pick that date. Rumors circulated that upon the arrival of a regiment of the 38th Chinese Division the unit would go back to India for rest and recuperation.

The Chinese soon arrived, and the Marauders were pulled back. For the next two weeks the Marauders rested in place. As the weeks went on, signs began to appear that all was not going to continue as pleasantly as they were expecting. Rumors now changed from returning to India to another mission. Men became angered over any talk of additional combat before a rest period in India. Arguments broke out. Yet the rumors persisted, and they always focused on the Japanese stronghold of Myitkyina. Staff officers from the Northern Combat Area Command appeared and observed the troops, asking how the men felt. Colonel Henry L. Kinnison Jr. reported that despite the recent hard fight the Marauders were in good shape. Colonel Hunter, who already knew that a drive on Myitkyina was under consideration, sent out a reconnaissance party under his intelligence officer, Captain Laffin. Word came down that General Merrill, well again after his rest in the rear, would soon assume direct command. More Chinese units appeared in the area, and appearances of a combined effort being planned grew daily. On 22 April came the word: there would be a third mission. And of course the objective was Myitkyina.

Colonel Cannon also reviewed the unit and was given what Colonel Hunter referred to as the Hancock treatment. When Major Hancock, Galahad's excellent supply officer, had visited the front, he had asked to spend the night with a frontline unit to get a feel for the situation. The Japanese having only recently departed, Colonel Hunter could not resist the temptation to show the major exactly what combat was like. He arranged with Major Briggs to have one of his patrols simulate an enemy attack at Major Hancock's post, with an appropriate Marauder response. So successful was this charade that it was replayed for Colonel Cannon, Colonel Kinnison, and others.[15]

Preparations began immediately. The 2d Battalion absorbed its Kachin elements. The 1st and 3d Battalions retained their combat-team organizations. The 1st Battalion would combine with the Chinese 150th Regiment, 50th Division, and a battery of pack artillery from the Chinese 22d Division to form H Force. Colonel Hunter commanded H Force, with Colonel Osborne remaining in command of the 1st Battalion. The 3d Battalion would combine with the Chinese 88th Regiment, 30th Division, and the 5307th Pack Artillery Battery to become known as K Force, under the newly assigned Col. Henry L. Kinnison Jr. Colonel Beach remained in direct command of the 3d Battalion. General Merrill returned to full duty, along with his newly appointed executive officer, Col. John E. McCammon, a former operations officer on General Stilwell's staff at

Chungking who spoke fluent Chinese. Described as "a slender, good-looking, slightly gray-haired individual with a soft voice,"[16] Mc-Cammon found that his association with Galahad was to be rather brief. Colonel Hunter "evidently, had not made the Stilwell Team"[17] despite having led the command in its most difficult battles of the campaign.

General Stilwell flew in to discuss operations with General Merrill on 27 April. The objective was now officially the enemy base at Myitkyina. With all the changes and adjustments in place, K Force moved forward the next day.

6. Third Mission: Myitkyina

General Stilwell had originally believed that the farthest he could hope to push his campaign before the monsoon season would shut down operations was Shaduzup. The Japanese drive on Imphal, however, had begun to disturb the Allied high command and resulted in a meeting between General Stilwell and Adm. Lord Louis Mountbatten, the supreme Allied commander in the theater.

Meeting with Admiral Mountbatten, Gen. William Slim, commanding the British XIV Army, and their staffs on 3 April 1944, General Stilwell was interested in learning the British view of operations. He was worried that the Japanese offensive would cause the British to demand that he divert troops to assist them in defending Imphal. General Slim, however, was confident of eventual victory at Imphal, and Admiral Mountbatten authorized General Stilwell to continue his efforts at clearing the Japanese forces out of the Mogaung-Myitkyina area. In fact, so confident was General Slim that he eventually turned over control of Chindit operations to General Stilwell, something that General Wingate would have been appalled to learn. In this directive it was not the intent of the British to actually seize the enemy base at Myitkyina, but only to clear the surrounding approaches to that base in preparation for an assault once the monsoon rains had ceased. The British command did not believe it could be taken before then, had doubts about its importance, and was not prepared to commit reserves to seize and hold Myitkyina while the battle at Imphal continued.

General Stilwell felt differently. He knew that strong forces of British long-range penetration groups, Chindits, were already operating in the area around Mogaung and Myitkyina. He hoped that the activities of those forces would draw off enough of General Tanaka's reserves to weaken the Myitkyina garrison sufficiently to allow a depleted 5307th Composite Unit (Provisional), reinforced with Chinese infantry and artillery, to seize the base. Unlike his British counterparts, he viewed Myitkyina as a key to securing the entire Mogaung-Myitkyina area, his assigned objective. It would also aid his political objectives, increasing his ability to fly supplies to China as directed by both Washington and Chungking. An enemy base at Myitkyina deprived the pilots flying the "hump" to China of use of the shortest route. The base also enabled enemy interceptor pilots to strike those flights. Its seizure by the Allies would reverse those difficulties. The Americans could fly a shorter route, protected by Allied fighter planes flying from the captured airfield at Myitkyina. More flights would also be possible, providing a swifter solution to increasing supply levels to China than the land route, the Ledo Road, had been so far.

General Tanaka had his own objectives. As assigned to him by his area command, he was to hold the Kamaing area indefinitely. Once the Chindits had been driven off the Japanese lines of communication, the Japanese 53d Division would be attached to him for a counterattack to recover all ground lost to the Allies. That depended of course on the Imphal offensive succeeding. The Imphal offensive had now stalled, and he had steadily lost ground in the Kamaing area. The Chindits were still prowling around his rear, and he could expect little assistance until those problems were resolved. He did receive, however, two understrength regiments from other units. These were the 146th Regiment of the 56th Division, at the strength of one battalion, and the 4th Regiment of the 2d Division, with two battalions. Although the 53d Division did assemble in his rear area, higher headquarters wavered in its decision about where to commit these reserves, and so they were not committed decisively. Faced with these difficulties, General Tanaka counted on the monsoons to stop or slow the Allied advance and to give him enough time to construct new defenses in front of Myitkyina.

General Stilwell had ordered both the Chinese 22d and 38th Divisions to attack by envelopment. Both division commanders protested the orders. Denied their protest, the Chinese began their attack. They faced the depleted 4th Japanese Infantry, but the attack progressed slowly and envelopments were few. The 22d Division pulled units out for refitting, while others remained idle. It was then that Colonel Brown, commanding the Provisional Tank Group, was secretly advised by one of his Chinese officers that orders had been received from Chungking not to make the advance as directed by General Stilwell. Colonel Brown reported the conversation to General Stilwell.

General Stilwell directly ordered General Liao to move his 22d Division forward. The objective was Inkangahtawng, the village the Marauders had probed before being withdrawn to Nhpum Ga. General Liao reacted by moving his division headquarters a mile forward but not his frontline troops. He was now next to Colonel Brown's command post. Again General Stilwell ordered General Liao to attack, and again division headquarters moved forward into the lines of its 66th Infantry Regiment. But again there was no movement at the front. While this foot-dragging continued, Colonel Brown's tanks, without infantry support, continued to attack the Japanese positions, losing several American tanks in the process. Finally, on 20 April, and after the British relieved the siege of Kohima, the Chinese began to advance.

When the Chinese moved, they moved swiftly. A week later they had turned the flank of the Japanese 4th Regiment and had crossed the Kamaing Road despite heavy enemy resistance, which had included some of the heaviest artillery support yet seen in the campaign. On 4 May Inkangahtawng fell to the Chinese 22d Division. The advance continued, with the 22d Division pushing back determined Japanese opponents step by step. In one instance a special group was organized, code-named Purple Force, which consisted of the Chinese 149th Infantry Regiment from the 50th Division and a group of 250 Marauder evacuees. The assignment was to circle around the defending Japanese and cut the line of retreat. The attempt fizzled. Encountering mountains too steep for its animal transport, Purple Force had to send the mules back to base and carry all their equipment on their backs. Finally, the American officer leading the force became lost and had to be located by Lt. Col. Joseph W. Stilwell Jr., the general's son and intelligence officer, who directed the force back to its base. The commander of the Chinese 149th Regiment, considered a competent commander, refused to work with Americans again. Not only did this mission fail, but it deprived General Merrill of desperately needed combat veterans.

Nevertheless, the main attack continued to make progress, although much slower than General Stilwell would have liked. He was convinced that Generalissimo Chiang Kai-shek was controlling events from his far-distant headquarters at Chungking, and postwar evidence supports this belief. Despite the slowness of the advance, it was successful. Suddenly, on 19 May, General Sun announced to his American liaison officer, "We go on to take Kamaing now." With his 112th Regiment performing a Marauder-like envelopment and his 114th attacking to keep the enemy defenders occupied, the Chinese entered Kaimaing on 25 May, capturing thirty-five enemy trucks, a jeep, an automobile, warehouses of food and ammunition, a workshop, artillery and horses, and a motor pool. General Tanaka had been dealt a severe blow.

He reacted swiftly. He stripped his headquarters and support units of all available men and rushed them to the threatened area. He pulled in the 4th Regiment and ordered its commander, Col. Yusaku Ichikari, to attack the Chinese block. And once again, as he had done earlier, he ordered his engineers to cut a secret escape route in case it was needed. The Japanese struck promptly and with great determination against the 112th Regiment's block. Failure would mean that the 18th Division would surrender all its transportation and artillery and a major portion of its supplies, making the division ineffective and unable to defend the rest of the Mogaung-Myitkyina area.

Despite the fierce attacks, the 112th Regiment held its position, losing all but two of its officers in the process. The battle for the roadblock, known as the Seton Block, showed the Chinese soldier at his best. In addition, other Chinese commands hammered at General Tanaka's forces. With all restrictions off, the Chinese troops performed well and made life difficult for the Japanese invaders.

On 1 June a task force drawn from the 22d Division crossed the Kamaing Road and cut off the 4th, 55th, and 56th Japanese Regiments from the secret escape trail prepared by General Tanaka. Confusion reigned in the Japanese camp. For example, after the cutting of the road, the commander of the 55th Regiment could contact only one of his infantry companies. The Japanese were forced to turn off into the jungle, cutting trails as they went and carrying five hundred wounded men with them. As a result of the Chinese attacks, the 18th Japanese Infantry Division was in desperate straits. The normal rice ration, usually 860 grams per day, was now down to 100 grams. The loss of gasoline supplies immobilized transport, forcing equipment to be either hand carried or abandoned. Allied aircraft had destroyed 40 percent of the division's supply dumps. Infantry companies were down to an average of thirty men per unit. The Chinese 149th Regiment had captured all the artillery supporting the 56th Japanese Regiment and had killed the crews. Acting as rear guard, the regiment had been forced to sacrifice entire platoons as delaying forces while the balance of the regiment covered the withdrawal of the 18th Division.

The Marauders were busy during those weeks as well. On 28 April, K Force moved north to Taikri and then turned eastward from the Tanai Valley into the mountains. H Force followed at a two-day interval. The journey to Myitkyina was estimated to be sixty-five miles long, of which one-fifth was over the Kumon Mountain Range, which rose in places to over six thousand feet. The trail was not well known and had not been traveled in years. Captain Laffin and 2d Lt. Paul A. Dunlop went ahead of K Force, accompanied by thirty Kachin Rangers and thirty Chinese coolies, to repair the worst stretches of trail. To make matters more difficult, the monsoon season now began in earnest. The clouds made air supply more difficult, and the rains washed out the trail.

The Marauders who made up the enveloping force were an angry group. Convinced that high command had blundered in ordering them forward on yet a third mission after the recent successes, they made their displeasure known. As Lieutenant Ogburn later wrote, "We reasoned why with volubility and bitterness but also wearily, aware of the futility of it."[1] Despite their personal feelings, the Americans plodded forward, assured by their commander that this was positively the last effort to be asked of them. For many, Myitkyina became the end of the rainbow, the pot of gold after which they could rest and return to a more normal existence.

> This was positively to be the last effort asked of us. We had it from General Merrill himself that when we had gained our objective we would be returned at once to India, given a party to cause taxpayers a shudder, installed in a well-appointed rest camp, and given furloughs. It was this prospect more than anything else that gave the 5307th the resolution to surmount the obstacles that lay before it on the trail to Myitkyina.[2]

There were obstacles in abundance. General Stilwell's plan called for H and K Forces to cross the Kumon Range, while M Force remained in a position to cover the southern flank, the most likely area for an enemy counterstroke to originate. This plan, originated by General Merrill and altered by Colonel Hunter and the staff of the 5307th, was approved by General Stilwell and became his scheme for a swift conquest of Myitkyina before the monsoon rains came in strength. Knowing what he was asking of his only American combat unit, General Stilwell also advised General Merrill that once Myitkyina had been seized, Merrill would be authorized to begin evacuating the Marauders without further reference to higher headquarters. With all these promises in their heads, the Marauders and their Chinese and Kachin allies stepped forward on the trail.

It was little more than a trail. It was actually a path that the local Kachin natives used on occasion in places where no trail existed. In other places the trail was so steep that footholds had to be cut for the animals to negotiate the hills. In steeper locations the animals had to be unloaded entirely, the loads manhandled up the hill, and then the animals pushed up the hill to be reloaded. Twenty animals and their loads, mainly from the Khaki Combat Team leading the column, were lost over steep hillsides. After six days of this type of march the column reached Naura Hkyat, where a report came in from Kachin scouts that the enemy was in the vicinity. The intelligence and reconnaissance platoon of the Khaki Combat Team probed and found nothing, but the 1st Battalion of the 88th Chinese Regiment did have a brush with a Japanese patrol probing toward Ritpong, an intermediate objective. Apparently Ritpong was an enemy base.

Somewhere along this trail a decades-long mystery was created. The column had carried since before the first mission a large mount of silver rupees. These were what Colonel Hunter called "secret intelligence funds" to be used for buying intelligence information from local residents. While marching on the trail to Ritpong, Colonel Hunter noticed a soldier struggling up a steep hillside, carrying, in addition to his heavy pack, a pair of saddlebags. Inquiring what was in the bags, Colonel Hunter learned that these were the silver rupees. Colonel Hunter, fully aware now of the far reach of his OSS Kachin allies, ordered the soldier to toss the saddlebags down the steep hillside into the jungle. Astonished, the soldier did as he was told. For years afterward, Lieutenant Ogburn, who as communications officer for the column was responsible for these funds, worried over their fate, concerned that he would be billed by the army for the loss. And Colonel Osborne, equally unaware of what had happened to them, often chided the lieutenant about the fate of the funds charged to his care.[3]

On 5 May the column reached a trail junction about one mile from Ritpong. Here Colonel Kinnison began an envelopment by sending a combat patrol from the Khaki Combat Team to approach the village from the rear. The reported trail didn't exist, and the patrol was forced to cut its own trail around the village. The remainder of the Khaki Combat Team, followed closely by the Orange Combat Team, cut a trail toward the village. At the end of 6 May all units were in position as planned. In the interim the 88th Chinese Regiment had attacked the village from the north but had been driven back.

At 0530 on 7 May the Khaki Combat Team advanced toward Ritpong, while the Orange Combat Team protected the bivouac area in reserve. Barely off the start line, the advance elements came to a fork in the trail. Here a Japanese scout passed without noticing the Americans in the nearby jungle. A block was placed on the trail, and reconnaissance parties probed the area. One of these checked on a group of huts nearby and disturbed an enemy patrol preparing its breakfast. The enemy group fled before the Americans could engage them, but back at the trail block an enemy squad was wiped out as they approached. The Khaki Combat Team now moved forward to Ritpong but was halted by a wel-placed enemy machine-gun position that blocked their advance.

The 88th Chinese Regiment had also advanced again on 7 May and was making good progress. Rather than expend the Marauders' limited strength, Colonel Kinnison halted K Force and let the 88th Regiment attack while supported by the Marauders. He also made efforts to cover the force's rear and ordered out patrols. One patrol from the intelligence and reconnaissance platoon encountered a heavily guarded enemy supply column on its way to Ritpong, dispersed the guard, and left the abandoned supplies for K Force retrieval.

The 88th Regiment had made progress but had not yet cleared the village when night fell. During the night of 7 and 8 May the enemy garrison made several breakout attempts. These were repulsed by Marauder blocking parties with considerable loss to the enemy. The Chinese continued their attack, finally clearing Ritpong on 9 May. The time it took to secure Ritpong allowed H Force to overtake K Force.

H Force, under Colonel Hunter, the 150th Chinese Regiment, the 1st Marauder Battalion, the 3d Company Animal Transport Regiment, and a battery of the 22d Division artillery continued on to arrive 10 May at the village of Lazu. There, thirty-five miles from Myitkyina, preparations were made for the final thrust to the objective. Colonel Hunter's group was to be the assault force. Colonel Kinnison's men were to feint to the east, where at the village of Nsopzup a large enemy supply base was under attack by British-led Kachin and Gurkha guerrillas. The battle at Ritpong had alerted the Japanese to the presence of the American forces behind their lines, and a swift reaction could be expected from the direction of Nsopzup, the nearest enemy base. Colonel Hunter's group would head for Myitkyina, while Colonel Kinnison would move east to deflect any enemy attempt to intercept H Force. The western flank was already covered by Colonel McGee's M Force, which was cutting paths through the jungle toward the village of Arang, having pushed off an enemy probe along the way. Despite the fevers and dysentery suffered by most of his men and the loss of half his animal transport, Colonel McGee managed to keep his command within two days' march of H and K Forces.

Colonel Kinnison moved toward Ngao Ga on 11 May. As usual, the trail ran over steep hills and into deep ravines. The day was hotter than usual, with the heavy humidity of the monsoon weather ever present. Several men collapsed from the heat and humidity. The march continued early on 12 May, but at 0950 the leading elements ran into an enemy platoon about four hundred yards northwest of the village of Tingkrukawng. The Orange Combat Team immediately attacked but found themselves facing an entire enemy battalion. The Marauder attack soon halted. Enemy resistance halted all forward movement even after the Khaki Combat Team added its mortars to support the attack.

Colonel Kinnison sent a company of the 88th Regiment to outflank the enemy position, but the Chinese ran into heavy opposition and suffered severe casualties. The Orange Combat Team then tried a close outflanking maneuver around both sides of the trail, only to find that the enemy held the high ground with dug-in gun positions dominating all approaches. The attack was halted for the day. During the night Colonel Kinnison conferred with his commanders and decided to use Major Briggs's Khaki Combat Team to circle the village and attack the enemy from the rear while the Orange Combat Team kept them busy along the trail.

While K Force struggled at Ritpong, Colonel Hunter's H Force had caught up with them. It was there that Colonel Hunter was to turn off and head directly for Myitkyina. Upon arriving, however, he found the Chinese 88th Regiment blocking the trail. Conferring with Colonel Kinnison, Colonel Hunter received priority on the trail and managed to slip by Ritpong without being noticed by the Japanese, who were being kept busy by K Force.

The H Force continued on to the local OSS headquarters at the village of Arang, where they received an airdrop of food and supplies. Men unfit to continue were left there for evacuation. During the march Colonel Beach spoke with General Merrill, who was flying over the area, trying to locate Colonel Hunter. Hunter, who could both see General Merrill's plane and hear Colonel Beach "hogging the radio,"[4] was unable to reach his commander and proceeded without reporting.

When Colonel Hunter arrived at Arang, however, General Merrill appeared and discussed final plans for the last march to Myitkyina. Although most of the points discussed satisfied Colonel Hunter, he lacked confidence about what would happen once the airfield had been seized, because by that time his men would be low on all kinds of supplies. Told by General Merrill "Don't worry. I'll be there and take over,"[5] Colonel Hunter did worry. As it turned out, there was good cause.

For nearly six hours the Khaki Combat Team cut a trail around the village. The terrain was so steep that no mules or heavy equipment could be carried along. Finally reaching the approach to the rear of the village, they began to crawl up the steep incline leading to the village. As they came near the village they observed that the Japanese had a heavy block along the trail and that an enemy patrol based on that block was trying to work its way around their own flank to cut them off.

Two platoons were swiftly sent out to stop this threat. Despite several attempts, the Khaki Combat Team could not bypass the enemy trail block. About the only thing gained from this maneuver was that Major Briggs managed to reach a high point from which he could observe enemy positions and direct the Orange Combat Team's mortar fire.

After six additional hours of trying to outflank the enemy, the Khaki Combat Team had exhausted its ammunition. They had not eaten all day. Supply drops in the heavy jungle in close proximity to the enemy were out of the question. Colonel Kinnison ordered Major Briggs to withdraw, a difficult mission with wounded men, especially in darkness, but it was successfully completed by an exhausted column.

The following day a Chinese battalion was sent to the southwest to reinforce a Chinese company whose attack had also stalled. That effort achieved little. Meanwhile, the Orange Combat Team's frontal attacks were also stymied. Signs indicated that the enemy garrison was receiving reinforcements from the east. General Merrill and Colonel Kinnison conferred and agreed that further effort there was not warranted, as it was only intended as a feint and sufficient time had been given to Colonel Hunter's H Force to move toward Myitkyina. Colonel Kinnison pulled his force out of the battle and moved to follow Colonel Hunter to the objective. The battle of Tingkrukawng had cost the Marauders twenty-nine men—eight killed and twenty-one wounded—although Chinese casualties were considerably heavier. Among the Marauder casualties was Colonel Kinnison, who during the battle contracted the deadly mite typhus. Evacuated swiftly, he died in a matter of days with what has been described as "shocking speed."[6]

While K Force struggled at Tingkrukawng, Colonel Hunter was leading his group toward Myitkyina. At Arang they had been joined by a group of seventy-five OSS-trained Kachins under the command of Lt. William Martin. Together, Lieutenant Martin and the Marauders' Captain Laffin led the column toward Myitkyina. They followed a trail southward and crossed the motor road southwest of Seingheing, where an OSS Detachment 101–trained Kachin guided the column over a maze of native trails toward the objective. Although they had not engaged an enemy on this march, they had already lost 120 men to illness. Their luck held until 2030 hours on 15 May, when the Kachin guide, Nauiyang Nau, was bitten by a poisonous snake. The Kachin attempted to continue leading the column, but his foot swiftly swelled to the point where he could no longer walk and his life was in danger. The Marauders were lost in a maze of native trails, and only the guide knew the way. Captain Laffin and Lieutenant Dunlop took turns throughout the night sucking poisoned blood out of the guide's leg until, before dawn, he was well enough to proceed by riding Colonel Hunter's horse.

The column rested on the morning of 16 May at the village of Seingheing, where they took the last supply drop they would receive until Myitkyina. About thirty officers and men who could not go on were left at the village, under the command of Major Senff, commander of the Red Combat Team, who had seriously injured his back. Litter-bearing light aircraft were ordered in to evacuate the group. The drop was distributed, and then at noon the column resumed its march. Two natives who had been encountered along the way were kept with the column to preserve the secrecy of its mission.

Arriving at a point only four miles from the airstrip, Colonel Hunter ordered his attached Kachins to gather up the natives at the village of Namkwi, whose loyalty after years of Japanese occupation was open to question. Colonel Hunter refrained, however, from cutting either the telegraph or railroad lines to preserve secrecy. He sent out a patrol under Sgt. Clarence E. Branscomb of the White Combat Team's I&R platoon to reconnoiter the airfield defenses, and he set the following morning as the time of the attack.

Staff Sergeant Branscomb, an Oregon native, was an original South Pacific volunteer for the Marauders, having served with the 161st Infantry Regiment in the New Georgia campaign. He had been platoon sergeant in Lieutenant Wilson's I&R platoon throughout the campaign. When he was called by Colonel Hunter to take a patrol to the airport, the Colonel gave him his last fifth of Canadian Club and a radio to report his findings. Lieutenant Colonel Caifson Johnson told him the direction of the patrol and what to look for as to defenses. "I went back to the platoon and asked for a couple of volunteers. Finally got two and I'm not sure if it was Clarke and Frye but anyway we started off but didn't get far before we killed the Canadian Club and things got better."[7] For the next three hours the patrol scouted the airfield, noting enemy work crews, pill boxes, and enemy troops in movement.

> We crawled around in the grass and brush trying to work our way around the airport perimeter. After almost knifing each other a few times and at about 2:30 a.m., I picked up the radio and started walking down the middle of the runway, thinking if those emplacements were occupied we'd soon find out [and] besides our time was up.[8]

Because the radio was malfunctioning, Sergeant Branscomb used a basic code system of 1 for no and 2 for yes to inform Colonel Johnson that there were Japanese on the field, that the field was in usable condition, and that gliders could land there.

Meanwhile, H Force settled in with their backs to the Irrawaddy River. "I had a sound reason for placing my back to the river," Colonel Hunter later wrote. "I wanted them in a place where they would be hemmed in and forced, if necessary, to dig in and fight. I had previously ascertained a couple of useful pieces of knowledge; the Namkwi was unfordable, and most of the Chinese soldiers of the 150th could not swim."[9]

Colonel Hunter was aware that because of Allied planes strafing the airfield the Japanese normally kept to the jungle fringes of the area during daylight hours. Sergeant Branscomb's patrol provided him with an estimated number of Japanese defenders and Burmese workmen present. Colonel Hunter ordered Colonel Osborne to take his battalion, with the Chinese 150th Regiment following, to the southwest end of the field. There he was to leave the Chinese in position and continue on southwest to the ferry terminal at Pamati.

Thirty minutes later, at 1030 hours on 17 May, the attack began. Opposition was negligible, and both the Chinese and the Marauders gained their assigned positions by 1100 hours. At that time the Red Combat Team was ordered to hold the ferry site alone while Colonel Osborne and Major Johnson's White Combat Team returned to the field. Orders were received there from Colonel Hunter to seize Zigyun, another ferry site and the main point of entry to the Myitkyina area from the Japanese side of the Irrawaddy River. The Chinese 150th Regiment, under the watchful eye of Colonel Combs, accomplished its objectives as ordered.

The relative ease with which H Force had seized the airstrip would not last. Although General Tanaka knew that his main base at Myitkyina was bound to be an Allied objective, the actual timing of the attack came as a complete surprise. Strained as his resources were at this point, General Tanaka did manage to have two understrength battalions of the 114th Infantry Regiment under Colonel Maruyama in the town. Also, about 100 men of the Japanese 15th Airfield Battalion were present on the airstrips. An additional 318 men from other labor units were present, as were 320 patients in the nearby military hospital. A total of about 700 able-bodied Japanese troops were in the immediate area when H Force struck.

Colonel Hunter was not fooled by the ease of the initial attack. He immediately sent the prearranged code signal to General Stilwell's headquarters. The code, "Merchant of Venice," indicated that the reinforcement and supply process should begin immediately. Earlier signals sent at two-day and one-day intervals had alerted headquarters, and all preparations had been made. Because the strip had been captured intact, a flow of food, ammunition, and infantry reinforcements was scheduled to begin immediately.

Once again the weather took a hand. On 17 May a company of the 679th Engineer Aviation Battalion was flown in by glider, to repair and maintain the airstrip. A battery of .50-caliber antiaircraft guns also arrived for airfield protection, followed by the 2d Battalion of the Chinese 89th Regiment. Then the weather closed down the airfield. Interference by the army air corps also affected the build-up. Instead of continuing with reinforcements, the next shipment was two troops of the British 69th Light Antiaircraft Regiment, something not immediately vital to seizing the town of Myitkyina. Both General Merrill and Colonel Hunter expressed their disappointment.

Colonel Hunter was more than disappointed. He soon became furious. As the first liaison plane landed he went to greet what he expected to be General Merrill. "I was surprised to see emerge not Merrill but Moe Asensio, colonel of engineers, class of 1927, United States Military Academy. My greeting was not very cordial, for I was disappointed at not seeing Merrill, who had assured me at Arang that he would be the first man to come in."[10] As more engineers or support troops came in, Colonel Hunter became more concerned about his own support. Without the other Chinese and Marauder infantry forces, holding Myitkyina could be a dangerous if not impossible assignment.

A second liaison plane landed Gen. Donald Old, the troop carrier commander, onto the field, and he was soon directing dozens of gliders filled with airfield engineers onto the runway. Colonel Hunter asked him if he could talk to the aircraft about how to land on the field and was told he could not. "I am sorry to say I lost my sense of humor, respect for rank and most senior officers in general," Hunter later said, "for I asked, 'General, what are you doing

here if you can't communicate with your aircraft—and stop this fi-
asco.'"[11] General Old advised Colonel Hunter that his aircraft would
eventually bring the promised Chinese troops, but Colonel Hunter
saw no evidence of either reinforcements or the desperately needed
supplies he had been promised upon arrival at the field.

General Stilwell, however, was exultant. He had heard time and
again how the taking of Myitkyina was impossible in that campaigning year. Even if it could be taken, he heard, it could not be held.
And if it could be held, it was not worth the effort it would take to
hold it. Now he had it, and he intended to both hold it and make it
a valuable base for future operations. So anxious was he for success
that he flew over the field on 15 May while Colonel Hunter was still
sheltering in the nearby jungle and preparing to seize the strip. After Colonel Hunter secured the strip General Stilwell flew in, together with a number of correspondents, to relish his triumph. He
recorded his satisfaction in his diary, including a soon-to-be-famous
reference to his allies who had considered his task unimportant.
"Will this burn up the limeys," he wrote after talking to General
Merrill about the resupply flights.[12]

Indeed, the seizure of Myitkyina was as much a surprise to the
British as it had been to the Japanese. Prime Minister Churchill
wired Admiral Mountbatten, asking if he was aware of the U.S.-Chi-
nese effort at Myitkyina. Admiral Mountbatten was forced to reply
that he had heard only incidentally that General Stilwell was planning an attack on the town and airfield. He planned to write to General Stilwell, expressing his concerns that the retention of the base
would require unacceptable numbers of British troops.

In fact, although both commanders were aware of it, considerable numbers of British and Commonwealth troops had been involved in the capture of Myitkyina. The efforts of the Chindit
brigades behind enemy lines had distracted enemy reserves and
had cut vital supply lines. Additional troops had been committed to
guarding lines of communications. As General Tanaka had noted,
critical reserves for his division had been held back by area command because of the activities of those British troops. Additional
British assistance would soon come into play.

Immediately upon securing the airstrip, Colonel Hunter had

called for his reinforcements from Galahad. Colonel Kinnison, before his fatal illness, had ordered his command to Myitkyina. Colonel McGee was already en route, having successfully protected the right flank of the entire force. While awaiting their arrival General Merrill flew in and established his headquarters. Colonel McCammon then ordered Colonel Hunter to seize the town of Myitkyina. The newly flown-in battalion of the 89th Chinese regiment would defend the airstrip while two battalions of the 150th Chinese Regiment attacked the town. The third battalion remained in reserve on the airfield. The White Combat Team of Colonel Osborne's battalion would move to seize Zigyun while the Red Combat Team continued to hold the ferry point at Pamati.

The White Combat Team seized Rampur and discovered several warehouses of clothing and other enemy supplies. Colonel Osborne then led off to Zigyun, which they took without opposition. When they radioed Colonel Hunter for further instructions, Colonel Osborne was told to await the arrival of a company of Chinese infantry and then return to the field. Expecting the Chinese relief force within hours, the White Combat Team garrisoned Zigyun for two full days before the Chinese force, which had encountered several groups of Japanese stragglers and had dug in nine times in five miles, arrived. The 150th Regiment was initially more successful, seizing the Myitkyina railway station before encountering severe enemy opposition and retiring to a line about eight hundred yards outside of town.

The American liaison officers—Lt. Col. William H. Combs, Capt. Thomas L. Kerley, Maj. Fred Huffine, and Maj. Frank C. Hodges— led the battalions in the attack. During that action the two battalions lost direction and, believing each other the enemy, fired upon each other before Colonel Combs could stop the slaughter by risking his life between the two warring factions of the same regiment. Major Hodges was not as fortunate. Shot in the back, his body was later found by an American patrol.

With daylight on 19 May, K Force found itself bivouacked within fifty yards of the Myitkyina-Mogaung motor road and marched along the road to the Allied perimeter. While they were en route General Merrill radioed them and ordered an attack on the village of Charpate, a suspected enemy strong point. The attack succeeded against minimal resistance. The 3d Marauder Battalion secured the village while its companion 88th Chinese Regiment garrisoned a line from the village to the railroad. Marauder patrols blocked the Mogaung Road and all trails leading to Charpate. Later in the day several groups of Japanese trying to get into Myitkyina along the Mogaung Road were pushed away. On that date the 3d Battalion, 42nd Regiment, 14th Chinese Division, arrived by air along with the rest of the 89th Chinese Regiment.

Some of the other units that continued to arrive by air to reinforce the garrison showed how little the situation was understood at the various headquarters that had sent them forward. On 17 May 1944 the 504th Light Pontoon Company was stationed near Ledo, in India. "Early that morning the Company was alerted and told to draw their assault boats and motors and proceed to the Ledo airfield for air transportation to an unknown destination. We loaded the first C-47 with six assault boats and three motors, eight E.M. and one 2nd Lt."[13] The aircraft took off, but a few moments into the flight they were recalled. One plane, however, failed to receive the recall message, "so we went on and landed at Myitkyina much to the surprise of Col. Hunter. He seemed rather upset, and told us to dig in next to Col Seagraves Med. Station."[14] Later the platoon leader, 2d Lt. James Watson, took his platoon and its equipment to the Irrawaddy River and ferried Marauder patrols back and forth across the river. Some of the platoon eventually relieved elements of the Marauders at a blocking position near the river.

The toll that the march and battle were taking on the Marauder contingent was highlighted when General Merrill, checking his men, noted that one platoon had cut out the seat of their pants, so tormented were they by dysentery. Despite this, he reported that his men "were [a] pitiful but still splendid sight."[15]

Once again, on 18 May, the 150th Regiment attacked and once again repeated its error of the previous day by attacking itself. This time casualties were so severe that the regiment had to be withdrawn for refitting and replacements. The continuing strain brought on another heart attack for General Merrill, and he was evacuated. Colonel McCammon assumed command, with Colonel Hunter as his deputy.

The Americans believed that Myitkyina was lightly held and were frustrated by the failure of their Chinese allies to seize the critical town. In fact, the Japanese commanders at Myitkyina had been ordered to hold the town at all costs into the month of August, when preparations for additional defenses to the rear should be completed. Colonel Maruyama had brought his 1st Battalion, 148th Regiment, of the 56th Japanese Division across the Irrawaddy and into Myitkyina. Other groups of Japanese managed to gain access to the town despite the Allied cordon around it.

By 31 May there were an estimated 2,500 Japanese troops in the garrison. In addition, there were the several hundred sick and wounded who could not be counted on to contribute to the defense. Shortly afterward Maj. Gen. Genzu Mizukami, the infantry group commander of the 56th Division, arrived and took command. He brought with him not only additional units of the 148th Regiment but two pieces of artillery as well. A total of about 4,600 Japanese were eventually to participate in the defense of Myitkyina. More would have arrived, but a British Chindit attack at Mogaung diverted an entire regiment en route to Myitkyina. The Kachin Rangers were also blocking the enemy access to Myitkyina.

Several Japanese guides had managed to slip past American, Chinese, and Kachin positions to reach Japanese reinforcement units approaching the town. The Kachins, chagrined that the enemy guides had bypassed them, set up a listening post along the Sumprabum Road. Within hours a large group of Japanese soldiers were marching past the listening post, which they could clearly see, toward Myitkyina. British Lts. Bert Butler and Bob Tanner swiftly used their radio to call in the outlying Kachin Ranger companies, who arrived in time to prevent this particular group of enemy soldiers from joining the garrison.[16]

At about that time the Japanese area command, 33d Army, assumed command, freeing General Tanaka to concentrate on his operations still under way around Kamaing. The Japanese command, however, committed the opposite error from the Allies, in that they grossly overestimated the attacking force, estimating the number of attackers at thirty thousand.

Indeed, the issue of intelligence was to be a matter of future controversy for both sides. Central to this aspect of the campaign was

Capt. Won-Loy Chan, of Colonel Stilwell's staff. A twenty-seven-year-old Chinese-American who happened to hold a commission in the army reserve at the time of Pearl Harbor, he by chance had been selected as a Japanese language expert, although his chosen vocation was law. Combined with his knowledge of Chinese, he was selected to serve on General Stilwell's staff, where his knowledge of the three key languages—English, Chinese, and Japanese—would be critical. In the early stages of the campaign for northern Burma he had consistently made estimates of enemy strength and intentions that the Chinese commanders in the field had contradicted. After the war Captain Chan, known inevitably as Charley Chan, investigated and determined that almost without fail, his estimates were on or close to the correct strength of the enemy. The Chinese officers simply refused to believe them or were instructed to use them as an excuse to preserve their assets by their government.

One difficulty in verifying contemporary intelligence estimates was the reluctance of both Chinese and Americans to take prisoners. On 7 February, for example, Captain Chan learned that the 114th Regiment had captured four prisoners. Together with nisei interpreter Tom Ichimura, he raced to 38th Chinese Division headquarters to interview the prisoners. The four men, all low-rank enlisted men, at first refused to speak. But Captain Chan argued that they were facing two men of the same race as their own, and that confused them. They soon spoke of what they knew, but little of value beyond order of battle information could be expected from these men. More usual was the oft-repeated experience of prisoners being reported but upon arrival finding that they had "been shot while trying to escape."

The question of how much information General Stilwell's staff, at least, had about the condition of the Marauders is also highlighted by Captain Chan. He shared a tent with General Stilwell's other son-in-law, Maj. Ellis Cox, and was aware that even before the seizure of the Myitkyina airstrip "they were a physically spent force whose effective strength was about half of what it had been when they first hit the trail out of Ledo back in February."[17]

During the battle for Myitkyina the Fourteenth Evacuation Hospital had sent forward about half its staff to a new airstrip built near the Ledo hospital. Arriving in May, their primary duty was to care for the sick, wounded, and injured Marauders. They recorded how many had not eaten in days and were suffering from Naga sores and dysentery. The sick were defined as anyone with a temperature of 102 degrees for three or more days, and only those could be flown out to hospitals in Assam. The Fourteenth Evacuation Hospital history records that "many of them were seriously ill and they were so tired, dirty, and hungry that they looked more dead than alive. They suffered from exhaustion, malnutrition, typhus, malaria, amebic dysentery, jungle sores, and many other disease[s] resulting from months of hardship in the tropical jungle."[18]

The nursing personnel and all members of the Fourteenth Evacuation Hospital worked eighteen hours a day to care for those wounded and ill Americans. The other half of the hospital was fully occupied with wounded and ill Chinese soldiers, also resulting from the Myitkyina campaign. Between the two groups, they were caring at one point for more than 2,800 wounded or sick soldiers. Each nurse, aided by one or two corpsmen, was responsible for 120 to 130 patients. Combined with the miserable conditions brought on by the monsoon season, which sometimes brought several inches of water into the wards, the nurses did the best they could to deal with the wounds, malaria, typhus, dengue fever, amebic dysentery, and other illnesses, one of which was called AOE, accumulation of everything.

The inability of the attacking force to seize the town of Myitkyina caused concern at General Stilwell's headquarters. He considered asking for a British division to be flown in to complete the operation. The British 36th Division was both available and trained for flight operations. Yet Stilwell decided against the request. It has been claimed that having gone to such lengths to deceive the British, he could not now turn and ask for their assistance. Instead, he ordered to the Myitkyina front American engineer units then working on the Ledo Road.

Requests were sent to the camp at Dinjan for Marauders convalescing in hospitals after evacuation from Burma as casualties. About two hundred such convalescents were rushed to Myitkyina by air, and upon arrival at least fifty were put right back on the plane as unfit to enter combat.

This incident gave rise to an accusation that tarnished the General's reputation permanently. Many veterans of the campaign believed that General Stilwell gave orders to refuse evacuation to wounded or ill Marauders in order to maintain his strength at Myitkyina. Reports of nonmedical officers tearing off the evacuation tags of sick and wounded Marauders appeared.

However, with one possible exception this did not occur, as proven by an investigation by several medical officers of the command. What occurred was that so many Marauders were being evacuated that there were not enough hospital beds for them all. As a result, those less in need of constant medical treatment were classified as outpatients and quartered outside the hospital. These men were soon selected for return to the battle area by nonmedical officers who in ignorance believed they were fit to return to duty. Eventually this situation was corrected, but not before serious damage was done to the Marauder morale and to General Stilwell's reputation, as he was blamed for being the source of the order to return unfit men to combat.[19]

The 209th Engineer Combat Battalion was also rushed forward, having recently completed a number of bridging tasks, including a 960-foot span over the Tarung River and a 1,200-foot-long bridge over the Tawang. General Stilwell also restructured the command structure at Myitkyina. Colonel McCammon was now placed in command of the recently created Headquarters, Myitkyina Task Force. This task force consisted of the 88th and 89th Chinese Regiments of the 30th Division, and the 150th and parts of the 42d Regiments of the 50th Division. Also included were the survivors of Galahad under Colonel Hunter, the Seagrave Hospital Unit, and the 42d Portable Surgical Hospital. Colonel McCammon was instructed by General Stilwell to assume the rank and insignia of a brigadier general while his staff rushed through a recommendation for promotion. Colonel McCammon stuffed the general's insignia into his pocket and carried on, assisted as always by Colonel Hunter. What had begun as a lightning attack had now degenerated into a partial siege in the worst sense of the term.

General Joseph Warren Stilwell (1883-1946), Commander, U.S. Forces in the China-Burma-India Theater of Operations, 1942–1944.

Generalissimo Chiang Kai-shek (1887–1975), political and military leader of the Chinese Nationalist Forces in China and Burma. Although technically allies, the Generalissimo and General Stilwell disliked each other intensely.

Field Marshall and Mrs. William Joseph Slim (1891–1970). General Slim led the British Fourteenth Army alongside the Chinese and American forces under General Stilwell. He was one of the few British officers General Stilwell respected.

Brigadier General Frank Dow Merrill (1903–1955). Commander of "Merrill's Marauders" on the march during operations in Burma, 1944.

Tanks of the 1st Provisional Chinese-American Tank Group ford a stream approaching Bhamo, Burma. This unique formation fought alongside the Marauders during much of the Myitkyina campaign.

Colonel Low, Commanding Officer of the 66th Chinese Regiment, confers with his Vice-Commander, Colonel Liu. As a part of the 22d Chinese Infantry Division this unit fought alongside the Marauders during the Myitkyina campaign.

This 10-year-old Chinese soldier is a member of a Chinese division which is boarding a plane at the North Myitkyina airstrip, December 5, 1944.

Brig. Gen. Frank D. Merrill (left) and Lt. Gen. Joseph W. ("Vinegar Joe") Stilwell confer at Naubum, Burma, May 5, 1944. This was the period when General Stilwell was planning his secret march on Myitkyina. Both men look determined.

C-46s dropping supplies and ammunition to the Marauders. Air supply kept the Marauders in action throughout the campaign which was the first "Long Range Penetration" experiment by the U.S. Army conducted under combat conditions.

Marauder Cpl. Bernard Martin and a Chinese soldier inspect each other's weapons near Nphum Ga, Burma, April 28, 1944.

American and Chinese soldiers fill their canteens at a waterhole near Myitkyina. Diseases which decimated Marauder ranks were traced to poor water purifying discipline.

General Stilwell presents the Legion Of Merit to Major General Liao Yao Hsiang, Commander of the 22d Chinese Infantry Division which fought alongside the Marauders in the Myitkyina campaign.

Men of 3d Battalion, 5307th Composite Unit (Provisional) train with a flame thrower against pillboxes. Pictured are from left Pvt. Dominick J. Baracani, Sgt. Harold C. Shoemaker and Pfc. Kenneth L. Keith, 13 January 1944.

Column of Marauders with the essential mules crossing the Tanai River protected by Kachin Ranger patrols, 18 March 1944.

Men of the 209th Engineer Combat Battalion enjoy ice cream after 59 days of intense combat at Myitkyina.

Brigadier General
Theodore Wessels,
Commanding
Myitkyina Task Force,
7 August 1944.

Soldiers of the First Chinese (Separate) Infantry Regiment training at Myitkyina, December 8, 1944. Although a part of Mars Task Force, it never joined the Task Force in combat.

Men of the 3d Battalion, 475th Infantry, at the Nalong River crossing, November 22, 1944.

Lieutenant General Daniel I. Sultan, commanding the India-Burma Theater after General Stilwell's recall, inspects the 613th Field Artillery Battalion (Pack), a part of Mars Task Force, at Mong Woi, Burma.

Soldiers of the 124th Cavalry Regiment on a training march near Ramgarh Training Center, October 25, 1944.

Mule skinners attached to the 2d Battalion, 475th Infantry Regiment, Mars Task Force, struggle across a swift river on the march to Bhamo, Burma, November 17, 1944.

Soldiers of the 3d Battalion, 475th Infantry, repairing the bamboo bridge over the Shweli River to strengthen it enough for the pack animals. January 2, 1945.

In Burma everything was more difficult. U. S. Army Nurses undergoing jungle training carrying full field equipment in the Burmese jungles.

General Sultan and General Sun Li-jen, Commander of the Chinese First Army, examine captured enemy equipment at the headquarters of the 38th Chinese Infantry Division.

Men of "F" Company, 475th Infantry Regiment advance towards an enemy trail block southeast of Tonkwa, Burma, December 17, 1944.

Major John E. Lattin, Executive Officer of the 2d Battalion, 475th Infantry, receives Christmas packages near Tonkwa, Burma, December 20, 1944.

Officers and men of the 2d Squadron, 124th Cavalry, watch an airdrop of supplies near Tun Hong, Burma, January 21, 1945.

Lt. Col. Loren D. Pegg, Executive Officer and later commander of the 124th Cavalry inspects damage with Lt. Col. Earl F. Ripstra and Maj. William T. McDaniels near Nammpakka, Burma, 21 February 1945.

Two soldiers of Mars Task Force in the brush of the ridge leading to Loi-Kang Hill, January 18, 1945.

Ammunition and supply dump of the 3d Battalion in the valley named "Dead Mule Gulch" in honor of the sixteen mules killed in one night by enemy artillery fire.

Artillery observers of Mars Task Force direct fire on enemy targets along the Burma Road. This was expected to close the road to enemy traffic but many groups of Japanese did manage to pass either on the road or on trails built on the far side.

Even in the Burmese jungles, army paperwork must be completed. A headquarters clerk hard at work during the Burma campaign.

7. New Galahad

The lightning strike to seize the critical Japanese base at Myitkyina was quickly turning into trench warfare remarkably similar to the First World War in France. General Mizukami's men dug themselves into the terrain with all the usual skill, dexterity, and speed for which the Japanese soldier was known. Trenches began to appear around Myitkyina, along with bunkers, snipers, and the ever present ambush sites. To ensure that the town was held at least until August while a new line of defense was being established, General Tanaka was relieved of responsibility, and from early June the Myitkyina garrison reported directly to 33d Army Headquarters.

The Allies had one advantage given to them by the enemy. The Japanese, unlike the Allies, consistently overestimated the strength of the attacking forces and therefore refrained from any large-scale counterattack. Such an attack—particularly in the early stages of the battle, when the Americans were exhausted and the Chinese severely disorganized—had a possibility of success. To offset this perceived strength a regimental combat team of the 53d Japanese Division was ordered to reinforce the Myitkyina garrison. They were en route when the British seizure of Mogaung canceled the operation.

Indeed, the British operations had several beneficial effects on the battle at Myitkyina. One of the original Wingate Chindit operations called for a small force under Lt. Col. J. R. Morris to land along the Shewli River and then march inland to establish a base in that area. The force, which quickly became known as Morris Force, consisted of the 4th Battalion, 9th Gurkha Rifles. Once established at its base the force was to harass Japanese communications along the motor road between Bhamo to the Irrawaddy ferry at Myitkyina. They were not to block the road but to use the typical guerrilla methods of demolitions, mines, and ambushes to accomplish the mission. Morris Force landed successfully and marched off to accomplish their mission as scheduled. This they proceeded to do until General Stilwell's forces appeared.

The increasingly difficult struggle to secure Myitkyina caused General Stilwell to seek assistance from all available quarters. Seeing the situation developing into a siege-type struggle, he sought to cut off the enemy's supply and reinforcement routes. One such route ran through the area covered by Morris Force. Colonel Morris soon received orders to seize two villages through which enemy reinforcements and supplies passed. The two villages, Waingmaw and Maingna, lay on the east bank of the Irrawaddy, directly opposite Myitkyina.[1] This would close off the ferry points from which enemy troops and supplies crossed into the developing fortress of Myitkyina.

Believing that the village of Myitkyina had already been seized, Colonel Morris began his attack. Rushing his men forward into what he believed was a mopping-up operation, he launched his first attack against Waingmaw. There the 4/9th Gurkha Rifles[2] actually attacked a garrison that not only outnumbered them but defended from prepared defensive works. The outcome was predictable. Three times the Gurkhas attacked, each time breaching a portion of the defenses and each time eventually being repulsed. Several bunkers were taken by two Gurkha corporals who crawled into enemy machine-gun fire to hand-carry grenades close enough to destroy those bunkers. But Morris Force had too few men and soon also ran out of ammunition. Colonel Morris pulled his battalion out of the attack and flew to Myitkyina to confer with the American command.

General Stilwell had also considered using the British 36th Infantry Division but discarded that idea in the interests of national pride, both American and Chinese. Instead, he called up two battalions of American combat engineers. And once again he turned to Galahad. This time the Marauders, those that were left, took the key village of Charpate. The 88th Chinese Regiment consolidated its lines along the railway. The depleted 150th Chinese Regiment held the airfield. Marauder battalions held strongpoints north and west of it. Additional Chinese reinforcements came into the arena as well. Yet supplies remained a problem. Entirely dependent upon air supply, Headquarters, Myitkyina Task Force, as Colonel Mc-Cammon's command was now known, had at best a two-day reserve of critical supplies. They were faced with overcoming defenses compared to those on the Western Front in World War I but without tanks and with never more than fourteen artillery pieces available. Even air support was limited to twelve P-40 fighter aircraft of the 88th Fighter Squadron, which was now flying from Myitkyina Airfield. As one official historian has put it, "It was Cassino on a shoestring."[3]

The initial efforts to secure the town fell to the 3d Marauder Battalion. On 21 May they attacked from Charpate to Myitkyina, believing that the town was still lightly held. They advanced only several yards when enemy fire forced them to halt and dig in well short of the objective. That night they were attacked from the rear and were forced the next day to retire to Charpate. General Stilwell called 22 May Black Monday in his diary, learning that the 150th Regiment "ran away and had to be taken out."[4] This Chinese regiment, having suffered 671 casualties since entering the battle, was relieved and sent to the rear for rest and recuperation. No such reprieve was granted the Americans, however, who had lost far more men during their campaign.

It was at about that time, 19 May, that Capt. Tom Senff staggered into the American perimeter, accompanied by Sgt. Frank S. Drolla. Captain Senff had been left in charge of the evacuees back along the trail. Colonel Hunter had called for air evacuation and had left just as the first liaison litter planes lifted off with the first few casualties. Now, more than a week after those planes had left, Captain Senff appeared, limping along on a bamboo cane, to report that no other planes had ever appeared and that the casualties were still alone in the jungle. The captain, whose left leg was paralyzed and whose throat had closed up due to infection, had limped twenty-five miles, following Colonel Hunter's path, to Myitkyina, avoiding the trails and any sign of the enemy, until he arrived to report. Colonel

Hunter was furious. "My unofficial remarks concerning this incident were and are still unprintable."[5]

On 23 May Japanese forces attacked the Marauder battalion and only with great difficulty was that attack repelled. During the attack, Marauders were observed falling asleep under fire, and Colonel McGee fainted three times while directing his battalion. The following morning still another attack pushed the battalion farther back. Losses mounted alarmingly. Between seventy-five and one hundred Marauders were being evacuated daily after proving that they had a fever of 102 degrees or higher for three days. An additional fifteen to thirty men were showing signs of the deadly mite or scrub typhus each day, while at least 80 percent of the Americans clearly suffered from dysentery. As General Stilwell would soon record in his diary, "Galahad is shot."[6]

Yet General Stilwell kept them at the front. He had little choice, in his view. He was keeping the Chindits in the battle despite their demands for relief, as they too had overstayed the allocated time in the Burmese jungles and were in the same shape as the Marauders. He had committed to securing Myitkyina and was now in the spotlight, with British and Chinese critics waiting for him to fail. He continued to look for support to end the battle.

Colonel McCammon continued trying to resolve the battle. He scheduled a full-dress assault on Myitkyina for 25 May. The attack was to be made by two Chinese regiments, who were to drive right through Myitkyina and reach the riverbank, where defenses would be established.

After a day of battle the 88th Chinese Regiment reported that it had straightened its lines, although the 89th Regiment had nothing to report. Colonel McCammon, who was suffering from pleurisy, reported failure to General Stilwell. The general noted, "Disturbing news from Mitch. McCammon gloomy. Decided to go down."[7] General Stilwell did visit Myitkyina, complaining about the rain, the all-night firing, and very little sleep. It may have been at that time that one of the Marauders commented about General Stilwell, "I had him in my rifle sights. I coulda squeezed one off and no one woulda known it wasn't a Jap that got the son of a bitch."[8]

It was also about that time that Colonel Hunter, making a reconnaissance in a jeep that his orderly had "acquired" from the Chinese, was strafed by an enemy plane. His orderly was seriously wounded and later killed in the strafing of his ambulance at the field. Colonel Hunter escaped unhurt.[9] The orderly, Pfc. Barlow G. Coon, received a posthumous Silver Star for saving Colonel Hunter and other passengers despite being seriously wounded.

The immediate result of General Stilwell's visit was the relief of Colonel McCammon and his replacement by Brigadier General Boatner. Another unexpected result was a report written and presented to General Stilwell by Colonel Hunter. The colonel, who had served throughout the muddled history of the 5307th Composite Unit (Provisional), without complaint as a dedicated and loyal career army officer, had finally had enough. According to Lieutenant Ogburn, who heard about it later, Colonel Hunter wrote that from the start the Marauders had been treated as a visiting unit for which theater headquarters had no responsibility and that despite repeated requests the Marauders had not been named a standard army organization but had remained a provisional unit, and thus had been refused designation, honors, and guidons. All these factors reflected on the morale of the command, wrote the colonel. He noted also that General Merrill had ordered that no officers would be promoted until the operation's end. In addition, no awards or decorations had been awarded to any individuals other than the normal award of the Purple Heart for wounds. He argued that the morale of Galahad was sustained only by the promise that it would not be used as a spearhead for Chinese units, and there at Myitkyina that was not the case. Galahad had also been promised that immediately upon arrival at Myitkyina it would be evacuated as a whole for rest and recuperation. Yet it was still expected to fight on, despite several adverse reports on the health of the command. Colonel Hunter concluded that Galahad should be pulled out for recuperation, awards, and promotions to be provided as deserved and that the unit be disbanded. He further advised that any future units such as Galahad be treated in such a manner as to instill pride of unit and a link to the overall campaign.[10]

While General Stilwell digested Colonel Hunter's report, there was indeed another unit coming in to assist, not replace, the 5307th Composite Unit (Provisional). Based on a War Department decision in October 1943 that individual replacements for the 5307th

Composite Unit (Provisional) would not be practical, it was
arranged that new units would be formed in the United States and
shipped intact to the China-Burma-India theater in time for the
next campaign season. It was assumed that once in the theater, veterans from the original Galahad would be used in command and
key leadership roles to bring combat experience to the new unit. At
Fort George Gordon Meade, in Maryland, the replacement unit was
established as an infantry unit with four platoons to a company.
There were no headquarters or headquarters staff provided, based
on the assumption that these would be provided by Galahad veterans upon arrival in Burma. As often happens in orphan units such
as these, the intention of the War Department became lost in execution, and no companies or battalions were ever actually established in the new unit. Instead, the shipping structure for trans-
porting these men overseas became the ad hoc structure of the
command. Despite several pleas for better organization made at
Fort Meade, at the port of embarkation, and aboard ship, no
changes were made. Nor was the China-Burma-India theater headquarters advised of the situation.

.   Most of the new volunteers came from the 33d Infantry Regiment then in Panama, and others came from the 71st (Pack, Jungle) Division training at Camp Carson, Colorado. A number of officers, including one future battalion commander, came from the 2d
Filipino Infantry Regiment (Separate), which was one of two regiments formed to assist in the liberation of the Philippines. Consisting of men of Filipino heritage living in the United States, the 2d
Regiment could not be kept up to strength and was reduced to battalion strength. Several officers were excessed and given the choice
of going into a replacement pool or volunteering for what was then
known only as GH 770, another unit organized for a dangerous mission. After traveling around Africa into Bombay, they were flown
forward to Myitkyina. "Not one officer or enlisted man of GH 770
received one minute of briefing, indoctrination, or unit training—
they were not even organized except on paper—before being
thrown into combat against the battle-hardened Japs, veterans of
the Malayan, Burma, and Singapore campaigns."[11]

A total of 2,600 men were provided in the replacement unit. Of
these, 400 were intended to form two quartermaster pack units. The

rest were either infantry or artillery trained. Unfortunately, most of the artillerymen were grouped together. Many of the men had volunteered from the training cadre of several replacement centers.

The unit arrived in Bombay on 25 May, just as the battle for Myitkyina reached a crisis, and they were speeded to Ramgath by trains they later dubbed Toonerville Trolleys. Upon arrival some men were rushed forward as individual replacements, and the entire unit spent about a week in the training camp before being flown to Myitkyina in two hastily formed battalions. For lack of a better designation, they were soon known as New Galahad. In spite of Colonel Hunter's admonitions to General Stilwell, these men had even less of an organizational structure than had the 5307th Composite Unit (Provisional). And they had almost no training in the kind of warfare they were about to enter.

When they arrived at Myitkyina, General Boatner formed three battalions, the first composed of Marauder veterans still on their feet, and the second and third composed of the newly arrived replacements. An exchange of men among the battalions was activated in the hope that by mixing veterans among the new men, some of their experience could be used to speed the adaptability of the new command to its hostile environment. As they prepared to go into combat the 1st battalion contained 300 men; the 2d and 3d had 950 each. As a token of training, these replacements were taken to the area of Namkwi, where the Japanese remained in passive defense, and were allowed to shoot at live targets.

General Boatner was also visited by Colonel (now Brigadier) Morris at about that time. Morris explained the reasons for his failure at Waingmaw, citing the strong Japanese defenses, the flooded countryside over which he had to advance, and the fact that his command was wasting away at the rate of a third of a platoon per day. He also noted that his men, like the Marauders, were falling asleep under Japanese fire. Despite the problems, Morris Force remained in action, harassing the Japanese on the opposite bank of the Irrawaddy until mid-July, when it was down to a total of twenty-five officers and enlisted men from the 1,301 it had in early May and was allowed to withdraw.

Like the Chindits, the Marauders continued to disintegrate as individuals. Lieutenant Sam Wilson—who had led so many dangerous patrols, had earned two Silver Stars, and was counted on by every field officer in Galahad—took his platoon down to the riverbank for a brief rest. As he was seeking a place to lie down, he noticed a wooden cross with a dog tag on it. Only by reading the tag did he learn that Captain Laffin, a close friend who also led from the front, had been killed. Captain Laffin, gathering intelligence as always, had been flying over the front in a liaison plane when a flight of enemy fighters shot them down. Lieutenant Nellis I. Johnson succeeded him as S-2. Lieutenant Wilson, who had been defecating blood for the past two weeks, did not argue the next time the unit's surgeon ordered him evacuated. As he gave the news to his platoon, the only good-bye was a request by one of his men for his tommy gun. As Lieutenant Ogburn noted, "There was never much ceremony when the end came for another Marauder."[12]

General Stilwell, having declined to call up British reinforcements, now turned to American resources to aid in the continuing campaign for Myitkyina. It had long been U.S. Army policy that engineer troops could be used as infantry in emergency situations. Indeed, the campaigns in Italy and Western Europe would see several combat engineer battalions thrust into combat situations in place of infantry units. With his only dependable combat unit rapidly disappearing before his eyes, and its replacement not yet in place, General Stilwell turned to his own combat engineers for aid. Although construction on the Ledo Road was the primary mission of his command, he ordered to the front two of the engineer battalions working on or along that road.

The choice fell upon the 209th Engineer Combat Battalion and the 236th Engineer Combat Battalion. Lieutenant Colonel Leslie E. Sandvall's 209th Engineer Combat Battalion was dispersed on various tasks when on 24 May the call came to assemble and proceed to Myitkyina for a combat mission. Immediately the line companies A and C, with the medical detachment, left the airstrip at Tingkawk and flew to Myitkyina. Headquarters and Supply Company and Company B arrived the following day, so that on 25 May the entire battalion of 26 officers and 552 enlisted men were available for duty.

Little time was wasted, and on 26 May Companies A and C took up defensive positions in and around Namkwi. Headquarters and the remaining troops soon established a position along the Myit-

kyina-Mogaung highway about two and a half miles north of Myitkyina, alongside the Orange Combat Team of the Marauders. Patrol action began immediately, and Company C was the first to encounter the enemy, losing one man killed and one wounded against
an estimated enemy loss of twelve killed.

The battalion spent the next few days learning the skills of the infantryman. While holding static positions they patrolled and observed. But that respite ended abruptly on the night of 31 May. During the day, Company C and the 2d Battalion of the Marauders had
moved against Charpate, from which the Americans had recently
been ejected. The company took up a position at the edge of the village and dug in for the evening. The rest of the battalion had been
relieved at the "railroad block" by the 236th Engineer Combat Battalion and had moved to attack along the Myitkyina-Mogaung road,
intending to establish a roadblock there. After sighting only one
enemy soldier the battalion established its position. Within swift
succession they encountered an enemy patrol, a truck of enemy soldiers, and two additional trucks with enemy soldiers and ammunition. Immediately afterward the battalion found itself involved in an
enemy attack that soon became hand-to-hand.

The 209th Engineers had walked into an enemy attempt at evacuation. Colonel Maruyama later reported that on that evening he
had attempted to break out of the Myitkyina garrison with three
battalions. This had been planned for 30 May and approved by
General Tanaka at division headquarters but had later been canceled at the order of General Honda, who ordered reinforcement
of both Myitkyina and Mogaung. Whether all the Japanese commanders knew of the cancellation is uncertain, and doubtful, considering the heavy fighting between the 209th Engineers and the
enemy. This struggle went on all night, ending only at 0500 hours
as the sun rose. The engineers later recorded casualties of four
killed and five wounded against an enemy loss of eighty-six dead
and three trucks destroyed. Later that afternoon the enemy struck
again at the battalion with heavy artillery and mortar fire. No
ground attack developed, however.

Lieutenant Colonel Harold E. Greenlee's 236th Engineer Combat Battalion received its call the day after its sister battalion. The
battalion had arrived in the China-Burma-India theater on 6 Janu-

ary 1944 after training in the United States. Since then it had been engaged in bridge and road building. It had also constructed some military bases. Upon arrival its men were assigned as base engineers for Base Section Three, Service of Supply, United States Army Forces in the China-Burma-India theater. Assigned on 28 May 1944 to "Northern Combat Area Command per letter orders, Headquarters N. C. A. C., 15 November 1944, for duty with 5307th Provisional Brigade, under the command of Brigadier General McCammon,"[13] the battalion would spend the next fifty-nine days fighting as infantry.

The battalion assembled at the southeast corner of the airstrip on 30 May, after which it proceeded to relieve units of both the 209th Engineer Combat Battalion and some Chinese troops northwest of the field. They noted that the observant enemy had shelled the positions they had just vacated. In the new position they were joined by Lieutenant Harris and two enlisted men from the Marauders who would train them in mortar fire procedures. Private First Class Casimir Cytrynowicz, of Company A, 209th Engineers, spent a night learning about mortars from a Sergeant Clubb, of the Marauders. During the training, Sergeant Clubb also traded Private Cytrynowicz his compass, trench knife, ponchos, and spoon for all his East Indian money. The next morning Sergeant Clubb was evacuated, and Private Cytrynowicz was returned to Company A, the local expert in mortars.

On 1 June the battalion was ordered to send out a reconnaissance in force to determine enemy strength at the village of Namkwi. Companies A and C, less one platoon, under the command of Capt. James G. Tice, moved on the village. Included in the plan was the training opportunity that this would provide to the inexperienced battalion. The two companies succeeded in entering the village, during which the two commands became separated from each other. Company C lost communications with Captain Tice and returned to its roadblock position. Company A, according to Colonel Hunter, fell out for a break instead of consolidating its position. Sometime after that it renewed its advance, only to be caught in an ambush within the village.

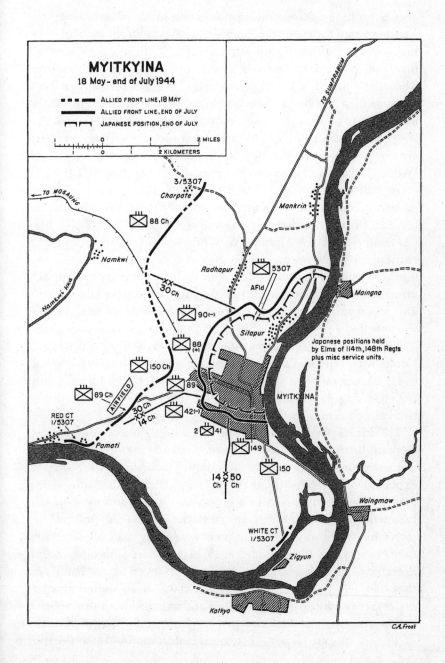

MYITKYINA
18 May - end of July 1944

▪▪▪ ━━ ALLIED FRONT LINE, 18 MAY
━━━━━ ALLIED FRONT LINE, END OF JULY
⊓ ⊔ ⊓ JAPANESE POSITION, END OF JULY

1   0   1   2 MILES
0   2 KILOMETERS

Japanese positions held
by Elms of 114th, 148th Regts
plus misc service units.

C.A.Frost

A bitter battle developed for possession of the village. American wounded had fallen in the open, and several attempts had to be made to rescue them. Staff Sergeant Tim L. Bradley led another man well forward in front of an enemy position to rescue three wounded comrades. During the rescue Sergeant Bradley was himself wounded and had to be left behind. He was subsequently listed as missing in action and posthumously awarded the Silver Star.

Private Durad L. Wright led two other men forward to assist several men who were trapped under enemy fire. Led by Private Wright, the group killed the two enemy soldiers manning the machine gun that had trapped their friends, and they forced others to withdraw, thus saving the trapped engineers. Private Wright later received a Bronze Star for that action.

Private First Class Alpheus W. White was first gunner on a machine gun. While setting up his gun to repulse the enemy he was mortally wounded. Despite his wounds he continued to feed ammunition to his assistant gunner, saying, "Go ahead and fire the gun, never mind me." Private White died a few hours later. He too was awarded a posthumous Silver Star.[14]

The Americans could not hold the village and soon retreated. Company A returned to the airstrip. This episode marked the end of formal operations to seize the Myitkyina garrison by a rush, and the following day, 2 June, the Chinese began formal siege operations aimed at eliminating the enemy garrison.

The initial performance of the combat engineers disappointed General Boatner and Colonel Hunter but was not unexpected, because the men had not practiced infantry tactics in years. More was expected of the New Galahad replacements now arriving at the front. Those men arrived in a group on 28 May and were rushed into action immediately, because of General Stilwell's fear that a recent Chindit withdrawal from an enemy supply road would enable them to increase the pressure at Myitkyina. The Chindit concept, now that General Wingate was dead, had changed dramatically, and they had held the block at Hopin in a classic defense that now was no longer possible due to casualties and exhaustion of the troops.[15]

The condition of New Galahad was little better than that of the engineers, despite General Boatner's expectations. Captain Arthur

W. Wilson had come in earlier as an individual replacement and had been assigned to Company A of the Red Combat Team. He knew many of the men in New Galahad, however. "Most were fresh from the States, right off the boat, thrown in without infantry training or any attempt at structure. Most did not know the names of officers. They had few NCOs and zero training as units. Most men did not even know the names of their squad mates."[16]

Staff Sergeant William S. Brader recalls volunteering for a heavy weapons assignment at Myitkyina.

> They took us to an airfield, loaded us on a C-47, flew over the Taj Mahal at Agra, India. Then flew us to 'Mitch.' Landed on the strip about 2-3 p.m., and got shelled as we stepped off the plane and the pilot told us to 'get the hell away from the plane' and he took off as fast as he could. Dug fox hole about 50 yards from strip and settled in for the night with water buffalo at night running into us and our 'lines of tin-cans' warnings.[17]

Like the engineers before them, they also practiced at Namkwi, shooting at live targets. This initial contact produced fifty psychopathic cases, and several officers were transferred as unfit. General Boatner reported to General Stilwell on 15 June that "reports continue to indicate the complete disorganization and fear in U.S. Units. They are in many cases simply terrified of the Japs."[18] There was also concern that the Chinese troops were suffering continuing casualties, at least 121 per day, while the Americans trained out of contact with any sizable enemy force. The NCAC also believed that the Americans would tip the balance because it still believed that they were facing fewer than a thousand Japanese defenders. In fact, as postwar testimony would show, there were more than four thousand Japanese troops defending the Myitkyina fortress.

Nevertheless, General Boatner continued trying to reduce the enemy garrison without delay. On 3 June the 42d and 150th Chinese Regiments made yet another attack on the town. They were bloodily repulsed, losing 320 men in the failed attack. That attack also drained most of the critical supplies necessary for any new attacks. Artillery ammunition fell to a total of six hundred rounds. General Boatner bowed to the inevitable and delayed any major attacks until his supplies could be built up again and his American units acclimated to combat conditions. He ordered the two engineer battalions to be mixed with Marauder units to give them confidence. He also placed them in a provisional regiment under the command of Lt. Col. William H. Combs, who had previously advised the 150th Chinese Regiment in combat and had earned a Distinguished Service Cross for his exploits while with the Chinese.

General Boatner prepared for his next attempt to begin 10 June. Artillery supplies were built up, and the plan called for all Allied units to attack simultaneously, the Chinese from the south and the Americans from the north. The attack progressed slowly and spread over several days. On 13 June a platoon of New Galahad was hit by an enemy counterattack and abandoned its positions, falling back onto an adjacent company. Two of the men, however, stayed in position and using an automatic rifle and a machine gun, repulsed the counterattack alone.

On the same date a veteran Marauder, Pvt. Howard T. Smith, took over his platoon when his lieutenant was killed and the platoon pinned down under enemy fire. "Pvt. Smith immediately took charge of the platoon, disposed the men in advantageous positions, and then alone crawled up to the enemy gun position. Armed only with hand grenades, he crawled under vicious enemy fire and succeeded in destroying the pill box and the machine gun."[19] Credited with saving the lives of his platoon and advancing the attack, Private Smith was awarded a Distinguished Service Cross.

The engineers were also involved in that attack. The 209th Engineers had led off on 10 June. By 13 June the battalions were well involved in pushing the enemy back. During the early morning hours of that day Company B moved forward approximately one thousand yards in front of its battalion position to surprise the enemy. They encountered over two hundred enemy troops, who immediately engaged them. The company fought back and established positions where they had first discovered the enemy.

Company A was ordered forward to assist. As they advanced they were attacked as well, and one platoon of about twenty-eight men became separated and returned to the battalion perimeter. The rest of the company joined with Company B and dug in to fight. For the balance of the day the position of the two companies was shelled and snipers were active. Toward noon communications were lost between the embattled companies and the rest of the engineer battalion. That afternoon H&S Company and Company C moved forward to join the others. They had proceeded barely five hundred yards when they were stopped by a strong enemy defense. The two forward companies were isolated.

During the night the two separate parts of the 209th Engineer Combat Battalion received incoming fire from Japanese, Chinese, and American sources. At dawn the Japanese attempted to break the forward perimeter, but despite heavy fire the two companies held their position. Later that same date, 14 June, the rest of the battalion received orders to withdraw to more secure positions. Patrols were sent out in advance to secure the route of withdrawal. It was during this phase of the operation that Colonel Combs advanced into enemy fire to warn one of the 209th patrols about an enemy ambush. The colonel uncovered the enemy ambush site but was mortally wounded in the process. He received a second Distinguished Service Cross, his first having been awarded for service with the adjacent 150th Chinese Regiment.

The engineers withdrew successfully. Later that day two men came into the new perimeter from the surrounded companies, bringing a situation report and requesting food, ammunition, and medical supplies, all of which were critically needed by the forward companies. Attempts to airdrop the supplies later that day were unsuccessful. Orders also went out to the 236th Engineers to attempt to reach the surrounded companies.

Having survived three enemy attacks designed to destroy them, the two companies successfully held their advanced position even though neither supplies nor relief had arrived. Colonel Greenlee now assumed command of the provisional engineer regiment, while Maj. Mahlon E. Gates moved up to command the 236th Engineer Combat Battalion. It was quickly determined that the efforts of the 236th to relieve the 209th's companies were unsuccessful despite the use of 37mm guns by Company A of the 236th and repeated attacks to outflank the enemy. Orders were given that the two surrounded companies were to break up into small groups and withdraw as well as they could to the main perimeter, bringing their wounded and any equipment they could carry with them. At 0430 hours on 16 June the first large groups arrived at the battalion perimeter.

Another Marauder veteran, 1st Lt. Melvin D. Blair, also distinguished himself that day. On 13 June while he led a patrol, enemy fire pinned the group down. Lieutenant Blair "alone crawled across the trail under enemy machine-gun fire to the rear of the enemy position and silenced the gun by killing the crew with his carbine."[20] A similar incident occurred on 16 June. After rescuing wounded men trapped under enemy fire, Blair advanced alone and destroyed an enemy machine-gun position, permitting his platoon to advance unopposed. Like Private Smith, he survived to wear his Distinguished Service Cross.

But the veterans had not finished showing the newcomers how it was done in Burma. On 14 June Pfc. William J. D. Lilly was in command of a heavy machine-gun position when it came under direct fire from an enemy automatic weapon. Ignoring his personal safety, Private First Class Lilly and his platoon sergeant advanced against the enemy. When the sergeant was wounded, Private Lilly advanced alone. Using hand grenades and his pistol, he destroyed the enemy gun and crew. He too survived to wear his Distinguished Service Cross.[21]

These examples to the new men were soon copied. Technical Sergeant Richard E. Roe, of one of the New Galahad battalions, crawled forward alone under intense enemy fire to destroy an enemy machine-gun position that had caused casualties in his platoon. Although fatally wounded, he succeeded in destroying the enemy position and freeing his trapped comrades. His Distinguished Service Cross was awarded posthumously. Staff Sergeant Alvin O. Miller of the 209th Engineers earned his Distinguished Service Cross when he saw three members of a machine-gun crew wounded by enemy hand grenades. He charged into the enemy attack and with rifle and grenades stopped and turned it back. He then turned to save the lives of the wounded gun crew. Captain John C. Mattina of the 209th also noticed wounded soldiers lying out under enemy automatic weapons fire. Despite the risk, he advanced alone under that fire to rescue the wounded. He survived to wear his Silver Star. During the attack Sgt. Fred N. Coleman, of the 236th Engineers, saw a hand grenade land between two men of his squad. Without hesitation he threw himself on the grenade, taking the full blast but protecting his men from injury. His Distinguished Service Cross was awarded posthumously.[22]

Others also aided their comrades at their own expense. Technician Fourth Grade William H. Miles was a medical corpsman who worked both in front of and behind the lines. Although he knew he was seriously ill he refused evacuation and continued to aid his fellow soldiers until he fainted from exhaustion. He died while being evacuated and was awarded a posthumous Silver Star.[23]

American soldiers continued to distinguish themselves throughout the battle. Second Lieutenant John W. Travis was a Signal Corps officer who earned the Silver Star by leading wire-laying details under enemy fire, sometimes going well in advance of Allied positions. First Sergeant Worth E. Rector earned his Silver Star on 14 June by crawling out under intense enemy fire and directing mortar fire on enemy weapons harassing American positions. At least two enemy machine guns were credited to Sergeant Rector. Also on that date T4 Lewis E. Day crawled forward of the lines to aid a wounded man. Although he was a medical corpsman, he seized a rifle and killed an enemy soldier who was attacking his patient. He also received a Silver Star. Privates First Class Marvin H. Anderson and Everett E. Hudson received their Silver Stars for leading five wounded men out of a surrounded position into Allied lines despite being under direct enemy fire.[24]

All of this effort did advance the Allied lines from one to two hundred yards and seized some critical points. But for all the effort and heroism expended, the gains were still not decisive. Once again General Boatner, with General Stilwell's permission, halted all attacks until the forces under command were better prepared. Incredibly, high command still believed the intelligence reports that the enemy garrison numbered about five hundred men.

Having halted all main force attacks, the Allies went back to patrolling. General Boatner now also directed that tunnels should be started to approach the enemy defenses. General Stilwell again flew in for a look around and concluded that a new commander was necessary, as General Boatner had too much to do to spend sufficient time with the troops. General Stilwell sent back to headquarters for Brig. Gen. Theodore F. Wessels to come forward and take command of ground operations, while Colonel Hunter remained in command of troop operations. Meanwhile, events continued as before at Myitkyina.

Even patrol actions could be costly, however. On 20 June Pfc. George C. Presterly, of the engineers, was on patrol when it was hit by enemy fire. Moving forward alone, he assaulted the enemy strongpoint, drawing all the enemy fire onto himself. Despite being mortally wounded, Private First Class Presterly continued his attack until the enemy was destroyed. His Distinguished Service Cross was posthumously awarded.

By this time the Marauders were finished. General Stilwell had already recorded their demise in his diary, but the statistics tell the story in more detail. One hundred twenty-three had died in battle or nonbattle instances. Another 8 were missing in action and presumed dead. Two hundred ninety-three were wounded severely enough to require evacuation, while dozens of others carried on with lesser wounds. In addition to these 424 battle casualties, they had suffered another 1,970 cases of disease requiring medical treatment and evacuation. This total loss of 2,394 literally wiped out the 5307th Composite Unit (Provisional), leaving barely 500 men able to remain on active duty, many of whom were rear-area personnel in support positions at the airfields.

New Galahad was now acclimated to the conditions at Myitkyina as a result of weeks of combat, and on 18 June the 3d Battalion managed to cut the Maingna ferry road, a main Japanese supply route. During this same time the Chinese 150th Regiment managed to advance five hundred yards by using flame throwers and seized a key enemy defensive position. Despite these successes the enemy defenses remained strongly held, and again attacks were called off. The situation had developed into one in which both sides held battalion- and regimental-sized strongpoints with wide gaps between them. The experienced enemy soldiers could use those gaps to great advantage, while the Americans were less experienced and less likely to use them. These circumstances resulted in the surrounding of the two 209th Engineer Combat Battalion companies described earlier and also to the destruction of two companies of the Chinese 2d Battalion, 42d Infantry Regiment, on 14 June.

General Wessels had been on the staff of the infantry school at Fort Benning, Georgia, before coming to the China-Burma-India theater as a part of General Stilwell's plan to train the Chinese army in American tactics. Once it became clear that the Chinese had little interest, General Wessels was assigned as a staff officer at Southeast Asia Command (SEAC) headquarters. Now he had been called forward to replace General Boatner at Myitkyina. Captain "Charley" Chan had recently arrived to serve in the Myitkyina Task Force intelligence section and noted, "General Boatner looked very tired. His desk was strewn with maps and papers." Captain Chan was tasked with monitoring avenues by which the Japanese were bringing in reinforcements, a clear indication that the idea that there were only a few hundred defenders was at last past.[25] On 26 June, after General Boatner had fallen ill with a recurring bout of malaria, General Wessels assumed official command.

Described by Colonel Hunter as "a rugged, robust, hearty officer of good infantry military background who possessed the rare (in CBI) quality of being able to think along orthodox military lines,"[26] General Wessels had every reason to be pessimistic about his new command. Events, however, caused him considerable good fortune that had not been made available to his predecessors. Once again the British had provided assistance. The key enemy position at the town of Mogaung had been seized. Brigadier General Michael Calvert's 77th Brigade—consisting of remnants of battalions from the 6th and 9th Gurkha Rifles, The King's Regiment, The Lancashire Fusiliers, and The South Staffordshire Regiment—had fought nearly an identical battle to the one fought by the Marauders. Instead of Myitkyina, their rainbow ended at the town of Mogaung. Surrounded on the west and north by impassable rivers, the exhausted British and Gurkha soldiers were forced to attack along a narrow road built up on a causeway. The defenders, the same regiment of the 53d Japanese Division that had originally been directed on Myitkyina, held numerous strongpoints in and around the town, much the same as at Myitkyina.

Yet another similarity was the losses suffered by this brigade during the campaign. They were nearly identical to those of the Marauders. Starting with 2,355 men, as he approached Mogaung, Brigadier Calvert could field barely 800 men. Even these men were so tired that, according to records, officers leading attacks walked forward, too tired to crawl. Chinese regiments promised to Brigadier Calvert were delayed, leaving him no choice but to carry on with his depleted command. On 18 June, when the Chinese 114th Regiment arrived, the town was sealed off against additional reinforcements and the attack to seize the town began. Much like what happened at Myitkyina, the Chinese fell short of their objectives, leaving the British to do the best they could. The Victoria Cross, Britain's highest award for valor, was awarded to Capt. Michael Allmand posthumously and to Rifleman Tulbahadur Pun, of the 3/6th Gurkha Rifles, during that battle. After sixteen days of continual assault, Mogaung fell to the remnants of six British and Gurkha battalions. Its fall, however, nearly caused another battle when the NCAC headquarters announced that fall to the Chinese, ignoring the British. Brigadier Calvert, one of those endearing characters so common to British military forces, immediately dispatched a message to General Stilwell's headquarters, stating, "The Chinese having taken Mogaung 77 Brigade is proceeding to take Umbrage." Legend in British military circles has it that Stilwell's staff wired back asking for the map coordinates of Umbrage.

Brigadier Calvert's seizure of Mogaung released several Chinese units for use at Myitkyina. It removed the threat of a Japanese advance based upon Mogaung to relieve Myitkyina. It also opened up the formerly Japanese controlled area between Mogaung and Myitkyina, removing the feeling of being surrounded that the Allied forces at Myitkyina held. Finally, it removed one of the two areas that provided General Mizukami with supplies and reinforcements.

General Wessels, enjoying his good fortune, made a round of visits to all his combat troops. His purpose was to get to know his new command, instill confidence, and improve morale among them. General Stilwell placed Colonel Hunter in command of all ground troops at Myitkyina, although General Wessels remained in overall command. Before the general and the colonel could get to know each other, they faced a joint crisis as the result of General Stilwell's direct intervention into the battle.

During his latest visit to Myitkyina, General Stilwell had ordered Colonel Hunter to send one battalion of the Chinese 42d Regiment on a specific azimuth to cut off the Japanese defenders from the north. The 1st Battalion, consisting of 250 men, did as ordered, driving deep into the enemy defensive system on 28 and 29 June. General Stilwell was thrilled, feeling that the decisive breach had been made. However, on 29 June the battalion ran into enemy resistance and dug in, well out of reach of any ground support. Air supply was called in, and General Wessels, under direct orders from General Stilwell to support the Chinese, ordered Company G of 2d Battalion, New Galahad, to advance to support the trapped Chinese.[27]

Company G started forward under an inexperienced commander. "On our way we came to a big, deep rice paddy. We started across and were very heavily fired upon and we withdrew to the edge of the paddy. Stayed there all night. Just before daybreak we crossed the paddy again. Just on the other side I heard a Jap say the word 'Myrone.' Then he disappeared."[28]

The company then observed an Asian soldier beckoning them forward. The company commander took them for the Chinese he had been sent to meet and moved forward.[29] As they met the Asian group the leader suggested to the company commander that he and his men lay down their arms. It was only now that the company commander realized that he and his command had been ambushed. He immediately gave the alarm and then was killed by a bayonet. The lead scout was shot as the others raced to give the alarm. Hidden Japanese machine guns ripped through the column of Americans, and heavy losses resulted. Thirty-five survivors, many of them wounded, managed to make their way back to Allied lines, but so badly decimated was Company G that it was never reconstituted, and its survivors were distributed among other New Galahad commands.

During the retreat Pfc. Anthony S. Firenze fought a vicious eight-hour rear guard action to save as many of his comrades as possible.

On 1 July he continued to man his machine gun despite being wounded early in the action. It was this weapon that broke up and disorganized the last enemy attack, forcing the Japanese to withdraw with considerable losses. Private Firenze continued to fire after all his gun crew but one had been killed, and he fired until the gun barrel burned out. Although he was in great pain from his earlier wounds, Private Firenze volunteered to act as a scout for the rear guard's withdrawal. He was later awarded the Distinguished Service Cross.[30] The trapped Chinese battalion later successfully withdrew on its own.

General Wessels's luck now began to turn bad. After the loss of Company G the monsoon rains struck in full force, bringing low visibility, swamp conditions, and increased illness to the troops. However, troop performance improved as the shock of combat wore off. Training programs were expanded to troops both on and off the front lines. Two Chinese battalions, the 3/88th and 1/89th were pulled out of the line to practice for a set piece assault on a small portion of enemy defenses. A support plan of thirty-nine B-24s and fighter cover from the 88th Fighter Squadron was included. The attack, which took place on 12 July, failed when American bombers dropped their loads short—an occurrence that was not unusual—and they fell among Allied troops waiting to go into the attack. Once again attacks gained only a few yards each day.

The attacks were whittling down the enemy defenders, however. By mid-July 790 enemy were dead and another 1,180 were wounded. The Japanese were now compressed into a smaller perimeter and no longer had the freedom of maneuver that they had previously taken advantage of so expertly. So the attacks continued. On 21 July a patrol in which Pfc. Marvin H. Dean, a veteran of the Marauders, acted as first scout was ambushed and pinned down by enemy machine-gun fire. Advancing alone, Private First Class Dean took out the enemy position and freed his trapped patrol. He was one of six Marauders to be awarded a Distinguished Service Cross for the Myitkyina campaign.

The first signs that the Japanese were finished at Myitkyina appeared in the last week of July. Kachins operating under Detachment 101 ambushed some rafts floating down the river from Myitkyina. Although most of the Japanese occupants were killed, two were captured. They revealed that the rafts held hospital patients being evacuated from the garrison by the simple method of floating them down the river to Japanese lines. A day or two later, on 26 and 27 July, the 3d Battalion, New Galahad, finally seized the northern airfield that had been a mainstay of the enemy defenses. The 209th and 236th Engineer Combat Battalions were now pulled out of the line, replaced by newly arriving Chinese units, and sent for rest and recuperation. These two battalions had suffered severely, with losses in the 209th Battalion at 41 percent of its original strength.

By August, Allied gains against a decreasing enemy resistance had increased noticeably. The defenses were still formidable, as when on 28 July a group of wounded were trapped under direct machine-gun and rifle fire. Marauder veterans T5 Russell G. Wellman and Pfc. Herman Manuel teamed up to rescue the wounded despite the intense fire that wounded both men, each of whom won a Distinguished Service Cross.[31] At about this time Colonel Maruyama made a request that the remnants of his regiment be allowed to withdraw.

As early as 24 June signs began to appear that the enemy garrison was at least preparing for a withdrawal. Captain Chan noted that natives reported being ordered to build rafts for the Japanese. They were also required to make one thousand Pungee sticks, dipped in poison, for use in booby traps. Native refugees escaping the fortress reported morale problems and occasional suicides among the garrison. The problem was that there was also conflicting evidence, as when two Chinese men were captured who claimed to have been impressed into Japanese service. Captain Chan, who was amazed that the captured Chinese had not been summarily executed by their Chinese captors, learned from them that there were no plans to withdraw and that additional supplies were expected by the Japanese.[32] Broadcasts across the lines by General Stilwell's political officer, John Emmerson, and Marauder veteran Sgt. Henry ("Horizontal Hank") Gosho were increased, but in at least one instance were answered by Japanese broadcasts calling for the Allies to surrender.

General Mizukami had decided that the garrison would fight to the bitter end. However, with Colonel Maruyama's request in front of him he relented and gave permission for the surviving defenders to withdraw. As usual with Japanese commanders in this war, General Mizukami atoned to his emperor for his supposed failure by committing ritual suicide on or about 1 August.

The enemy decision to withdraw did not become immediately apparent to the Allies, however. Fighting continued for several days but with lessening resistance from the evacuating enemy defenders. New Galahad continued to be in the thick of the fighting. On 31 July Capt. Shields A. Brubeck was commanding a heavy weapons company. Together with two infantry companies they were separated from American lines. Ordered to take joint command, Captain Brubeck set up covering fire and then led the infantry attack. When a section of the attack was held up by accurate enemy fire, Captain Brubeck "rushed the enemy, firing his submachine gun. Inspired by this action the line rushed forward and their combined fire overcame enemy resistance,"[33] allowing the attack to succeed.

Captain John J. Dunn led his company on 30 and 31 July with equal distinction. After leading from the front, he recovered the body of an officer while the area was still under the enemy fire that had felled that officer. Captain Dunn later ordered his men to remain behind while he advanced alone against enemy snipers that had inflicted casualties on his command. He eliminated that threat and allowed his command to continue the advance unopposed.[34] Together with 1st Lt. Donald W. Delorey, who displayed equally distinguished leadership, Captains Dunn and Brubeck won Distinguished Service Crosses during the closing days of the battle.

Sometime after General Mizukami's suicide a patrol from the 236th Combat Engineers located his bunker. "The underground dugout that the general was found in was about as big as a house and was his headquarters, supply depot and hospital," according to the men who found him.[35] A detail led by T5 Howard P. Horton carefully entered the bunker and collected the usual souvenirs. Upon leaving, however, they were less cautious and set off a forty-four pound bomb that had been placed at the entrance as a booby trap. Fortunately for the souvenir hunters, the bomb had a ten-second delay fuse, which prevented any casualties. Lieutenant Colonel Greenlee later had a few select words for his souvenir hunters.

The Japanese had some difficulties in their own command structure during the battle. While Colonel Maruyama believed that his duty lay in denying the general area of Myitkyina to the Allies, thus allowing him some room for maneuver, his commander, Major General Mizukami, had other orders, and they were strangely worded. Normally, Japanese commanders were ordered to defend a location for a specific time, or for a purpose, or to "the last man." General Mizukami's orders, however, read: "Major-General Mizukami will defend Myitkyina to the death."[36] This order allowed General Mizukami to authorize Colonel Maruyama's request for the withdrawal of the remnants of the garrison when further resistance was pointless. Indeed, it saved the Americans from additional weeks of savage combat should the survivors fight to the death instead of withdrawing. The general, however, could not retreat. As the garrison withdrew during the first days of August he received a signal from the southern area army, the highest Japanese command in Southeast Asia, that he had been promoted to full general. This was one more signal that he was expected to die in Myitkyina.[37]

On the first night the Japanese walking wounded, singing the popular Japanese soldier song "Shina No Yoru" ("China Nights"), the regimental records and battle flags, and the garrison's "comfort" women crossed the river safely. General Mizukami, with his headquarters, left the town but stopped at a midstream island known to the Japanese as Nonthalon. Technically, he was still within the limits of the town of Myitkyina and had obeyed orders. Sometime during the second night a gun shot was heard, and General Mizukami's orders had been fulfilled. He had died in Myitkyina. The remainder of the garrison crossed on the second and third nights.

When Colonel Maruyama appeared at 18th Division Headquarters some days later, he was berated by a noted Japanese staff officer, Col. Masanobu Tsuji. General Tanaka put a swift halt to the reprimand, protecting the defender of Myitkyina from his own high command.[38]

The comfort women who escaped with the Myitkyina garrison were some of the 3,200 women employed through private contractors by the Japanese armed forces in Burma. These included 2,800

Korean women, almost all of whom had been coerced into the prostitution business by private contractors who provided the service to the armed forces. There were also significant numbers of Burmese women, many of whom had volunteered, believing the Japanese promises of freedom for their nation at the war's end.

Three "comfort stations" had been established at Myitkyina, two staffed by Koreans and one by Chinese. These were assigned to the 114th Japanese Infantry Regiment. Colonel Maruyama set the prices and was universally hated by the women, being described as "the most notorious officer in the Japanese Army."[39] He kept a favorite, a Korean woman named Ha Ton Ye, for himself. In the retreat it was reported that he ordered that the comfort women be given priority even over Japanese wounded. Of the sixty-three women present at Myitkyina[40] during the retreat, most of them floated down the river on small boats. Several were caught in a skirmish with Chinese troops, and a number of Chinese comfort women surrendered to them. The Korean women continued with the retreating Japanese until they were exhausted, so they stayed at a deserted house along the river while their contractor tried to construct a raft. But before the raft was ready they were captured by Kachin Rangers. Among them was Colonel Maruyama's favorite, Ha Ton Ye. Out of the sixty-three women, four had died on the march, two of whom had been shot when mistaken for Japanese soldiers.[41]

During the morning hours of 8 August Captain Chan was asked to help interrogate some of the captured women. Assisted by Sgt. Grant Harabayashi, another Marauder veteran still on his feet, he showed them several pictures of Japanese officers known to be in the garrison. The women could identify only Colonel Maruyama and had no information of military value.

As the interrogation ended, the women became agitated and Captain Chan asked Sergeant Harabayashi to ask what was upsetting them. They were concerned about their fate now that they were captured. Captain Chan assured them that they would be sent to safety in India and then returned to Korea after the war. Some sixty years later, the issue of the conscripted comfort women would still be a matter of concern to both the Korean and Japanese governments.

Myitkyina was officially declared secured on 3 August 1944, after the last few die-hard rear guards were overrun. Colonel Maruyama managed to escape with about 600 men, leaving his seriously wounded behind to delay pursuit. One hundred eighty-seven enemy had been captured, the rest killed. For the Allies, Myitkyina cost 972 Chinese killed, 3,184 wounded, and 188 sick and evacuated, for a total of 4,344 casualties. Of the Americans, 272 were killed, 955 were wounded, and 980 were evacuated due to sickness, for a total of 2,207.

The figures for the Chinese must be considered in light of the traditional Chinese soldier's ability to care for himself, boiling all his drinking and cooking water, for example, as opposed to the American habit of filling canteens while crossing a stream. Another factor affecting the statistics is that after the war numerous Chinese deserters were uncovered in the area of Myitkyina, causing something of a criminal and political problem. Many, if not all, were not included in the preceding figures, because carrying them on the roles increased the graft available to Chinese unit commanders.

Nearly six hundred of the American sick were from Galahad, which had brought them into the battle already weakened from the preceding campaign.[42] And there was one final casualty on 3 August. Colonel Hunter, who had led, guided, and cajoled Galahad throughout its long trials, was relieved of command by a slip of paper ordering him back to the United States by the next available water transportation.

Despite the removal of Colonel Hunter, the scandal over the treatment of the Marauders could not be covered up. Colonel Hunter was not the only Marauder officer irate about the treatment of his men. Two of the regiment's medical officers, Major James E. T. Hopkins, M.D., battalion surgeon of the 3d Battalion, and Captain Henry G. Stelling, of the 2d Battalion, wrote scathing reports of the circumstances that devastated the Marauders. Combined with a report by Col. Tracey S. Voorhees, of the Judge Advocate General Corps, these became known collectively as the Hopkins Report, under the title "The Marauders and the Microbes: A Record of Righteous Indignation."

The reports decry the treatment of the Marauders after Nhpum Ga. The medical officers believed that after that campaign the entire unit should have been declared medically unfit for further combat without a long rest and recovery period. Major Hopkins wrote of the 3d Battalion after Myitkyina, that "it can only be kept on even a moderately efficient garrison status with the greatest effort of the surgeons and other officers." He reported that "by the 31st of May all but 13 men and one officer of the 3d Battalion had left Myitkyina on EMT tags. These men were held up several days because of General Boatner's verbal order to Major Schudmak that none but very seriously ill would be evacuated." In commenting on the history of the Marauders, Major Hopkins remarked that "many will agree that it holds more dynamite than the Patton Incident."[43]

Captain Stelling commented in his report that "confidence in Theater commanders became zero." He was critical of other Marauder medical officers, saying, "The Regimental surgeon in his administrative capacity did not undergo the hardships of the entire campaign. He rarely carried a pack and was flown by air from place to place. Yet he dared to pose as an authority upon the condition of the men and made only token protests against the treatment they were receiving."

Having served with the hard-hit 2d Battalion, Captain Stelling reported:

> Our battalion commander was so set on reaching Arang and being ready to push on to Myitkyina and so blind in his stubborn determination that he walked off with his usual very light pack and left most of his staff far behind and started pushing the leading platoon at full speed. Some units of the outfit were trailing near the end trying to keep up.

At Myitkyina Captain Stelling recalled:

> The men were so completely exhausted by then that they were literally on their last legs. All alertness and all will to fight or even move had left them. When ordered to dig in, many fell from exhaustion and went to sleep by their partially dug foxholes. Others fell without attempting to dig. Those on guard fell asleep from sheer exhaustion.

Colonel Voorhees was sent by the judge advocate general's office to investigate the theater's medical supply system but quickly became drawn into the Marauder controversy by Major Hopkins, whom he met at the airfield upon arrival. Colonel Voorhees's interest resulted in his own report on the reaction of the theater command to the medical critics. He reported that the acting theater surgeon, Col. George E. Armstrong, had a copy of the report and had tried to discuss it with General Stilwell, who refused him an interview. Furthermore, Colonel Voorhees had been promised that all hospitals now recommended that malaria cases be returned to the United States rather than treated and returned to combat. In addition, the rotation policy of two years overseas and then a return to the United States would be immediately applied to the surviving Marauders, most of whom qualified for this program. He recorded that General Boatner had promised that the Marauders remaining at Myitkyina (this was written in July) would be relieved as soon as replacements arrived and that they would be sent to the rear for recuperation.

As a result of the promises he received, Colonel Voorhees declined to forward the Hopkins Report to the surgeon general in Washington. "I took this course with some reluctance as the document was a most remarkable one and contained a most informative statement with persuasive internal evidence of being an accurate and fair review of the circumstances."[44]

Perhaps the best and most impartial estimate of the quality of Galahad's leaders was written by one who served with them but had no American or military bias. Jack Girsham had served with the Marauders throughout its combat career and would continue to serve until the Burma Road was cut in 1945 with its successor organizations. As a British citizen with neither American nor British military connections, his evaluation was the most objective to be found in the convoluted atmosphere that prevailed in the China-Burma-India theater. He recorded, "Two things impressed me about Merrill: First, he was a cool, clever, and tough fighting man, the type who would never lose his temper or his nerve. Second, as I came to learn, he cared for his men."[45] Of the others, he saw "the finest officers you could want, in my opinion. Colonel C. N. Hunter, the second in command, was much like Merrill, but with more of a temper, and not at all hesitant about stating his opinion when the higher-ups blundered."[46] Finally, "Colonels William Osborne and George

MacGee [*sic*] were great field commanders, willing and anxious to get up where the shooting was going on, which made the GIs respect them more than anything else."[47]

One issue that surfaced continually in reviews of the Myitkyina campaign was the value of the intelligence information provided by and to the Myitkyina Task Force. The original estimate of 500 Japanese in the garrison is cited as a gross underestimate by the official history. Captain Chan, however, points out that this figure was a "roundup" given by the 5307th Composite Unit upon arrival in the area and that it referred only to the forces of that unit's immediate front, not to all enemy forces in the area. The responsibility for providing an overall intelligence estimate rested with the NCAC, which apparently relied on frontline estimates and simply accepted them at face value. Captain Chan reports that when he left for Myitkyina on 12 June the NCAC estimate for the "Myitkyina area" was 3,000 enemy troops. At the conclusion of the battle, 4,075 enemy troops were estimated to have been killed. Allowing for reinforcements known to have arrived during the fight, this is not a bad estimate.

However, it appears that for reasons unknown, much of the early decision making about how to reduce the Myitkyina fortress was based on the rosier early estimates of only 500 enemy defenders, and that is where the problem lies. When it was known at least to the intelligence officers of the Myitkyina Task Force that additional enemy forces had arrived, why were these outdated estimates used to plan offensives?

In his postwar interrogation, General Tanaka confirmed that he ordered the 114th Infantry Regiment—less one battalion, about 3,000 men—to defend Myitkyina. The regiment's 3d Battalion was ordered to join the garrison in May, and in June another battalion of the 56th Division infiltrated into the town. This was in addition to the service troops and wounded already present. General Tanaka gave an estimate of "peak strength" as 4,600 soldiers and in turn estimated the Allied force as consisting of three thousand Americans and twelve thousand Chinese. He guessed that the British (Chindit) forces numbered another two thousand, and totaled the attacking force at thirty thousand men.[48] Clearly the art of intelligence on both sides of the battle for Myitkyina was seriously flawed.

With Myitkyina-Mogaung in Allied hands, the supply effort to keep China in the war could improve. The use of the airfields, and their denial to the enemy, allowed the air transports to fly a more southerly, and therefore shorter and safer, route over the Himalayas. This allowed a faster turnaround of aircraft, increasing the amount of tonnage carried over a long term. Indeed, between May and July of 1944 hump tonnage actually doubled. It would continue to rise as the Myitkyina area was developed into a firm base for air transport. Another advantage was the ability to advance the Ledo Road and its accompanying pipeline to China. Myitkyina provided a useful supply base for the continued reconquest of Burma and China. Finally, the loss of Myitkyina-Mogaung combined with the loss of the Imphal-Kohima battle, put the Japanese in Burma firmly on the defensive, a position from which they would not recover.

8. From Galahad to Mars

As the battle for Myitkyina wound down, efforts turned to the rehabilitation of the fighting units. There were serious problems in the maintenance of morale among those who still could function within the old and new Marauders. As Lieutenant Ogburn would later record, "What destroyed the 5307th was the imputation of inadequacy. The Marauders were made to feel that it was lack of courage and stamina on their part that necessitated sending unprepared troops into combat."[1]

Yet they knew that without their efforts the Allied forces would never have reached Myitkyina that campaign year. They knew little of General Stilwell's difficulties in getting the Chinese forces to obey his instructions, and so pointed to the thirty Chinese divisions known to be sitting in Yunnan and doing nothing as further evidence of General Stilwell's duplicity. As more and more Marauders were released from the hospital or came back from Myitkyina to the rest camp set up at Dinjan, fifty miles south of Margherita, the resentful attitude toward all things military began to show itself.

The military police preferred to stay out of any altercations after a few unpleasant episodes with stray Marauders. Nurses at the 14th Evacuation Hospital stopped calling the police to try to settle outbreaks of violence within the wards. In addition to attitudes of hostility, the veterans managed to concoct what was termed "bullfight brandy," which upon analysis was found to contain marijuana along with the alcohol. This combination often made the men uncontrollable. Lieutenant Ogburn, one of the few officers at the camp, was called to a Red Cross canteen one evening to recover two Marauders who were tearing up the place after drinking bullfight brandy. "Two horrified Red Cross girls were backed against the far end while the two drunks hurled plates and shouted obscenities as extreme as I had ever heard even in the 5307th. My intervention merely provided a new target for them and I had to swing a chair to get them out of the place."[2] Significantly, of the many other enlisted Marauders in the club, not one of them either intervened to stop the disorder or testified later against the offenders.

Some Marauders were sent back to Myitkyina as individuals to re-inforce the few Galahads still there. Lieutenant Philip S. Weld received ten such men one morning and within moments of their leaving for frontline positions he heard a shot. One veteran, a staff sergeant, had shot himself through the toe. He made no secret of it and advised Lieutenant Weld that others would soon follow suit if they were not relieved. The lieutenant managed to quell the potential revolt, and no outbreak occurred, but clearly the attitude of the surviving Marauders was that they were entitled to a rest and would not settle for anything less.

Ironically, while the unit was falling apart internally its external reputation was such that it was one of the most respected units in the American army at the time. Again, Lieutenant Ogburn records one illuminating episode.

> We heard with amusement of a group of rear-echelon types in New Delhi who, one day on a street corner, desisted from their congenital pastime of deriding the British to bait a Japanese-American enlisted man standing by himself. The object of this attention merely made a quarter turn, bringing into view the 5307th's well-known shoulder patch. And that was that.[3]

However, Lt. Nellis I. Johnson, who had replaced Captain Laffin as the unit's intelligence officer, had a different experience with respect to the unit's shoulder patch. After being ordered out with a high fever by General Merrill, Lieutenant Johnson was later evacuated to the United States by way of Natal, Brazil. As he walked into the airport terminal during a layover he was approached by a couple of military police led by a lieutenant. He was escorted to the colonel commanding the base and advised that he was to be confined to quarters during his stay. When asked why, he was told that a group of Marauders had recently come through on their way home and had "wrecked" the colonel's base. Henceforth, anyone wearing a Marauder patch was restricted the entire time he remained on that base.[4]

Private Clyde Blue, of the African American 518th Quartermaster (Truck) Battalion, recorded the feelings of respect that others felt for the Marauders. A soldier with no love for the army, he felt no patriotism except at the sight of the Marauders when they came through Assam after being relieved. "The men of this unit I will never forget. Their camouflage clothing was torn and dirty; their boots worn. With all of the loot stashed around our area these men were not even offered new clothing or boots." He looked closely at those veterans and remembered:

> Around the eyes, all of Merrill's men looked alike no matter what their coloring; they had the eyes of dead men. A smart MP grabbed one of them when they first arrived. The Marauder just looked at him and the MP loosened his grip like he had grabbed the heated end of a soldering iron. I suspect he realized he had come about as close to death as possible without dying. These men had become professionals in the art of killing, working behind enemy lines. They had been at it too long, killing and being killed. They had seen too much violent death, and in turn had become messengers of death. An overzealous, immaculate officer snapped one of them up for not saluting. For his trouble he got a contemptuous visual sweep from toe to head and was brushed aside like so much dirt! Talk about a red-faced Major![5]

Private Blue also related that many Marauders spent time with the African American soldiers, because they were the only ones the Marauders could relate to in regard to their joint disgust with the treatment received from the United States Army.

In the interim there were other events occurring beyond the limits of the American infantry that would soon affect them. On both sides of the battle lines the opposing high commands were taking steps to express the dissatisfaction with the events in Burma. The failures at Imphal, Kohima, and Myitkyina had been severe blows to Japanese intentions. During the battle Lt. Gen. Renya Mutaguchi, commanding the Imphal operation, had relieved all three of his division commanders for what he felt were failures in accomplishing the missions assigned to them. Now at the end of August 1944 he himself was removed, transferred to the general staff in Tokyo, and replaced by Lt. Gen. Shibachi Katamura, who had formerly commanded the 54th Japanese Infantry Division.

Others were similarly removed, along with their staffs who were scattered across Asia, and were replaced with combat veterans proven in battle. The new head of the Burma area army was Lt. Gen. Kimura Hyotaro, who was described as flexible, shrewd, and skilled in strategy. Coming from the Ordnance Administration Headquarters in Tokyo, he had formerly been vice-minister of war under General Tojo. For his chief of staff Tokyo headquarters appointed Lt. Gen. Shinichi Tanaka, the commander of the 18th Japanese Infantry Division, who had given General Stilwell so much trouble during the past months. It was believed that Tanaka's persistence and toughness combined with Kimura's skills would solidify the Japanese position in Burma.

Japanese plans also changed. As early as 2 July 1944 the southern area army issued Operation Order 101, which instructed the armies under its command to continue fighting the British west of the Chindwin River and Stilwell's forces in northern Burma, eliminating all discussion of an advance into India. The objective was to continue to cut communications and supplies to China. As Japanese fortunes continued to decline, even this plan was outdated, and by September a new directive ordered the Japanese army in Burma to ensure the security of southern Burma, ignoring northern Burma, as the new flank of the Southeast Asian defense zone. Included in this latter order was an indication that whatever could be done would be done with resources already at hand. No help could be expected from Japan, which was already struggling with stretched resources all across the Pacific. The recent losses in India and northern Burma had also put a strain on the loyalty of those Burmese who had joined with the Japanese in exchange for their independence, and they could no longer be counted on in anything more than an internal police role.

Events elsewhere were also showing signs of Japanese stress in maintaining a grip on Burma. To the north of the Salween, Chinese forces numbering more than seventy-two thousand had attacked in response to American statements threatening the cessation of supplies unless Chinese forces took a much more active part in the clearing of northern Burma. This operation, known as the Salween offensive, struck the understrength 56th Infantry Division. Numbering barely eleven thousand men, that division held off the Salween offensive from April until late June.

After they withdrew due to lack of supplies, which had forced some of them to resort to cannibalism, the Japanese left behind one regimental group defending the walled city of Tengchung. It took five Chinese divisions until late September to clear Tengchung. Even then American air power played a major role. Using the delay to reorganize and re-equip, the Japanese even managed a successful counterattack, which returned Japanese control to that section of the Burma Road. But despite this impressive performance, the 56th Japanese Infantry Division was denied reinforcements, and its men were exhausted. As on other fronts in Burma, they were soon forced to surrender the area they had defended so valiantly. By the end of the year this division would be in full retreat, facing another American Long Range Penetration force as it made its withdrawal down the Burma Road.

The Americans and the Chinese also shuffled their command structure. The long antipathy between Generalissimo Chiang Kai-shek and General Stilwell finally resulted in Stilwell's recall. He was replaced by Lt. Gen. Albert C. Wedemeyer as adviser to the generalissimo, while the NCAC was to be commanded by Lt. Gen. Daniel Sultan. Only the British kept the commander, Lt. Gen. William Slim, who had finally brought them a significant victory at Imphal. Even there a sordid incident occurred when for a few brief weeks General Slim was relieved of command due to internal British military intrigue.

Upon hearing of Stilwell's recall, General Slim remarked, "I liked him. There was no one I would rather have had commanding the

Chinese Army that was to advance with mine. Under Stilwell it would advance."[6] General Slim's opinion was a personal one and was not shared by many other British officers serving in Burma.

Lieutenant General Albert Coady Wedemeyer was born on 9 July 1896 in Omaha, Nebraska. He graduated 270th out of a class of 285 at West Point in 1919. He later served in China with the 15th Infantry Regiment, attended the German War Academy, and was assigned to the War Plans Division when the United States entered World War II. Described as tall, suave, able, and ambitious, he saw his career nearly end when he fell under suspicion of leaking secret war plans to the press. His German ancestry and recent attendance at a German war academy lent itself to these suspicions. Despite intense investigation by the Federal Bureau of Investigation, no evidence was ever produced linking Wedemeyer with the press leak. As a result, he survived professionally and was sent to Asia to get him out of the public eye. Originally assigned as assistant to General Mountbatten, he was selected to succeed General Stilwell.

At the same time, new organizations were ordered for the China-Burma-India theater. Part of the reason for the recall of General Stilwell was the American insistence that he be given actual command of the Chinese armies, under Generalissimo Chiang Kai-shek. Included in this plan was the separation of the CBI theater into two separate theaters. One was to concern itself with the India-Burma campaign while the other was focused on China. General Stilwell would command one and Lt. Gen. Daniel I. Sultan the other. However, Generalissimo Chiang Kai-shek refused to consider any plan that included General Stilwell. The antipathy between the two men had by this time become so acute that rather than accept this proposal the Generalissimo again demanded Stilwell's recall. In Washington General Marshall, having finally conceded the impossibility of Stilwell's position with the Chinese leader, agreed.

Despite the loss of General Stilwell, the plan to divide the theater was adopted. While General Wedemeyer commanded in China, General Sultan took over command in the new India-Burma theater. As an engineer and administrator his talents were uniquely suitable in that theater.

Born in Mississippi in 1885, Sultan graduated ninth in a class of 111 at West Point in 1907. He served in the Philippines in World War I and in various engineer and administrative posts during the interwar years. He competed with General Marshall for the post of army chief of staff and later commanded an infantry division in training. Sent to be General Stilwell's deputy, Sultan was highly regarded by the latter, who said, "Dan Sultan is the best thing that ever happened to the theater."

Other events changed the way the war was conducted in the new theaters. President Roosevelt had now appointed a personal representative to the generalissimo. This relieved the army, usually in the person of General Stilwell, from delivering messages from the president to the generalissimo, a source of friction between the two. Another factor was that the number of interactions between the president and the generalissimo decreased significantly as the war now clearly entered a final phase. While it was still American policy to keep China in the war, it was no longer necessary that much be accomplished. The promises of the Soviet government to commit to fighting the Japanese on the Asian continent immediately after the fall of Germany also reduced the urgency of the situation in China.

As September approached, the monsoon rains in Burma began to subside and plans began to be made to continue the campaign. The great British victory at Imphal-Kohima, which had nearly wrecked the Japanese 15th Army, had changed the entire situation in the theater. As the Allies followed the Japanese retreating from Imphal, they encountered increasing evidence of Japanese weakness. Abandoned equipment, unburied dead, and disorganization of units clearly indicated that the Japanese army in Burma was ripe for a major offensive by the Allies. The problem was now how and where to conduct that offensive.

Two plans were prepared. Plan X directed NCAC forces in northern Burma to drive south from the Myitkyina-Mogaung area to seize Katha and Bhamo. Included here were plans to conduct an airborne operation in the Wuntho area. The goal of Plan X was to seize all of northern Burma to align Kalewa and Lashio. Plan Y, in contrast, called for IV and XXXIII British Corps of the XIV Army to cross the Chindwin River and debark on the central Burma plain, where they could best use their superior armor and artillery assets. Plan Y included an airborne assault, this time on Kalewa, with Mandalay as the ultimate objective. A third plan, Plan Z, suggested an air and sea assault on Rangoon. This plan, although kept alive for some time, failed to materialize due to lack of adequate resources, particularly landing craft.

The Northern Combat Area Command was ordered to protect the east flank of the XIV Army by destroying any enemy forces on that flank and securing a general line of defense at Lashio-Mongmit-Thabeikkyin. The date for the establishment of this line was February 1945. Protection of the air supply route and overland communication routes to China was also a primary concern. In effect, Plans X and Y were to be joined and put into operation.

Because the advance entailed moving across country similar in nature to that just seized in the previous campaigning season, another long-range penetration group was to be formed to lead the new advance. The War Department had known of General Stilwell's strong desire to have an American division–sized force under his command to lead the Chinese forward. As a result of these requests and several alternate suggestions, such as brigading American and Chinese soldiers together under American officers, a new force was formed. Once again a provisional designation was used, this time the 5332d Brigade (Provisional). It was to consist of the 475th Infantry Regiment, formed largely of veterans of the Old and New Galahads, the 124th Cavalry Regiment, and the 1st Chinese Separate Regiment. This force, which became known by the code name of Mars Task Force, was to lead the NCAC in the campaign.

The 124th Cavalry Regiment was organized as a part of the Texas National Guard at Houston, Texas, in March 1929. It was a horse cavalry regiment and had its individual troops stationed at various cities and towns across Texas. It practiced the usual weekly training programs and encampments, as did all National Guard units between the wars. The regiment was inducted into federal service on 18 November 1940 and ordered to Fort Bliss, Texas, where it was attached to the regular army's 1st Cavalry Division. Here it entered into prolonged training. Men over the age of twenty-eight were discharged and replaced with inductees. After its year of mandated service the regiment had just begun to send its members home when the Japanese attacked Pearl Harbor. Instead of spending the holidays at home, the regiment spent it along the Mexican border, guarding against border crossings from a country that had neither declared war on the axis nor had broken diplomatic relations with them. During this phase the regiment trained many new men who were then shipped to other units. By early 1943 the 124th was the only mounted regiment left in the entire U.S. Army.

In December 1943 Col. Milo H. Matteson of Carmel, California, took command of the regiment. Shortly thereafter, the 124th Cavalry Regiment (Horse) was transferred to Fort Riley, Kansas, where they surrendered their horses. Sent to the New York POE, they were convinced they were bound for Europe. Instead, they arrived at the Los Angeles POE and soon loaded onto the USS *General H. W. Butner*. After a miserable thirty-one-day journey they arrived in India on 26 August 1944. There the regiment's designation was changed to 124th Cavalry Regiment, Special, indicating its transformation from mounted cavalry to infantry. By that time only 27 percent of the original Texas National Guardsmen remained with the regiment.

Their companions in the 5332d Brigade (Provisional) were barely in official existence when the cavalry arrived at Ramgarh. The 475th Infantry Regiment (Long Range Penetration Regiment, Special) was not activated until 5 August 1944. Its commander was Lt. Col. William Lloyd Osborne, the same officer who had commanded the Marauders' 1st Battalion through the previous campaign. Many of its men were veterans of Galahad or New Galahad.

New Galahad's 2d and 3d Battalions had completed mopping up around Myitkyina and Sitapur on about 3 August. The battalions had been fighting constantly for sixty-five days and were disorganized and exhausted. On that day Colonel Hunter turned over command to Colonel Osborne, who combined the Old and New Galahads. Most of the 2d and 3d Battalions were sent back to Dinjan for a rest. The new campsite, Camp Landis, was selected, and preparations were made to bring the new unit together and to begin training for the next season. As the new site took shape many of the Old Galahads were given furloughs. Yet even during a supposed quiet period, ten enemy soldiers were killed in the immediate vicinity of Camp Landis, and Sergeant Young, of Company E, captured another nearby.

Between 10 and 14 August the men alternately rested and built Camp Landis. Then a series of officers schools were conducted under regimental supervision. The series included classes on small-unit problems, scouting and patrolling, rifle squad in the attack, security patrolling, rifle instruction, and practice firing. These classes ended on 7 September, after which the two battalions began a cycle of training that included marches, range firing, military sanitation, first aid, map reading, familiarization of enemy weapons, and firing of American weapons.

To both fulfill the training cycle and plan future operations, Maj. Benjamin F. Thrailkill led his 2d Battalion out of Camp Landis on 27 August and marched to meet a large force of Chinese troops to the north to determine if that route provided a shortcut to China. The Montana-born major led his battalion, reinforced with Chinese, Kachin Rangers, medical personnel, and an engineer officer, to the area successfully. No enemy opposition was encountered, and the expedition returned without incident.

Once all the units had been integrated into the battalion, each unit practiced from 2 to 31 October in ambushes, road blocks, trail blocks, marches, airdrops, and river crossings. As new men joined the force additional training continued until all the men were brought up to the level of most of the force. From a low strength of 40 percent in early August the 475th Regiment was at full strength by October. November was spent cleaning up before departure and testing the skills they had learned during the past training cycles. On 15 November the first serial of the regiment left Camp Landis for the last time.[7]

Mars Task Force was activated on 26 July 1944. Brigadier General Thomas S. Arms assumed command that day of a unit that was still assembling its far-flung units. A native of Cleveland, Ohio, and a graduate of the Virginia Military Institute, class of 1915, General Arms was an infantry officer. He had served in China in the 1920s and later had taught at the infantry school and at the Ohio National Guard. After graduating from the Command and General Staff

School and fulfilling additional instructor assignments, including one under General Stilwell's command, General Arms commanded an infantry regiment before returning to China at General Stilwell's request in November 1942. After he was promoted to brigadier general in April 1943, Mars Task Force was his first combat assignment.

While the 124th Cavalry was in transit and the 475th Infantry was being formed, the third component of Mars Task Force was still undergoing training in India. This was the 1st Chinese Separate Infantry Regiment. Commanded by Col. Lin Kuan-lsiang, the regiment had been specially trained in long-range penetration tactics by American instructors at Ramgarh for the purpose of participating in a joint Chinese-American operation. Although formally included in the 5332d Brigade (Provisional), this regiment would never actually participate in operations, another holdout for the generalissimo's coming war for the control of China.

Unlike the original Marauders, Mars Task Force was provided with artillery support from the outset. The 612th Field Artillery Battalion (Pack) was one of several battalions of light artillery that the army had formed while experimenting with specialized units early in the war. Several of these division-sized units included light (or pack) artillery units for jungle and mountain warfare. The 612th Field Artillery Battalion was activated 17 December 1943 at Camp Gruber, Oklahoma, with a contingent of officers transferred from the 71st (Light) Infantry Division then training at Camp Carson, Colorado. Under the command of Maj. William G. Stephenson, the battalion continued to accrue officers and enlisted men to arrive at assigned strength. Major John W. Read assumed command on 21 December 1943.

The battalion trained under the command of the 413th Field Artillery Group, Second Army, at Camp Gruber. At the end of February 1944 it received about 280 mules for transportation use. A week later, on 1 March 1944, the battalion relocated to Camp Carson and later that month had its first overnight bivouac with the newly received mules. Training, including participation in the close combat and night infiltration courses, continued into April. In May excess officers were transferred out and several enlisted men went to the 613th Field Artillery Battalion (Pack). In June the battalion began departing, three detachments leaving for Camp Pleuscha, Louisiana, each with sixty men and 320 of the mules now assigned to the battalion. The bulk of the unit went west to Camp Anza, California.

The trip was a nightmare. The battalion's mules were carried by three ships: USS *Dearborn*, USS *C. W. Field*, and USS *W. S. Halstead*. Departing from New Orleans, the ships sailed around Florida to Norfolk, Virginia. This was to be a departure point for a sail across the Atlantic and around Africa to India. The *Halstead* hit a storm off Florida and had to lay over for four days of repairs in Norfolk. The ships then joined a convoy for the Atlantic crossing. During the crossing of the Gulf of Suez the *Dearborn* rammed a British ship and had to put in for repairs. The *Field* was hit by a dud torpedo that cracked its bow, but it managed to struggle along, arriving at Calcutta, India, on 23 September 1944.

The human contingent of the battalion was more fortunate. It loaded onto the USS *General H. W. Butner*, which sailed from Los Angeles alone, zigzagging across the Pacific. Five thousand soldiers were on board, making food service and labor details, particularly kitchen duty, especially difficult. An enemy submarine scare on 1 August 1944 resulted in such a sharp maneuver that every man aboard was thrown off his feet or out of bed. After a brief layover in Melbourne, Australia, the ship proceeded to Bombay, this time escorted by two British corvettes. After a journey of 14,564 miles the battalion was in the combat area. Shortly afterward it arrived at Camp Landis, near Myitkyina, and continued training under Lt. Col. Richard A. Knight, Major Read having been transferred to NCAC headquarters.[8] Lt. Col. James F. Donovan soon joined the command, bringing his 613th Field Artillery (Pack), which had arrived by a similar route.

The brigade also included several quartermaster pack troops, a veterinary hospital, and a portable surgical hospital. It was to be supported by the 10th U.S. Army Air Force, a part of the overall eastern air command then operating in the India-Burma theater. It had under command nine bombardment squadrons, seven fighter squadrons, four combat cargo squadrons, and three troop carrier squadrons. The major assignment of the 10th Air Force was to stop

Japanese supply and reinforcement efforts. Bridges, roads, and railroads were the prime targets. More than half of the efforts were devoted to this task, while about one quarter were devoted to ground support. Even this included the more numerous Chinese and British forces fighting in Burma. Air evacuation of wounded men, a process perfected in the earlier campaigns, was now a matter of course, and subsequently the claim would be made that every wounded soldier, American or Chinese, who was evacuated from a forward area was evacuated by air.

Once it was confirmed that a new long-range penetration brigade was being created for the continuing Burma campaign, a training area ten miles north of Myitkyina along the Irrawaddy River was established. Designated Camp Robert W. Landis, in honor of the first Marauder casualty of the campaign, it began receiving its first tenants in mid-August 1944. These men, who were soon to form the 475th Infantry Regiment, were gradually joined by other elements of the brigade, including the 1st Chinese Separate Regiment, which arrived in the fall. Because of various difficulties the training schedule placed the 475th Infantry Regiment in training in September and October, while the 124th Cavalry, which could not arrive until October, trained in October and November. It was during the October training that General Arms was injured in a motor vehicle accident. He was succeeded by Brig. Gen. John P. Willey on 31 October 1944.

John Perry Willey was born in Hampton, Virginia, on 22 April 1902 and received his bachelor of science degree from the Virginia Polytechnic Institute in 1924. Commissioned into the cavalry the same year, he later graduated from the Command and General Staff School before resuming instructor duties. He was promoted to brigadier general in September 1944. General Willey was an armor /cavalry officer who had earlier served on the NCAC staff and commanded the Myitkyina task force from 1 June to 3 August 1944.

During the training period, arrangements were made to supply the 5332d Brigade with improved rations for the coming operations. Three to four days' allowance of K or C rations, D (chocolate) ration bars, fruit juice supplements, dehydrated soup, coffee, sugar, peanuts, halazone tablets, vitamins, canned heat, and salt were combined into a cloth sack measuring thirty-two inches by fourteen inches. Weighing between thirteen and seventeen pounds, the sack was easily carried in a combat pack. The Services of Supply had noted that the earlier rations for the Marauders of constant K and C rations were woefully inadequate in the conditions expected of long-range penetration forces, and the new allotment was designed to improve on past experience. Consideration was also given to the animal members of Mars Task Force. The mules, horses, and ponies accompanying the task force would be fed by a premixed load of cereal fodder and salt in proportion. Twenty-five-pound sacks of this fodder were easily shoved out of the supply aircraft with minimal loss.

For the Japanese the concept of moving into China and holding Burma as a flank guard was now reversed. They had had recent success in China, causing General Chennault to lose several of his precious airfields. But that had not changed anything, because the capture of Myitkyina allowed the Allies to continue supplying China by means of air transport, which could now fly a shorter and more protected route. Clearly, Burma was now the main theater. There was no longer any intent to expand the Japanese hold on Burma, but only to hold what they still controlled. Even this, General Kimura knew, would be very difficult.

In order to hold his front, General Hyotaro had three armies—the 15th, 28th and 33d—all of which were sadly depleted as a result of the recent campaign. He had received his last reinforcements, the 49th Infantry Division, and although promised reinforcements totaling sixty thousand men and forty-five thousand tons of supplies, he already knew that few of these would reach the fighting troops. In fact, only about two thousand reinforcements reached each infantry division, and most of the supplies were soon redirected to Japanese defenses in the Philippines and French Indo-China. Disaffection in the Burmese auxiliaries was also showing itself, and even the morale of individual Japanese soldiers was beginning to deteriorate due to a feeling of abandonment by the homeland.

Nevertheless, the traditional defensive strength of the Japanese army remained present, as the Allies would soon learn in the coming campaign. The ten divisions under General Kimura numbered over one hundred thousand men, nearly all trained and experienced soldiers who would not give way easily.[9] Kimura knew he had no air support and little in the way of supply or transport. Indeed, the Japanese air force numbered only sixty-four planes against more than twelve hundred of the Allies. Japanese supplies, like those of the Allies, were road bound, thus making them targets for Allied air strikes. General Kimura had little to hope for other than the strength of his individual Japanese soldiers.

The Allies began the campaign in two parts. The Chinese advanced the 22d Division late in October 1944. To assist and support this drive, the American long-range penetration force would move with this attack. Farther south, the British XIV Army, once again under General Slim's command, would attack the main Japanese defensive positions along the Irrawaddy River early in December.

The first to move was the 475th Infantry Regiment, which was now commanded by Col. Ernest F. Easterbrook, who replaced Colonel Osborne after Osborne fell ill due to his earlier experiences with the Marauders. Colonel Easterbrook had served on General Stilwell's staff since 1942. He had one other qualification: he was another member of the Stilwell family, a son-in-law. General Stilwell, who had not yet left Burma, was still making assignments based on his very limited sphere of trust.

The newly promoted Lt. Col. Benjamin F. Thrailkill led his 2d Battalion and the 31st Quartermaster Pack Troop out of Camp Landis on 15 November. The force headed south and was followed the next day by Lt. Col. Arthur K. Harrold's 3d Battalion. The 612th Field Artillery Battalion (Pack), now under the command of Lt. Col. Severn T. Wallis after Colonel Knight was evacuated due to illness, left the next day, and finally the 1st Battalion under Lt. Col. Caifson Johnson, another veteran Marauder officer, left on the fourth day. Each unit moved to the assembly area on the Myitkyina-Bhamo Road twenty miles northeast of Bhamo. There the battalions reorganized themselves into battalion combat teams and moved down the road toward Bhamo.

As always in the Burma campaign, casualties began at once. In the 612th Field Artillery Battalion, for example, the first day's march cost them two heat-exhaustion casualties, and the next day they lost a man who was kicked by a mule. That same day, 18 November 1944, they were reviewed and addressed by General Sultan. Over the next few days they would suffer another seven casualties without ever meeting the enemy.

Bhamo was under siege by the Chinese 38th Division, so the Americans bypassed it by marching west until they reached Shwegu, where they turned south once again. For the first time in months an American long-range penetration group was in motion.

Once again they faced the Japanese 18th Infantry Division, this time under the command of Lt. Gen. Eitaro Naka, who had assumed command early in September after the promotion of General Tanaka. Previously, General Naka had served as vice minister of war (April 1941 through March 1943) and chief of staff to the Burma area army. He had been an opponent of the attack into India, and in the command and staff reshuffle that followed the defeat of that invasion, he and General Tanaka essentially reversed roles. General Naka now led the division west from around Namhkam to Mongmit, a road center southeast of Myitson. There they were to ensure that the Allied attack did not separate the Japanese 15th and 33d Armies, which were operating against the British and Chinese in that area. As a result of these Allied and Japanese assignments, the Americans would once again face the same old enemy, the 18th Division. That division, up to full strength due to the arrival of the final reinforcements, would again send its 55th and 56th Infantry Regiments to block Mars Task Force. Fighting alongside and behind the Americans was an old ally, the Chinese 22d Infantry Division. It was much like the campaign that was just concluded, with a few cast changes, except that this time the Americans were stronger and better prepared and the Japanese had fewer resources than it had had previously.

General Naka first became alarmed by movements of the 22d Chinese Division toward the village of Tonkwa. Although he did not know it, these were simply outposts sent from the division to protect its main positions. The 3d Battalion, 66th Infantry Regiment, had located itself in the area around Tonkwa as a part of these security precautions. General Naka, viewing this as a preliminary to an attack, decided to use aggressive defensive tactics and pushed his 55th and 56th Regiments, supported by artillery, forward to Tonkwa on 6 December.

That same day, the 2d and 3d Battalions of the 475th Infantry Regiment received orders to relieve the Chinese around Tonkwa. This came as a result of General Wedemeyer's plans to strengthen the central Chinese government by returning combat-experienced troops to the main Chinese army in China. As a result, he had ordered that the 22d Chinese Division be returned by means of airlift to China. The 475th Infantry Regiment would replace them in the positions they held, one of which was at Tonkwa.

General Naka's task force struck Tonkwa on 8 December and quickly forced the outnumbered Chinese battalion out of its positions and back toward the north. The Chinese dug in again at the village of Mo-hlaing. There the Chinese and Japanese prepared to duel once again, when on 9 December the Chinese were joined by the intelligence and reconnaissance platoon of the 2d Battalion, 475th Infantry. After a lull of four months Americans and Japanese were once again fighting for Burma.

9. Tonkwa

The 124th Cavalry Regiment (Special) was still back at Camp Landis. They had arrived after the 475th Infantry, and as such were forced to use U.S. Army pyramidal tents rather than the more comfortable British army tents being used by the infantrymen. Twelve miles from the Myitkyina airstrip, they found themselves often neglected in the distribution of supplies. The mechanics among them soon put their skills to work in creating mule litters for hauling supplies, modifying metal pack frames for use on the mules, and repairing two wrecked Japanese army trucks for use by the cavalry. These two trucks—made up of Ford, Chevrolet, and Dodge truck parts—also bore tires from India, Ceylon, Yokohama, Tokyo, Canada, Australia, and the United States. Combined with other vehicles borrowed or stolen, the 124th Cavalry soon had its own motor pool.

Other changes soon occurred in the 124th Cavalry. On 2 November Col. Thomas J. Heavey, a regular army cavalry officer, relieved Colonel Matteson, who had been given an assignment in China. The attached 612th Field Artillery Battalion (Pack) also experienced three of the six command changes it would undergo during the campaign, when Colonel Wallis assumed command from Lt. Col. Richard A. Knight, who had in turn relieved Maj. John W. Read earlier.

Another problem was the need to bring the units up to full strength. Many men had fallen out along the way due to illness, injury, or reassignment. There were no infantry replacement centers anywhere in the theater for American army units. Indeed, there were only two American army infantry units in the entire theater. Men were combed from the numerous Service of Supply units in the area. Many joined from port battalions out of boredom. Others, including military police, volunteered simply for some excitement. Some even agreed to demotions in rank so that they could join a combat unit. Here the reputation of Galahad almost certainly had an effect by encouraging men who still believed in the excitement of war.

Training remained the primary function of the 124th at Camp Landis. Trained to move on horseback and to hit and run, the cavalrymen had to learn from the start how an infantryman operates, particularly in long-range penetration operations in enemy controlled jungles. Training was as realistic as possible, and the inevitable casualties resulted. Injuries due to the use of live ammunition, along with physical breakdowns and mental conditioning, caused so many casualties that it soon became a joke in the regiment that the Japanese hoped the cavalrymen would continue training until they wiped themselves out.

There were brief episodes of relaxation. Twice a week movies were shown at the Camp Landis theater. Hunting was allowed when time permitted. In fact, the loss of two of the brigade's K-9 war dogs to a leopard[1] caused an official hunt that succeeded in eliminating the threat to part of the unit's roster. Swims in the frigid river alongside the camp were another pastime. A USO troupe featuring celebrities Jinx Faulkenberg, Pat O'Brien, and Ann Sheridan was welcomed.

But training continued to be the main occupation. British officers appeared to impart years of knowledge of Burma, with its perils and beauties. The Americans were taught how to live off the land and how to curry favor with the native population. They continued practicing hard marches with full field equipment. The need for strict malaria and typhus discipline was drilled into the cavalrymen so that few, if any, would be caught without boots or leggings for protection against typhus mites, and the men wore shirts or jackets regularly after dark, when the malaria-carrying mosquitos were about. On two occasions the bivouac area was sprayed with DDT. Foxholes were dug near each tent for protection against the occasional evening air raid by enemy planes.

Each of the two commands, the 124th Cavalry and the 475th Infantry, soon felt that the other had a different attitude. The 124th found the infantrymen proud, cocky, and arrogant. The 475th Infantry, however, found the cavalrymen too garrison bound and laughed at the way they still saluted their officers. The cavalry also came to resent the fact that due to an order issued at the Marauders' demise, every man in that regiment was advanced one grade. Thus a squad leader in the 475th might be a staff sergeant instead of a sergeant, while the cavalry regiment suffered because those promotions came under the rule that the brigade had to absorb the new promotions without any increase in the number of grades assigned. The cavalrymen felt that they were denied advancement because of the favored treatment the infantrymen received. As a result, in the cavalry, where a corporal was usually a squad leader, the men often found themselves limited to privates first class as squad leaders, simply because all higher ranks had been allocated to the infantry.[2]

Like its companion regiment in the brigade, the 124th Cavalry was never able to get up to full strength during the campaign. Its authorized allowance of 2,173 was never achieved, and replacements continued to arrive throughout its time in Burma. While completing its own training, the cavalrymen watched the 475th Infantry march out. Shortly afterward the 1st Chinese Separate Regiment also marched for the front lines, and the cavalrymen noted how the Chinese took along with them equipment such as trucks, jeeps, staff cars, and supplies that they themselves would not be able to carry on the backs of their mules when their turn came. For a brief while, the cavalrymen doubted they would ever be called to the front.[3]

Their concerns were relieved on 15 December, when orders came to the regiment to move forward. They were to start marching south the following morning. On 16 December 1944, just as the American forces in Europe were about to experience the German counterattack that became known as the Battle of the Bulge, the 124th Cavalry marched forward to battle, led by Col. Earl F. Ripstra's 1st Squadron.[4] The Chicago native's squadron was followed by the 613th Field Artillery Battalion (Pack) the next day. The following two days saw Maj. George B. Jordan and Lt. Col. Charles B. Hazeltine Jr. lead out the 2d and 3d Squadrons, respectively. Taking only essential equipment, the cavalrymen left behind barracks bags, many of which contained spurs and spit-shined cavalry boots.

Although the garrison-trained regiment was uniform in nearly all respects, one area stood out. It marched forward into combat in a variety of footwear. Some troopers wore cavalry boots with an inch or two cut off the top. Others wore GI shoes to which tops had been sewn on as makeshift leggings. Some had even managed to acquire paratroopers' boots on the black market, and they wore these into the jungles. The first steps from garrison troops to a combat outfit were evidenced in these varieties.

While the cavalry had been completing its training and preparing to move forward, the infantrymen of the 475th had already moved into combat. Following the orders to relieve the elements of the Chinese 22d Division around Tonkwa, the 2d and 3d Battalions arrived at Mo-hlaing on 9 December. There they found the Chinese locked in battle with the 18th Japanese Division. The Japanese, unaware of the newly arrived Americans, attacked off the march, expecting to once again drive the Chinese back. Instead they succeeded only in breaking the perimeter before being pushed roughly back by an American counterattack.

As the Japanese attacked, the two American battalions were marching toward Mo-hlaing along the Si-u Road, about three miles to the northeast. The regiment's 1st Battalion had been ordered to secure the area around Shwegu and therefore was not with the regiment. The 2d Battalion's intelligence and reconnaissance platoon, under Lt. Martin R. Smith, had already joined the Chinese and reported the situation back to Colonel Thrailkill. They had been attacked by three platoons of Japanese and had engaged in hand-to-hand combat in which Pvt. Walter C. Mink was killed and four others were wounded. Colonel Thrailkill ordered them to fall back on Company E, which was then leading the battalion's march. While Company E and the reconnaissance platoon held the road, the balance of the 2d Battalion began swinging around to the southwest, toward Tonkwa. This left the 3d Battalion facing Mo-hlaing while the 2d Battalion faced Tonkwa. The Americans now faced the Japanese at both locations.

As the Americans settled into positions the commander of the Chinese 66th Regiment asked that his unit be relieved, according to the plan for the Americans to replace his unit, which was about to leave for China. The 475th agreed and took over the Chinese positions. The Americans had arrived under orders to relieve the Chinese and hold their positions, not to advance. Therefore the 2d and 3d Battalions prepared defensive positions.

For the next two days, 11 and 12 December, the Japanese sent out patrols to feel out the American positions. Enemy artillery and mortar fire harassed the Americans as they waited to see what the Japanese would do about the situation. American patrols were also active, identifying several Japanese assembly areas, which were promptly shelled by Allied artillery. By the evening of 12 December the Chinese had left the area, and the Americans prepared for a Japanese attack.

Patrolling was the main activity before the attack. The regimental intelligence and reconnaissance platoon was ordered forward to the village of Cha-in, bypassing both Mo-hlaing and Tonkwa. There they found abundant signs of enemy occupation. Setting up a trailblock, the bulk of the platoon moved another eight miles into enemy territory to Hkawan. Still having no direct contact with the enemy, the platoon re-formed and returned to Mo-hlaing, arriving just in time for the first enemy artillery of the day.

The American positions were ideal for defense. They looked out upon open rice paddies bordered by jungle, which hid the enemy. At 0600 hours on the morning of the thirteenth the enemy attacked after a ten-minute artillery preparatory fire. This fire was ineffective, because much of it was fired over the heads of the entrenched Americans.[5] Attacking first one flank and then the other, the Japanese received the full fury of an American regiment's firepower. Both Companies E and F came under direct attack. Sergeant Wilbert A. Netzel's squad was particularly hard hit, losing four men wounded.

Within an hour the attack ceased. One enemy platoon tried to rush one flank but had gone no more than thirty or forty yards when they were cut down. Colonel Thrailkill and Maj. John H. Lattin, his executive officer, came up to Company F to view the situation. Noticing an enemy officer trying to escape from a trapped position in front of the company, the colonel began crawling forward, hoping for a shot at the enemy. Suddenly the Japanese officer threw a grenade, which bounced off the colonel's backside and landed nearby. The resulting explosion wounded Colonel Thrailkill in the back and neck. It also slightly wounded Major Lattin and Capt. Robert P. Maxon, the Company F commander. Major Lattin then shot the enemy officer, and immediately another enemy soldier jumped and ran from a nearby position. That soldier was killed by an alert Company F rifleman. Colonel Thrailkill was treated but not evacuated, and Major Lattin assumed temporary command. There were no further attacks that day.

The following day was a repeat of the attack that had occurred on 13 December, except that several more Americans became casualties and enemy artillery was much more accurate. One observer noted that the effect of combat on the new men was the increased depth of the foxholes they dug after the first action. Rather than repeat the attack, the Japanese resorted to increased patrolling. Ordered to defend the area, General Naka did not feel able to waste his resources on an entrenched enemy as long as that enemy was not moving forward into his protected area. The Americans requested an airdrop of 4.2-inch mortars, which would have helped with the close-in fighting. These were dropped as requested, but essential parts were missing, and so they were never used.

The intelligence and reconnaissance platoon was once again behind General Naka's lines. They had been ordered to investigate two trails that were believed to be enemy supply and evacuation routes. Opposed only by a sniper, they returned empty-handed but were immediately sent out again toward the village of Dandin Sakan, straight south from Tonkwa. Within two hours of leaving they encountered an enemy outpost position. The platoon leader, Lt. Alton M. Shipstead, fired off what he thought were three rounds at the enemy. Later investigation showed that in his excitement he had hit one enemy soldier six times, not three. The equipment of three additional enemy soldiers was found in the area, evidence that they had fled. Moving forward to the vicinity of Dandin Sakan, the patrol observed enemy vehicles along the main trail, indicating that this was an enemy supply base. The patrol reported back safely to the regiment.

Another patrol, this one from Company F, was not as fortunate and ran into an enemy trailblock, which killed Lieutenant Bachman and the two scouts leading the patrol. The patrol withdrew, and American artillery and mortars concentrated on the area of the trailblock. Later, six enemy dead, including two officers, were found in that area.

These constant patrols continued to bring on a series of sudden clashes between opposing forces, particularly in the vicinity of Company E, which had an enemy enclave near its positions. Ambushes once again played a major role. Lieutenant Lewis B. Mitchell took his patrol to establish a trailblock six miles north of Tonkwa and ambushed an enemy patrol of about twenty men. Enemy casualties were eight killed, including two officers, against American losses of two killed and six wounded.

Most of this activity hit the 2d Battalion, because the location of the 3d Battalion made it subject only to enemy artillery fire. This brought up the idea that the 3d Battalion could take the enemy that faced the 2d Battalion in the rear and remove the pressure on its sister battalion. Captain James K. Blocker's Company I drew that assignment. Reinforced with Lt. Alexander McFadden's platoon of Company K and Lt. Phillip Welsh's platoon of Company L, the combined force came down from Mo-hlaing to form an arc around an enemy force occupying a wood adjacent to Company E's position near Tonkwa. A bitter four-hour fight ensued, in which nineteen Japanese and three Americans were killed.

One of the wounded was Lt. Norman R. Berkness, of the 3d Battalion Headquarters Company. He was directing mortar fire when he was wounded in the ear by a sniper. Moments later another rifle shot gashed his leg several inches. Refusing medical treatment, he continued his duties. About an hour later, when his group was pinned down by an enemy machine gun, he made a one-man charge on the gun, only to be cut down with severe leg wounds. He later was rescued and awarded a Silver Star.

For the next week the Americans and Japanese skirmished in the area. Company F sent in a platoon to occupy the cleared woods. Patrol clashes continued in the area, and both sides gave and received casualties. On 18 December the 2d Battalion's intelligence and reconnaissance platoon, reinforced with an infantry platoon, tried to circle behind enemy lines to destroy a known artillery position. The ambushers became the ambushed and found themselves surrounded with evening approaching. Calling for assistance, they were told to escape by way of an azimuth to American positions. The platoon buried its radio, and two of its soldiers—Pfc. George Mozak and Pfc. Chester Gordon—blasted a way out by using a Browning automatic rifle. Colonel Easterbrook and Major Lattin went forward of friendly lines to fire tracer bullets that would guide the lost platoon to safety. Fortunately, only the platoon's pack mule and radio were casualties in this episode.

After one last spoiling attack on 18 December, the Japanese withdrew. The 3d Battalion began a pursuit but was halted on orders of the brigade at the village of Langu Sakan, about eight miles west of Tonkwa. Two strong combat patrols were sent to hurry the enemy along in their retreat. Returning on 28 December, they reported the enemy gone but the trail blocked in several places by fallen trees. The battalion's pioneer and demolition platoon went forward and cleared more than three thousand yards of trail.

On 20 December the regiment secured its first prisoner when a straggler was captured within the perimeter. Documents taken from enemy dead identified the 3d, 4th, 5th, and 6th Companies of the 56th Japanese Infantry Regiment, 18th Infantry Division, as well as elements of the 119th Infantry Regiment, along with at least seven pieces of artillery. One hundred seventy-one enemy dead were counted.

While the 2d and 3d Battalions had been fighting at Tonkwa, the 1st Battalion was having a battle of its own at Shwegu. Arriving on 5 December with orders to patrol one hundred fifty miles of territory until relieved by the British 36th Infantry Division, which would come down from the north, the 1st Battalion immediately set about securing its assigned area. On the tenth a patrol of Company A, commanded by SSgt. Wade Phillips, encountered a group of Japanese in possession of a local village. The patrol discovered that the enemy were preparing their midday meal. On the way back to the patrol base they met the rest of the platoon, under Lt. Paul E. Bouchard, who had been alerted to the enemy presence by local residents. The united platoon deployed around the village. Then one group fired into the enemy, driving them into another group, which also opened fire. By the time this action was over, thirty enemy were counted dead, and equipment for others was found abandoned. One Marsman sergeant was slightly wounded by knee mortar fire.[6]

Company B had reached the vicinity of Shwegu without its commander, Capt. David B. Lovejoy, who had left on 20 November to serve on a court-martial board. On 6 December, 1st Lt. William E. Holmes, the executive officer in temporary command, sent 1st Lt. Frank J. O'Brien's 2d Platoon out to place blocks on trails to the east of Shwegu. The company command post was set up in an old temple, and the weapons platoon, or 4th Platoon, also set up at that location. Using positions previously dug by the Chinese, the company prepared to patrol and secure its area. The 3d Platoon, under 1st Lt. Albert Davaust, went out and also established a patrol base to cover the Irrawaddy River up to the town of Katha, while 2d Lt. Othello V. Burr's 1st Platoon, reinforced with Kachin Rangers, patrolled along the river in the opposite direction. These bases were so far apart that contact often had to be maintained by radio relays from one patrol base to another and back to company headquarters. Company A's skirmish with the enemy caused Captain Lovejoy, who had by now returned to the company, to reinforce the 1st Platoon with the 2d Platoon. He sent Lieutenant Burr north to search out the area and to try to make contact with the 36th British Infantry Division. Again a radio relay had to be established simply to keep in contact with Lieutenant Burr's patrol. After several days, on 15 December, a 1st Platoon patrol made the first contact with the British.[7] Several days later, physical contact was established with the British, and the 1st Battalion prepared to rejoin its regiment.

The duties of the 475th Infantry were now simply to hold the area they had just secured to cover the withdrawal of the Chinese 22d Infantry Division, which was already being airlifted back to China. By Christmas 1944 there were few signs of the Japanese in the area. In the struggles around Tonkwa and Shwegu the regiment had lost 1 officer and 14 enlisted men killed. Another 7 officers and 49 enlisted men had been wounded. Against this cost the Americans claimed 220 enemy dead at the two sites.

The reason for the Japanese decision not to push the attack at Tonkwa was made clear after the war: the Japanese had broken the Chinese army's code and were reading all messages sent to and from frontline units at that time. As a result, they learned that the 22d Chinese Infantry Division was being withdrawn to China and that no Allied offensives were being planned in that area. That information fit in well with their new plan to defend against the main Allied thrust by General Slim's XIV Army toward Mandalay. Knowing that the Americans near Tonkwa were not under orders to attack, they pulled out their resources there for use elsewhere.

For the Americans the reasons behind the enemy's failure to continue attacking were unimportant. The Americans could now enjoy as good a Christmas as possible under Burmese jungle conditions. A recent airstrip built at Nansin, about twelve miles northeast of Tonkwa, allowed mail to be brought into the infantrymen's hands. Christmas packages arrived in considerable numbers. Replacements were also flown in and assigned to the command. Thirty-four officers and 217 enlisted men joined the regiment as replacements for the combat casualties and for the 329 men who had fallen from wounds, disease, or march fatigue.[8] Ironically, the greatest loss was in the 1st Battalion, as a result of the long arduous marches it had made while securing the area around Shwegu. For the week between Christmas and New Year's Day the regiment rested and relaxed. On 1 January they were again on the march.

10. The Burma Road

While Mars Task Force was fighting at Tonkwa and Shwegu, the battle of Bhamo continued. The Chinese 113th Infantry Regiment, heavily supported by the 10th U.S. Air Force, attacked and drove in the Japanese outposts, but the commander refused to follow the advice of his American advisers to coordinate his efforts against the main defenses.

Part of the problem was that this enemy position was one of the most formidable yet encountered in the Burma campaign. It had first been constructed in spring 1944 and had been continuously improved since that time. The area was divided into three self-contained fortress areas, each on high ground and well equipped with automatic weapons and supplies. Protected by sharpened bamboo stakes, barbed wire, and antitank ditches, the Japanese garrison in deep dugouts defeated every attempt to overcome the defense. The garrison, commanded by Col. Kozo Hara, had orders to hold the position until mid-January 1945. Although numbering twelve hundred men, fewer than at Myitkyina, they had much stronger and better-equipped defenses.

General Li, commanding the 38th Chinese Division, ordered his 114th Regiment to attack from the north. This unit made better progress, and so General Li allowed the 113th to keep the attention of the Japanese while supporting the 114th Regiment's attack in the north. The 3d Battalion of the 112th Regiment was added to the 113th's assets, which allowed another attack by the 113th—an attack that was better coordinated and supported than previous attacks. Throughout November the Chinese battered at the fortress of Bhamo.

Once again it was the 114th Chinese Regiment that made the most progress. Having used artillery to strip away enemy camouflage, the Chinese attacked each bunker one at a time. This costly but successful practice continued into December. Their progress alarmed the Japanese, and a task force was dispatched by the 33d Japanese Army to relieve the embattled garrison at Bhamo. That group, three thousand men under Colonel Yamazaki, advanced on Bhamo but ran into a reinforcing Chinese element, the 90th Infantry Regiment of the 30th Chinese Infantry Division. There a separate and equally bloody battle ensued between the two relieving forces. The Japanese attacked fiercely and broke through at one point, capturing a Chinese artillery battery. The 88th Chinese Infantry Regiment of the same division counterattacked with a ferocity unknown to the Japanese and restored the situation. In one instance a lone Chinese soldier continued to attack after all his comrades had been shot down. He nearly reached the Colonel commanding the Japanese force before he was killed. This type of aggressiveness by Chinese troops was disquieting to the Japanese, who were used to easy successes against untrained and unmotivated Chinese troops.

The continuing attack by the 38th Chinese Division on Bhamo and the aggressive blocking of the Japanese relief force by the 30th Chinese Division caused the Japanese to withdraw earlier than planned. On the night of 14 December the Japanese garrison of Bhamo successfully withdrew by charging through the Chinese defense lines. Once clear, they broadcasted a coded message to the Yamazaki detachment, which likewise withdrew from the front of the 30th Chinese Division. Bhamo had fallen.

With the fall of Bhamo there were only fifty air miles between the Chinese army in Burma and the closest Chinese main army elements in China, located in Yunnan. These fifty miles marked the last Japanese block across the Burma Road to China. To close that gap the Chinese army in Burma had a march of twenty miles across relatively flat terrain. Then it faced the western edge of the escarpment in which the Shweli and Salween Rivers cut their valleys. Across that plateau lay Yunnan.

The Chinese set out on the Myitkyina-Bhamo Road. It was an excellent road for the area. All it needed was to be paved and widened, and it would be ready for heavy traffic as the easternmost section of the Ledo Road. Crossing a series of ridges, it entered the Shweli Valley. Then it turned northeast for about thirty miles and linked with the old Burma Road at Mong Yu. East of the Shweli Valley, over fifteen miles of five-thousand-foot-high foothills, lay the Burma Road.

The Chinese now had to clear the Japanese 33d Army off this remaining fifty-mile stretch of Burma in order to open the new Ledo/Burma Road. Once that was accomplished, the two Chinese armies could link up and protect the road as vital war supplies were transported across it into China. The Japanese were under orders to defend the area, but the main concern still lay to the south, with the British drive on Mandalay. The Japanese purpose in covering the Burma Road was to hold any attack from the north toward Mandalay. Much of its assets faced the large Chinese force known to be in Yunnan. The 56th Japanese Infantry Division faced these Chinese and defended the fortified locality of Wanting–Mong Yu. The 168th Infantry Regiment of the 49th Japanese Infantry Division, under Colonel Yoshida, was ten miles behind, protecting the Burma Road. Protecting the left and rear was the Yamazaki Detachment, three thousand men who had just been defeated at Bhamo. Finally, the 4th Infantry Regiment of the 2d Japanese Infantry Division, under Colonel Ichikari, was located at Namhpakka, on the Burma Road where it intersects the road leading to Namhkam.

The withdrawal of the 18th Japanese Infantry Division and the sudden quiet in the area around Bhamo had convinced Lt. Col. Joseph W. Stilwell Jr., still the NCAC intelligence chief, that the Japanese had withdrawn leaving only modest rear guards to protect the rear. He estimated twenty-five hundred enemy troops around Namhpakka and another twenty-five hundred in the Shweli Valley itself. Armed with this information and faced with the loss of the 22d Chinese Division, General Sultan changed his plans. Originally he had intended to send the 22d Chinese Division around to the south to seize and cut the Burma Road in the Namhpakka area. This was expected to cut off the entire 33d Japanese Army from the rest of the Burma area army. By forcing the 33d Army to withdraw, he would clear that entire area. That in turn would clear the Ledo Road to link with the Burma Road.

General Sultan's revised plans called for the British 36th Infantry Division, under Maj. Gen. F. W. Festing, to move east of the Irrawaddy and then southeast by way of Mongmit to cut the old Burma Road in the Kyaukme-Hsipaw area, far south of Lashio. The 5332d Brigade—Mars Task Force, under Brig. Gen. John P. Willey— would make the difficult march across the hill country to the Mong Wi area and then cut the Burma Road near Ho-si. This was the original mission planned for the full 22d Chinese Division. The 50th Chinese Division, which had been following the British 36th Infantry Division down from the north, would swing east and move directly on Lashio. They would pass into the area currently occupied by the 5332d Brigade. A fourth force, the Chinese new 1st Army, would participate by clearing the upper Shweli Valley and opening the road to China.[1]

First to move off was the 30th Chinese Division, led by its 90th Infantry Regiment. Although no Japanese were found, the regiment, which led the advance, continually delayed. The regimental commander on several occasions abandoned his supplies and then demanded more by means of an airdrop. This conduct finally aroused the ire of Gen. Sun Li-jen, the army commander, and a new commander was appointed. The 90th now moved quickly and soon reached the hill dominating the entrance to the Shweli Valley. Expecting to fight their way into the valley, they were pleasantly surprised to find that the Japanese had withdrawn. The 33d Japanese Army, having conceded the Shweli Valley to the Allies, withdrew slowly to join the main Japanese forces to the south. They now used the Burma Road as their route of withdrawal, and as long as the Allies kept a distance, no serious combat developed.

The Japanese rear guards delayed but did not stop the Chinese advance, and on 20 January the first physical contact was made between the Chinese 30th Division and Chinese troops from Yunnan. Although the road was still not open, it could not be delayed for long. The Japanese had a reason to keep the road open: it was the only route of withdrawal for the 33d Army and for the 56th Japanese Infantry Division, which was opposing Chinese forces as it withdrew slowly along the road. While the Japanese were trying to decide how much longer they could delay the Chinese advance to open the road, they learned of American troops clashing with outposts that were protecting the road behind them.

The 124th Cavalry had received orders to assemble in the vicinity of Momauk. The regiment marched out and arrived there to find that their administrative section had arrived ahead of them by truck rather than on foot. They heard stories of the Bhamo fighting from those who had managed a visit to the battlefield site. The squadrons, however, were ordered to bypass the scene due to the presence of booby traps and mines in the area. Indeed, over the next three months engineers would continue to find all types of explosive devices in the area. At Momauk the regiment dropped the last of its nonessentials, including photographic and horseshoeing equipment. From that point forward they were to be in the combat zone.

Despite the equipment left at Momauk, the 1st Squadron commander, Lt. Col. Earl F. Ripstra, wanted to carry as much as possible and as far forward as possible on one remaining jeep. In order to learn if the trail ahead could accommodate the jeep, he sent Lt. Richard E. Wingreen, a Wisconsin native and former military policeman, ahead of the regiment with his platoon. Lieutenant Wingreen and his platoon sergeant, SSgt. Robert D. Smith, of Louisiana, led the patrol for two and a half miles, during which the group rose two thousand feet above sea level. There they arrived at the village of Jusai. The natives reported that two days earlier a squad of Japanese had passed through, taking food, clothing, and two hostages before moving out. The natives refused to lead the patrol from the village, fearful that the Japanese were still in the area.

The patrol went forward and soon found a dead native along the trail. After a scare by noisy monkeys, the patrol returned to report that the jeep would never get past the first mile of the trail. The regiment took one last airdrop, which provided standard rations for three days for each man. This three-day pack included three K rations, one 10- or 12-ounce can of fruit juice or fruit, three D-ration bars, fifteen salt tablets, fifteen halazone tablets, four multivitamin tablets, three packs of cigarettes, two boxes of matches, six silver packets of coffee or a can of soluble coffee, one tea ball, one ounce of sugar, one can of peanuts, one 4-ounce can of evaporated milk, and one pint of dehydrated soup. It was during this airdrop that Lieutenant Colonel Donovan almost became a casualty, when a parachute failure caused a free-falling case of rations to skin his knee and wreck his Thompson submachine gun.

During the training and early phases of acclimation a shoulder-sleeve insignia remarkably similar to the now famous "Merrill's Marauder" shoulder insignia had been developed and was worn by many of the men. Just as Mars Task Force was marching into battle a written order came from Col. Willis J. Tack, chief of staff to General Willey, that "the shoulder sleeve insignia for Mars Brigade has been disapproved by the War Department. CBI insignia will be worn by all personnel of the Theater. Immediate action will be taken to discontinue wearing of Mars Patch." This order, dated 19 December 1944, may or may not have been effective. The shoulder sleeve insignia was eventually adopted for the brigade.[2]

Despite the report of Lieutenant Wingreen's patrol, most of the cart drivers insisted that they could go anywhere the cavalry could march. As they started up the mountain trail, they fell out one by one, and by the time the cavalry reached the top not one cart remained with the column. As one member remembered, "Our introduction to the steep mountains with their narrow trails was abrupt. The first day's climb was rugged. The trail was winding, narrow and rough. Fallen logs that had not interfered with native traffic lay across it. Streams had to be forded."[3] The loss of the carts left more equipment behind until the regiment was finally stripped down to bare essentials for combat and survival. Although the cavalrymen had had several long practice marches, this actual march into combat was even more severe. "By the time the last serial had learned its own lesson in its own hard way, there was almost a solid trail of cast-offs on our route up that first mountain: carts and harness, field cooking outfits and ammunition, stationery, underwear, books and fatigues, toilet articles, mess gear, socks and jungle boots."[4]

The marches of the cavalry were typical of the marches that had worn down the Marauders and the 475th Infantry. The usual training pace of a fifty-minute march followed by ten minutes of rest were quickly abandoned, as the length of the column in the dense growth delayed both marching and resting. To make progress, the men often continued their marches into the evening. Each man had to hold on to the man or mule in front of him and literally feel his way along a narrow trail with steep drop-offs to the side. Exhaustion and injuries quickly mounted. Marches became regulated by the next water supply or airdrop. The mules often carried full loads twelve or fourteen hours each day with little or no food and water. Another unusual factor was that the task force was leaving Kachin country and was entering Shan and Palaung areas, known to be friendly to the Japanese. The normally helpful native populations that had so aided the Marauders were no longer available for Mars Task Force. About the only pleasant moment was enjoyed by the men of the 613th Field Artillery (Pack), when the air liaison officer, Lt. John Sittner, dropped their mail to them along the march.

The march took its toll at all levels. Colonel Thomas J. Heavey, who was forty-nine years old, had insisted on marching with his regiment every step of the way. By the time the unit reached the Shweli River he was ready to be evacuated as an exhaustion case. Colonel Ripstra, age forty-two, also marched with his squadron and was admired by the troops for his ability not only to march but to stay at the head of the column. Lieutenant Colonel Loren D. Pegg, the regiment's executive officer and a New Jersey native, assumed temporary command until a new commander could arrive. That new commander would be the recently promoted Col. William Lloyd Osborne, the former commander of the 1st Marauder Battalion and briefly the commander of the 475th Infantry before he fell ill.

The cavalry now arrived at the Shweli River Valley, where they were to join with the 475th Infantry for the march behind enemy lines. As they approached, the rain began—not the monsoon, but a heavy enough rain to cause problems. Indeed, the regiment remembers the episode as the Shweli Slide, because a well-worn path down the mountain to the river had turned into a mudslide. Colonel Heavey, still with the regiment at this point, had spent 4 January trying to find a better route to the river. Ordered by the NCAC to cross where he was, he simply slid down much of the mountain on his posterior and then reported to the evacuation point. Lieutenant Ralph Lee Cornwall reported watching a fully loaded mule start down, slip, turn completely over, catch a footing, and then proceed down the hill without disturbing its load. Several men tried to stop sliding in order to rest for a few moments, but few were able to do so. Once they started down, there was no stopping until they reached the bottom of the slide, right at the bank of the Shweli River.

While the cavalrymen struggled to join with the 475th Infantry, the planners continued to adjust to meet events unfolding. Once again they decided that the sole American contingent, this time Mars Task Force, would be used to force the Chinese to advance more rapidly in order to save face. As a result, Mars Task Force was to cut the Burma Road below Lashio, forcing the Chinese to seize that town in order to resolve the embarrassment caused by the American advance ahead of them. Colonel Easterbrook had suggested that the cut in the road be made at a suspension bridge about twelve miles south of Namhpakka. A good trail led to that spot, nearby hills were in range of machine guns, and the Japanese could not easily build a bypass in the area.

General Willey reviewed and approved the plan, but General Sultan had other ideas. He was concerned that the Chinese would not support an attack that deep into enemy lines, regardless of saving face. He also noted that there was no good area nearby for an airstrip, essential for the evacuation of casualties and for resupply. Instead, he directed Mars Task Force on the Ho-si area, farther north and closer to the Chinese main forces. This area had flatter ground, but the nearest hills were not close enough for direct fire upon the road, which was necessary to interdict enemy traffic. Another disadvantage was the availability of secondary trails for the Japanese to construct a bypass if Mars Task Force successfully closed the Burma Road. Nevertheless, the concerns outweighed the disadvantages, and Mars Task Force was directed on the Ho-si area. Later this series of decisions would raise a controversy about the effectiveness of the roadblock.

Apparently the discussion as to exactly where Mars Task Force was to establish its roadblock was not easily made. When General Willey later discussed the matter with the theater historian, Capt.

Edward Fischer, he surprised the captain by frankly disclosing the disagreement. Captain Fischer later recorded, "I was startled by his honesty when he told me that the Theater Commander had ordered him to cut the Burma Road, but that he had refused to do so." Captain Fischer, who describes General Willey as a handsome, forty-two-year-old cavalryman, remembered him as "the movie version of a fighting general" and "soft-spoken, kind and unbelievably honest."[5] He noted that General Willey told him, "I wanted to cut it here [Namhpakka]. Had I been given permission, I would have done it, because I could approach the road without exposing my men too much. But General Sultan said to cut it here [Ho-si] and I didn't do it because I would have lost too many men crossing the wide-open approaches to the road."[6]

The first step on the mission was to consolidate the two individual units of the task force into one complete group. With the 124th Cavalry moving forward to Bhamo on 16 December just as the 475th was engaged at Tonkwa, brigade headquarters moved to Momauk. At about that time an order was issued consigning the 1st Chinese Separate Regiment to the NCAC reserve, thus effectively reducing Mars Task Force to the 124th Cavalry and 475th Infantry with supporting units. While the 124th Cavalry struggled forward and endured the Shweli Slide, the 475th Infantry had an easier march from nearby Tonkwa, now turned over to the Chinese. The infantry regiment had moved out on New Year's day toward the Shweli River. A screen of Kachin Rangers preceded the marching column, and it was known that Chinese troops had also preceded them along that route, so danger from the enemy was relatively slight. Nevertheless, casualties resulted from the inevitable marching conditions of steep and narrow trails, disease, and exhaustion.

First to cross the Shweli River was the 475th Infantry. It found the four-hundred-foot-wide river relatively easy to cross because of a bridge built by the Chinese who had gone on ahead. Although it needed some repairs due to damage caused by the swiftly flowing river, the infantry managed a quick and trouble-free crossing. Once across, however, the march entered the usual steep mountains that rose into the clouds, making airdrops impossible. For many days thereafter the column went hungry. Then the same rains that had put the 124th Cavalry through the Shweli Slide hit the 475th Infantry in the mountains. The trails became slippery and hazardous. On 6 January alone the 475th Infantry evacuated twelve men as march casualties.

Back at the Shweli River the cavalrymen now faced another obstacle. The rains had swollen the river to flood stage. The Chinese bridge soon collapsed. The Americans immediately set to repairing and rebuilding the bridge. Bivouacking near the river, they, like the infantry regiment across the river, could not be resupplied by air, because the dense rain clouds obscured the drop zones from the pilots who repeatedly tried to make the drops. Hunting, previously banned, was now encouraged but had limited success. One cavalryman came racing through the bivouac area with a lasso around a bull he had found. Amid laughter from his comrades he raced the bull for his tent and then suddenly threw his end of the rope around a nearby tree, successfully capturing the animal.

Meanwhile a crew worked in shifts on the bridge. Mules had to be taken across one at a time. One of the artillery batteries unloaded its mules to allow them to cross unhindered by the weight of the equipment. The men hauled the guns across themselves. Several men were tossed off the bridge as they crossed, but fortunately none were lost. To make matters worse, once across, the column had to cross another, smaller stream with another shaky footbridge before arriving at the regimental bivouac. Some distance from the bivouac was a small evacuation airstrip, suitable only for the small L-1 or L-5 liaison planes, where march casualties from the 124th Cavalry joined those from the 475th Infantry in awaiting evacuation. Here, too, Colonel Heavey finally left his regiment. Colonel Osborne, then marching with the 475th Infantry as an "observer," would await the joining of the two regiments before taking command of the cavalry regiment. Colonel Pegg continued in temporary command. The casualties had to wait three days before the skies cleared enough to begin evacuations. The clear skies also brought the long-awaited supply drops and the cavalry's first fatality, when Pvt. Guy I. McNutt was hit and killed by a falling grain sack.[7]

It was not until 10 January that the cavalrymen were ready to march to join the infantrymen up ahead and unite Mars Task Force. The infantry had established two strong patrol bases as protection for the joint bivouac near Mong Wi. The 475th Infantry had received orders to move out on 8 January. They faced terrain as inhospitable as the terrain they had just crossed. The central portion of the Loi Lum Range separated Mong Wi and the Burma Road. It contained mountains from five thousand to seven thousand feet high, with trails so difficult that again some mules could not hold to them and fell over the side. Other stretches were so steep that a man became exhausted after a few minutes and had to rest after only a few steps upward. As the lead regiment, Colonel Easterbrook's infantry would take the lead in marching to and cutting the Burma Road. The 124th Cavalry would secure the Mong Wi area and protect the infantry's rear.

Before the infantry left Mong Wi, Lt. Vern Mahoney, a native of Washington State, took his patrol well up into the mountains to rescue a downed C-47 crew. The march took them fifteen miles deep into the hills, over wet paddy fields under dim moonlight. Soon one of his men began to suffer from fever and chills but continued to march. Natives directed the patrol to an area lit by torches held by other natives. Daylight began to break as they reached the mountaintop, where they found the downed airmen. Two were severely wounded and had to be carried on stretchers. With less than an hour's rest, the patrol started back. One of the seriously wounded airmen died on the return trip, but the rest were successfully returned for treatment and evacuation.

Later a similar patrol of the 124th Cavalry would move forward to recover the casualties of the 475th that they had been forced to leave behind on the trail. One of the party was CWO Joseph Doyer. As a teenager Chief Warrant Officer Doyer had fought with the Canadian army in World War I and then had insisted despite his age that he be allowed to fight with the Marauders. Finally, he argued he was fit to serve with Mars Task Force. As a result of this rescue mission, however, he contracted typhus and died in a rear hospital shortly afterward. After he had survived two of the worst wars in history, the jungle had claimed him.

General Willey reflected on his original dispositions and changed them. He was concerned that one regiment might not be sufficient to close the road. When, on 13 January, both regiments reported themselves ready for operations, he alerted both regiments to proceed to the road. General Willey then tried, without success, to have the 1st Chinese Separate Regiment returned to his command to secure his rear areas. Clearly, General Willey felt that nothing less than a division-sized unit could successfully accomplish the mission assigned to his brigade.[8]

The 124th Cavalry followed the 475th Infantry out of bivouac on 15 January. The infantry regiment had departed on 8 January and had taken the lead toward the objective. However, the cavalry was directed upon Kawngsong, which was to the north and ahead of the points that the infantry regiment had been ordered to seize. That meant that they had to catch up to and pass the infantry.

This time Colonel Hazeltine's 3d Squadron would lead the march. Colonel Ripstra's 1st Squadron would follow a day behind, and Major Jordan's 2d Squadron stayed behind to guard the brigade forward echelon and to be held in reserve.

The march across the same terrible mountains where the 475th was already marching began for the cavalry. Colonel Hazeltine bypassed a chance to call in a supply drop at a razed mountaintop village in favor of finding a more favorable spot farther along the march. No such spot presented itself, and he called for a drop on a steep mountainside. After the first few parachutes had drifted over the sides to hang in trees, the drop was called off. Rather than waste time recovering the lost ammunition and supplies, the squadron abandoned them and marched on. Colonel Ripstra's men received a drop at the bombed village but took nearly two days to assemble the new supplies and return to the march.

A report of possible Japanese ambush positions caused a change of route for the 3d Squadron, and this led them into a valley where they crossed the same stream sixty-two times within two miles of marching. In getting back to the original route the men had to cut a trail through the thickest jungle yet encountered.

During one march along a steep hillside Troop K lost mule number thirty-four. Loaded with 250 pounds of equipment, the mule was on a narrow ledge that suddenly gave way underneath him.

On the slope of a good 60 degrees, there was no hope for a footing as gravity took its natural course, and Number Thirty-

Four rolled, not easily nor gently, but head over heels with in-creasing momentum for 150 feet until he jammed between two trees. The topload jolted loose. The chests burst open. Records and supplies littered the path the mule had battered through the jungle.[9]

Staff Sergeant David H. Moore, SSgt. Amos A. Martin, and T5 Woodford D. Poling slid down the path and looked over the situa-tion. Sergeant Moore, who had not lost a mule yet, was dismayed. Clearly, number thirty-four was dead. The three men set about re-moving the straps holding the mule's cargo in place. As he was cut loose, number thirty-four fell the remaining thirty feet to the valley floor. Then, to the amazement of all watching, he calmly rolled over, gained his footing, and began munching on nearby bamboo. Sergeant Moore's record was still secure. As the remaining serials, including the 1st Squadron, passed the spot, another four mules would fall down the same slide. All but one would survive. Later the cavalrymen would learn that the 475th had lost a total of fifteen mules at this spot, of which only eight could be recovered.

Up ahead in the column of the 475th Infantry, Pvt. Harold "Chicken" Stringer, of Company B, was marching along when mes-sages began to be passed around that there was a gap in the column and that the lead serial should stop to let the rear catch up. This happened often in the march.

All night long the tail end of the column would pass the word to slow down "there's a gap in the column." Tension was mounting and fear of the unknown was in our hearts. Finally some smart GI passed the word up "there is a Jap in the col-umn" and the head of the column passed the word back "throw the son-of-a-bitch out." You could feel the laughter in the column, the tension was broken. The unit was ready to do its job that morning and they threw the SOB off the road.[10]

At some point in the march, in darkness and rain, the march of the cavalrymen bumped into the rear serial of the infantry. After some confusion and arguments, the mess was sorted out and each of the regiments went on their respective ways. As the 3d Squadron marched, the command group remained with the second troop in line. Some enemy soldiers, apparently very observant, let the first troop march by and then opened up with automatic weapons at the second troop and the command element. Captain Blair, the squadron operations officer, fell with wounds in his side and stomach. Private First Class William Null was ordered by Captain Blair to take his squad and find the enemy ambush. The group rushed into the jungle, firing as they climbed seven hundred feet to the top of the hill that the ambush position was believed to be on. By the time they arrived the enemy had gone, leaving no trace. The jungle prevented any pursuit, even if the Americans had had an idea about which direction to take. The squad returned to the column, and Captain Blair, his wounds treated, marched along to the objective.

By 19 January the regiment had run out of food, although some men had scarce reserves of D bars or other types. With no indication of when or where they might be resupplied, concern began to grow. The following day they arrived at the four-thousand-foot mountain that overlooked the Ho-si Valley, the brigade's destination. The valley was a flat expanse of paddy fields extending from a quarter of a mile to a full mile across. It was five miles long, and within it meandered the Nam Maw River, about thirty feet wide and not more than knee deep. On the east side of the valley was a steep mountain that rose forty-three hundred feet above the valley floor. This was the cavalry's objective. One smaller hill was already occupied by the 3d Battalion, 475th Infantry. Another forty-five-hundred-foot-high hill was about to be attacked by the 475th's 2d Battalion. Firing in that direction could already be heard.

Colonel Osborne assumed command there as the two command groups joined in the deserted village of Nawhkam, at the 1st Battalion, 475th's, objective. The cavalrymen swiftly secured some rations from the infantrymen and prepared their positions. The artillery was set up and was firing within moments of arrival. At dusk the cavalrymen marched across the valley and established positions atop their objective. As they dug in, they began to receive their first incoming enemy fire. Later they were amused to learn that "Tokyo Rose," the Japanese propaganda radio announcer, had claimed that

American paratroopers had landed behind the lines. Apparently the Japanese refused to believe that the Americans had made the march across country.

The march of the 475th to its nearby objective had been no less hazardous. They too had missed airdrops and had suffered from hunger and trail problems. The 2d Battalion spent the entire day of 11 January without food and having to watch airdrops to other battalions along the line of march. Not until 13 January did this battalion get a supply drop, and then the first supplies dropped were food for the animals. When the troops finally did receive food late on the thirteenth and the following day, there was a gorging from which several would suffer.

As they marched they could see signs of the enemy everywhere. On 15 January they bivouacked without fires but could see enemy campfires in the distance. The following day they followed a river instead of the trail and had to cross it eighty-eight times in knee-to-waist-deep water. Every man fell at least once. That night they again had a cold camp within three hundred yards of an enemy outpost. On 17 January they caught a Palaung spy and questioned him unsuccessfully. The 2d Battalion learned that the 1st Battalion was already engaged at the objective and hurried forward. The 1st Battalion, which had preceded the 2d, had just seized Nawhkam. Finally, on 18 January, they passed through the 1st Battalion and after crossing a two-mile-wide paddy, almost immediately came under fire. Company G, in the lead, was pinned down.

The area in which the coming battles would be fought was about four miles by four miles. It encompassed the village of Nawhkam, about forty bamboo huts on either side of a ridge-top trail. There both regiments established a headquarters group. One mile east of Nawkham was an alluvial valley about three miles long and half a mile wide. Along the eastern edge of that narrow valley was a string of three hills rising from 250 to 500 feet high. The southernmost and highest hill became known to the Americans as Loi-Kang Ridge, after the Kachin Village that lay on its crest. About one and a half miles to the east of those hills lay the Burma Road. On the road and behind a 4,250-foot hill, lay Namhpakka. The Burma Road was clearly visible from each of the dominant hills in the area.

On the ground, however, visibility was poor. Woods and under-growth covered the area, which made for poor fields of fire and provided easy ambush positions.

The 475th Regiment's first objective had been the high ground, 4,750 feet high, on which the Nawhkam village rested. This ridge dominated the small valley and in American hands would give them the needed observation to control the immediate area. The next step would be to seize Loi-Kang Ridge, across the valley. As a precautionary move, Company I and two companies of Kachin Rangers were sent five miles north to protect the route from the Shweli Valley to Namhpakka, in effect protecting the rear of the American force.

The march to the road had been led by two veterans of the Marauders, Staff Sergeants Ernest Reid and Chester C. Wilson. Leading the regimental intelligence and reconnaissance platoon as they approached Nawhkam, they left the trail and approached the village from the rear, moving cautiously down the one and only street. At the opposite end a Japanese soldier spotted them and opened fire on Sergeant Reid. Unhurt, Sergeant Reid watched as several Japanese scrambled out of the huts and tore off to the south end of the village. The Japanese, estimated at two squads, took up a position at the far end of the village at a slight knoll. The intelligence and reconnaissance platoon rushed forward at the sound of firing and covered the withdrawal of Sergeants Reid and Wilson. Lieutenant Colonel Caifson Johnson ordered Company B to clear the village, which they soon did, at the cost of one American wounded. The battalion continued to be busy, clearing another enemy outpost farther along the ridge at the same time that they were receiving a much needed airdrop of supplies and ammunition. That same afternoon the 612th Field Artillery (Pack) began firing on the Burma Road, about four thousand yards away and under excellent observation. The Japanese 56th Infantry Division's line of communication and supply was cut.

11. The Last Battles

The assault by the 2d Battalion, 475th Infantry, on the Loi-Kang Ridge had been led off by Companies F and G, with Company E supporting the attack from the east. Company G immediately walked into a hail of enemy fire. The battalion's objective was to seize the north end of the hill while the 3d Battalion would follow up and seize the rest of the 3,850-foot-high hill. The 3d Squadron, 124th Cavalry, would then move up to seize the hill, which overlooked Namhpakka.

As Company G moved up the hill it was met by the defenses of the 1st and 2d Battalions, 4th Regiment, 2d Japanese Infantry Division. This was the enemy's backup force to protect the road from exactly what was about to happen as Mars Task Force attacked to cut the road.

A bitter battle ensued for possession of Loi-Kang Ridge. The 2d Battalion managed to fight its way forward while struggling to evacuate casualties down the steep hillside and bring up supplies by the same route. Company F had begun the attack at 0730 hours by moving up the hill in single file to the military crest of the ridge, which was designated as the line of departure. The 2d and 3d Platoons led off the attack, followed by the 1st and 4th Platoons. They moved out at 0800 hours and advanced about fifty yards when they began receiving sniper fire from the high ground to the north. As they paused they were hit by automatic weapons fire and hand grenades, all coming from the same area as the sniper fire. The 3d Platoon faced thick underbrush in its advance, and any movement brought down machine-gun fire from the entrenched enemy. As the 1st Squad attempted to move forward, an enemy grenade killed Pvt. Arlie Bridges. Attempts to locate the exact position of the enemy grenadier were unsuccessful.

Private First Class Russell R. Moore then tried to locate the position. Armed with a Browning automatic rifle and grenades, he identified the enemy position and tried to knock it out. However, he was unable to reach the enemy position, so he went to Lieutenant Josefski and acquired a grenade launcher and antitank grenades. Firing uphill and into soft ground, he found that only one of his grenades exploded. He then returned to the platoon leader and picked up a bazooka team. Guarding the team while they fired three rounds, only one of which exploded, he once again remained in position to cover his platoon. Mortar fire directed by Lieutenant Josefski also had no effect.

On the west side of the trail the 2d Platoon was having the same kind of trouble. Despite several efforts to advance, they were stalled. Technical Sergeant Patrick W. Murphy managed to call in mortars from Company E, and these finally succeeded in silencing the enemy automatic weapons fire. With this fire quieted, the platoon assaulted up the hill "by leaps and bounds moving 25 Yds, then letting out a barrage of fire."[1] A sniper was eliminated by SSgt. Richard B. Archer, the leader of the 3d Squad, using antitank grenades. The attack succeeded in overcoming a strong enemy position armed with automatic weapons and 82mm mortars. The platoon reached the top without casualties and dug defensive positions. The 1st Platoon came up shortly thereafter and relieved them. Sergeant Murphy later received a battlefield commission and continued to lead the platoon as a second lieutenant.

Meanwhile, the 3d Squadron moved behind the 2d Battalion until it reached a spot where it could turn northeast toward its objective. Minor enemy resistance did not seriously delay the advance, but the cavalrymen's attack could not take place that day due to approaching darkness. During the advance one trooper was slightly wounded.

The 612th Field Artillery Battalion (Pack) had also arrived. On 16 January it had started the march to its assembly point at 0600 hours. As Pfc. Randal Colvin later remembered:

Many times [a] path had to be cut to allow mule traffic. C Battery marched long into the night, finally forced to rest in place. Many mules felled [sic] over the side of mountain. Mules and gun loads had to be retri[e]ved under very difficult circumstances. C Btry rested on trail from 0430 until 0615 then continued their march closed at 1710 hours on 17 Jan 45. C Btry set up their four 75mm howitzers and completed firing mission on the enemy, fired 27 rds. The men were exhausted, so very few fox holes were dug that day.[2]

The 1st Battalion had in the meantime seized its objective, Ho-aw Village, at the cost of two men wounded. Twenty-four abandoned enemy packs indicated a hasty retreat by the garrison. The Tenth Air Force joined with the 612th Field Artillery (Pack) Battalion in hitting the numerous targets in the area and bombing the village of Namhpakka. Transports came in for a supply drop, only to learn that the enemy was aware of the procedure and had prepared a welcome. From their end of Loi-Kang Ridge they could clearly observe the American rear areas much like the Americans could observe the Japanese traffic on the road. As a result, Japanese artillery and mortar fire, including at least two 150mm howitzers, shelled the drop zones during and after the supply drop.

In the last hours before daylight TSgt. Alfred T. Marti, of the 3d Battalion, led a patrol to the Burma Road—the first of any Allied troops to reach it in that area. The patrol celebrated by blowing a crater in the road to delay enemy traffic.

During these early successes General Willey again tried for the 1st Chinese Separate Regiment. Again the response was negative. He also asked for heavy Chinese artillery to be added to his force to counter the newly disclosed Japanese 150mm howitzers, which outdistanced the smaller 75mm pack howitzers of the brigade artillery. Once again he received a negative reply from General Sultan's headquarters. General Willey made these requests because of his growing concerns that he had to protect his supply drop areas in order to preserve the security of his force. Normally this was unnecessary for a long-range penetration unit, because a drop zone was always abandoned once it was used. Now, however, holding a stationary position required protecting the critical supply and evacuation doorway. Although General Willey continued to be unsuccessful in obtaining reinforcements, the Japanese managed to have the Yamazaki detachment arrive during the evening of 18 January to reinforce the 4th Infantry Regiment.

The next day, 19 January, the 2d Battalion renewed its attack to clear Loi-Kang Hill. As had happened the day before, the attack bogged down along the approach over which it had to be made. At about 1400 hours, after a day of frustrating setbacks, Colonel Thrailkill decided to charge the enemy positions. This tactic succeeded in clearing the Japanese from one of the strongest positions in the area at a cost to the 2d Battalion of seven killed and seventeen wounded. That day also saw the 612th Field Artillery (Pack) knock out four Japanese tankettes, two on the road and two moving near the positions of the 3d Battalion.

While the infantry was busy seizing critical positions, the cavalrymen were moving up to join them. In mid-morning the 3d Squadron's column came upon a twelve-man enemy patrol, which disappeared into the brush so fast that they could not open fire. At 1500 hours the squadron's intelligence and reconnaissance platoon spotted another patrol, this one consisting of nineteen enemy soldiers, and opened fire. A fire fight ensued in which the cavalrymen called down artillery fire from the 613th Field Artillery Battalion (Pack). After the fighting stopped, the scouts counted twelve enemy dead, the first for the 124th Cavalry. Not a single American had been hurt.

The 3d Squadron's objective was a large hill east of the valley and north of the 3d Battalion's hill. The squadron continued to move to its objective after its first fire fight under enemy artillery and mortar fire. The men reached the position as darkness was approaching and prepared what they believed were the correct defensive positions. At dawn on 20 January they realized that their maps did not match the ground as they actually found it. The defensive line was too long and had to be adjusted to fit reality. Expecting a flat-topped hill, they found instead a series of small hills joined into one.

First Lieutenant Hobart T. Kavel had led two small groups forward during the darkness of 19 and 20 January to try to determine the correct position of his command, Troop I. He and his men were pinned down the entire evening and suffered three casualties from heavy defensive fire. Private First Class Norman E. Meachan led his squad with such distinction during the night that the next day Lieutenant Kavel, himself a veteran Marauder who had won a Silver Star at Myitkyina, made Meachan a staff sergeant.[3] Lieutenant Kavel's action reinforced the fact that the cavalry had not yet secured its objective.

The cavalry's artillery support, Colonel Donovan's 613th Field Artillery (Pack), had by now also set up and made its presence known. Firing as a battalion group in contrast to the 612th's firing by batteries assigned to individual 475th Infantry Battalions, they managed to knock out one of the Japanese 150mm howitzers that had harassed the recent supply drop and had concerned General Willey. The 613th Field Artillery also used to good effect aerial observation provided by L-5 liaison planes. During the early morning hours, two enemy attacks on the 3d Battalion announced the arrival of the Yamazaki detachment.

Dawn on 20 January also saw adjustments in the Americans' dispositions alongside the Burma Road. The headquarters group of the 475th Infantry moved down from the hill at Nawhkam to the hill's base in the valley. This removed them from the immediate presence of the enemy and allowed them to continue to work without having to duck for cover every time an enemy sniper opened fire. It also allowed them to provide immediate protection for Maj. William C. King's 44th Portable Surgical Hospital, located in the same area. Major King had located his unit near a stream, which gave good protection from enemy artillery fire. The 3d Squadron, 124th Cavalry, also began to move against the enemy, which kept them from securing the rest of the hill that was their objective.

At about 0900 hours Troop K attacked and successfully seized their objective, counting twenty-six enemy dead. Troop I had to make two attacks after the first left them too extended to properly defend the area. They left twenty-four enemy dead as they finally joined with the rest of the squadron. Private William J. Green was a medical aid man with the squadron during this action. Already wounded in the leg, he raced forward to aid another wounded cavalryman. The aid man ignored his own wounds to treat others. By the time he finished his aid to others, it was too late for Private Green, who bled to death. Three Americans, including Private Green, had been killed and eight wounded. The starving Americans immediately searched the enemy dead for food, while taking over the enemy positions and arranging them for defense in the opposite direction. Later that afternoon, when food in the form of cold C rations did arrive, the men of the 3d Squadron were so hungry that they ate their food without taking time to heat it. After that meal, they took the time to heat their rations, using captured Japanese mess gear that served them better than their own.

While the 3d Squadron was advancing, the 1st Squadron arrived in their rear. Once the position had been secured, Troop A was called forward to act as reserve for the 3d Squadron, while Troop B joined the 3d Squadron in the defensive line because of its extended length. Troop C and the squadron headquarters troop held the 1st Squadron's positions, a hill about two miles northwest of Namhpakka.

The enemy did not ignore this threat to their vital communications link. Two enemy counterattacks were received by the 3d Squadron in the afternoon. The enemy concentrated on Troop I but inflicted only light casualties on the cavalrymen. The troop's mules, however, suffered much more severely. Held in a shallow gully near the troop's perimeter, they received the bulk of the enemy shelling. Artillery and mortar fire killed twenty-one mules. Shortly after the last enemy attack, a sign appeared, naming the area Dead Mule Gulch. That night enemy troops began a technique that they would continue until the end of the battle, a series of artillery and mortar barrages on the Americans' positions, in which they would move from one sector to another all night long. Both the 612th and 613th Field Artillery Battalions returned the fire in greater volume than it was received.

The following day the cavalry made another effort to clear its area. Just as darkness fell the night before, General Willey had radioed Colonel Osborne that the aircraft that had just made a supply drop had received enemy small-arms fire and that one of the kickers had been killed. General Willey ordered Colonel Osborne to clear the area of enemy who could fire at the supply planes.[4] In order to clear the hill Troop B was ordered to advance and push the remaining enemy off the hill occupied by the 3d Squadron. This they accomplished, and by 1815 hours the cavalrymen were asking for a mail drop on their positions.[5]

Other events were in progress on 21 January as well. The regimental headquarters of the 124th Cavalry was located on Nawhkam Hill. Like the 475th Headquarters the day before, they decided that they were too exposed in that position. During the day they relocated to the vicinity of the 3d Squadron, where they found themselves contesting the bivouac with the 49th Portable Surgical Hospital of Maj. Sidney Posner. Colonel Osborne ordered that the hospital be given priority, and so the cavalry moved to a spoon-shaped hill on the west side of the valley, opposite the 3d Squadron's hill. This was an open area of rice paddies directly in front of the hill that held the positions of the 613th Field Artillery Battalion. Unfortunately, while the headquarters troop could clearly see both the friendly and enemy positions, the Japanese had a good view of their positions as well.

The events of 19, 20, and 21 January had placed five American infantry battalions, supported by two artillery battalions, directly on the hills above the enemy's main line of supply, communications, and evacuation. Patrols from the 475th Infantry's 3d Battalion made several contacts on or along the road, placing mines and booby traps there. One patrol came upon a small enemy force, which withdrew before it. Up on Loi-Kang Ridge the 2d Battalion continued its unsuccessful fight to clear the enemy from their positions.

Indeed, Company G fought just to hold its positions. Sergeant Anthony Romano was pinned down in his foxhole, but he inched his Thompson submachine gun above the rim and fired blindly at the enemy. Although his stock was shot away, he continued to fire. At one point the enemy knee mortar fire ceased and a banzai charge was expected. Enemy officers could be heard giving commands. Staff Sergeant Broughton Monday heard one Japanese officer barely fifteen feet away. Despite being under heavy fire, Sergeant Monday inched up enough to hurl two hand grenades at the enemy officer. Important intelligence information would be recovered from that officer's body the following morning.

The enemy hesitated, and suddenly Company G's 3d Platoon found itself down to a few bullets per man. The platoon leader, 1st Lt. Richard E. Corvey, and a few men crawled down the hill under direct enemy fire and brought back a supply of ammunition. These bandoliers were handed from hole to hole, and once again Company G put out a devastating weight of fire. So heavy was this fire that one observer noted that it "threatened to clear the side of the hill of all its vegetation."[6] This sudden increase in fire and the loss of their officer caused the enemy to hesitate. Shortly afterward dawn approached and the enemy withdrew, leaving Company G intact.

Colonel Easterbrook wanted to take more positive action to cut the road. Although some enemy trucks continued to be destroyed as they tried to run past the American positions, enemy tankettes usually made the run without loss, although occasionally one was destroyed by the fire of the American artillery battalions. Clearly, the road was not truly cut but only harassed. It was known also that trails bypassing the American positions were in use by the enemy. Fears of nonsupport by Chinese forces were relieved when on 21 January leading elements of the Chinese 114th Infantry Regiment contacted patrols of the brigade to the north, indicating a joining of forces in the near future.

Colonel Easterbrook's request was denied by General Willey. As noted earlier, General Willey explained his reasons to Captain Fischer after the war. The concerns over the actual support to be expected from the Chinese, the ability to supply troops closer to the road, and coordination between Allied forces all combined to cause General Willey to refuse permission to physically cut the Burma Road.

Ordered to hold where they were while also doing everything possible to interdict the road, Mars Task Force spent the next week doing constant patrols. On 22 January a patrol from the 124th Cavalry, consisting of five Americans and sixteen Kachin Rangers, found an enemy trail block. They circled around to the rear of the enemy position, where they observed two logs blocking the road. The lieutenant leading the patrol crawled up to a nearby pillbox to see two enemy soldiers sleeping. First he fired at the Japanese soldiers with his M1 carbine; then he tossed in two grenades for good measure. Before the patrol could enter the pillbox to search for intelligence material, they observed another enemy group coming up the trail. The patrol withdrew unscathed.

That same day some of General Willey's fears were confirmed when a mortar crew from the 124th opened fire on a column of infantry and mules, only to discover that this was a Chinese group trying to join the Americans. The pattern of American patrols, ambushes, and booby traps by day and Japanese attacks and shelling by night continued. One patrol of the 124th Cavalry located an enemy ammunition dump near the 3d Battalion's positions, notified the 475th Infantry, and had the satisfaction of learning that a patrol from the 3d Battalion had blown up three thousand rounds of enemy 70mm, 75mm, and 105mm ammunition. Also destroyed were four hundred rounds of grenade discharger ammunition and eighteen drums of gasoline.

On 22 January the 3d Squadron received four flame throwers that they had requested in an effort to clear the area of undergrowth. Heavy 4.2 inch mortars were also airdropped and put to good use. Another supply drop introduced Mars Task Force to a new weapon, when they received night-sighting devices known as snooper scopes and sniper scopes. The men swiftly learned to use them by practical experience and put them to good use.[7] That same day also saw the cavalry's 2d Squadron, still held back at Mong Wi, begin to come forward, escorting brigade headquarters. Mars Task Force would soon be united alongside the Burma Road.

The patrols and ambushes continued with varying degrees of success. First Lieutenant Ernest Caine, of the headquarters company, 2d Battalion, 475th Infantry, led one such patrol on 22 January. Consisting of seven Americans and twenty-four Kachins, they left the 2d Battalion area to set up an ambush at a knoll overlooking the road. All the men were briefed and all the equipment was checked before departure. A rendezvous point was selected at the briefing.

Reaching the designated rendezvous point, the patrol waited for darkness and then proceeded by a covered route to the knoll. There they set up the ambush with a rocket launcher flanked by two Browning automatic rifles (BARs). Kachin riflemen provided all-around protection. At about 1915 they heard a truck motor, but apparently it was on one of the bypass trails to the north, where it could not be seen by the patrol. Fifteen minutes later the patrol fired two rockets at another vehicle that came up on the road. All the patrol's personal weapons, including the two BARs, also fired upon the target. After firing for two full minutes the patrol scattered and regrouped at the rendezvous point. There were no casualties to the patrol. The patrol leader fired a green flare to indicate both that his patrol was out of the danger area and that American artillery could now fire safely into the ambush site.[8]

While the Americans continued to harass the enemy around Loi-Kang Ridge, the Chinese of Col. Peg Ko-li's 114th Infantry Regiment closed to another section of the road, north of Mars Task Force. Colonel Ko-li conferred with Colonels Easterbrook and Osborne. Later Colonel Ko-li claimed that he did not clearly understand Mars Task Force plans. This led to confusion and recriminations between the Chinese and Americans. The Chinese command believed that the Americans did not block the road. Instead, they simply had five battalions lined up alongside the road and were harassing it from a distance. They also believed that the Americans had refused Colonel Ko-Li permission for his regiment to pass through their positions. As a result of these misunderstandings, the 3d Battalion, 114th Chinese Regiment, placed its own block on the road to the north, at the eighty-mile road marker, on 22 January.

American liaison officers reported, however, that this actual block was not placed until 27 January and that the interim period was used to close the regiment to the area of the road. The 3d Battalion, 114th Regiment, seized a hill at the eighty-two mile marker, five miles north of Mars Task Force. The 1st Battalion, 114th Regiment, put one understrength company actually on the road at the eighty-one mile marker and an artillery battery nearby in support.

The Japanese reaction was swift and fierce. The 3d Battalion was attacked day and night for five consecutive days. By the end of the fight the Chinese soldiers could not even stay awake in their foxholes. On the night of 29 January the Japanese attacked both the solitary company on the road and its supporting artillery battery. Both were destroyed, the artillery pieces being shattered by demo-

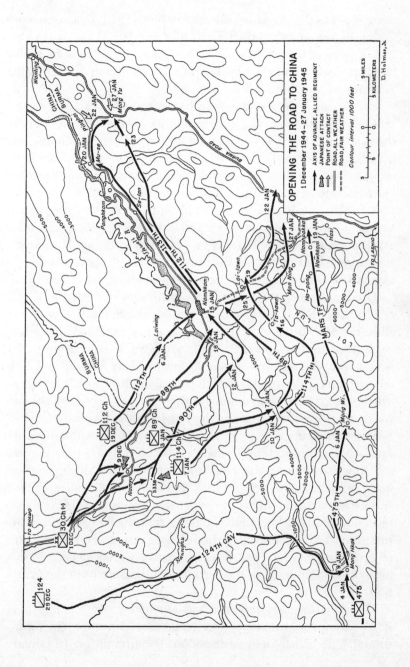

OPENING THE ROAD TO CHINA
1 December 1944 – 27 January 1945

AXIS OF ADVANCE, ALLIED REGIMENT
JAPANESE ATTACK
POINT OF CONTACT
ROAD, ALL WEATHER
ROAD, FAIR WEATHER

Contour interval 1000 feet

D. Holmes, Jr.

lition charges. All the while, the 3d Battalion, 114th Regiment, continued under attack on the nearby hill. The fate of the 114th Chinese Regiment lends credence to the concerns that General Willey had expressed about placing Mars Task Force directly on the Burma Road instead of above it.

The Japanese were actually withdrawing at this time. They knew that Mars Task Force and elements of the Chinese were on or along the road, and they believed that additional airborne elements, supply drops erroneously reported by the 2d Japanese Infantry Regiment as paratroopers, had arrived. They wanted only to keep the road open long enough to withdraw the advance elements of the 56th Infantry Division and its critical supplies. Hearing the reports of enemy forces to his rear, the 56th Infantry Division's commander asked permission to destroy his supplies and withdraw. His request was granted, but only if he withdrew with all his supplies and casualties. To accomplish this a relief convoy was sent to his aid.

The Japanese headquarters, 33d Army, sent one of its staff officers, a Major Kibio, north with forty vehicles filled with gasoline to allow the 56th Division to retire. Moving past the Mars Task Force road block on the night of 24 January, the trucks were heard by the Americans, who promptly brought down a heavy artillery and mortar barrage on the road. Major Kibio made the trip in a tankette, which was hit by a 4.2-inch mortar shell and destroyed, but he survived and made the rest of the trip in one of the trucks.

The bulk of the convoy got through, and the 56th Infantry Division began its withdrawal. This was a difficult process of moving past the Americans along the road and bypass trails. Moving only at night, while the Americans were kept on their hills under shelling and infantry attack, the troops progressed in their withdrawal over several nights. The bulk of the attacks struck the 2d Battalion, 475th Infantry, which would suffer the heaviest casualty toll of the campaign. The Chinese 114th Infantry, having been given a bloody nose in its attempt to cut the road, remained quietly on the nearby hills.

The American artillery also was a primary target of the Japanese attempt to keep the Americans from stopping their withdrawal. The 612th Field Artillery was the first hit on 19 January, when it lost an officer and four enlisted men wounded. The worst day was 26 January. In what the battalion history describes as "an artillery duel," they lost forty rounds of ammunition, one gun destroyed, one gun severely damaged, in addition to one man dead and four others wounded. The next day, seven more men of the battalion were wounded. The following day, 28 January, Colonel Wallis was transferred to Z Force, and Major Stephenson assumed command of the battalion. Another man was wounded by enemy fire.

Again, on 30 January, an artillery duel developed. In the afternoon, enemy shell fire destroyed fifteen rounds of ammunition, and A Battery lost one gun destroyed. One man was killed, with four others wounded. Eight liaison planes were in the air, trying to pinpoint the enemy pieces for counterbattery fire but having limited success. This type of battle continued until 2 February, when another 612th Field Artillery gun was destroyed. By the end of the battle the 612th would suffer more casualties than the 1st Battalion, 475th Infantry Regiment.

The 613th Field Artillery was also shelled on 27 January, with no casualties, but the following day they lost one man and one mule to enemy shell fire. The 29th of January saw Colonel Donovan slightly wounded by shrapnel, but he refused to be evacuated, and after treatment at the battalion aid station he returned to command. Shelling continued and on 2 February 2d Lt. Patrick E. Murphy and Cpl. Charles B. Hooper were killed and several others wounded by an accurate enemy fire. The battalion continued firing missions until the enemy withdrew, and unlike its sister battalion, lost no guns to enemy action.

These actions by the Japanese to pin the Americans down while they conducted that most difficult of military operations, a withdrawal across an enemy's front, were costly to Mars Task Force. The 475th Infantry, a prime target of the enemy fire, lost 32 men killed and 199 wounded during that period. As we have seen, the artillery battalions suffered severely. Most of the losses were in the 2d Battalion and the 612th Field Artillery. Nevertheless, the Americans continued their efforts to block the road. The artillery battalions kept up a constant fire on every target identified along the road.

The infantry and cavalry battalions continued with patrols to block the road.

On 23 January, Troop A sent out a patrol that discovered an enemy blocking position. The patrol withdrew and called down artillery fire, which destroyed the block. Also on that day a patrol from the intelligence and reconnaissance platoon, 3d Squadron, was the first cavalry unit to reach the Burma Road. Led by 1st Lt. Edwin M. Rhoads, the patrol reached the road, and each man made a personal obscene gesture to celebrate. Among the patrol was Colonel Donovan, the commander of the 613th Field Artillery, who was "officially" looking for targets for his guns. It was also on that date that Major Jordan radioed that his 2d Squadron would join the regiment on 28 January. That night a patrol under Lt. John W. Jones, of Company E, 2d Battalion, destroyed two trucks and two tankettes with rockets and demolitions.

Lieutenant Jones's patrol consisted of his own 2d platoon, E Company, reinforced with a bazooka team and a light machine-gun squad. They left the company perimeter at 1650, 23 January, and moved down the mountain, using a pack trail on the west side. Upon reaching the base, they circled around the mountain to the east until they arrived at the designated assembly area at 1730 hours. Using the cover of trees and a shallow gully, they advanced to within seventy-five yards of the road. There they set up a perimeter defense and sent a two-man listening post forward. At 2030 hours the listening post reported hearing sounds of enemy traffic.

Lieutenant Jones moved his patrol to within fifteen feet of the road and waited until they could plainly hear the vehicles. The vehicles then stopped about six hundred yards north of the ambush site. After a three- or four-minute pause they started south again, until the lead truck became visible to the bazooka team. At a range of about twenty yards, the rocket team opened fire and got a hit at the front of an enemy tankette. The tankette continued to roll, and every weapon at the patrol's disposal opened fire. The tankette rolled to a stop just past the patrol's perimeter. A second tankette sped past the rocket team. They fired into the rear of the vehicle and hit it just below the turret. Then the first tankette opened fire with its small-caliber cannon. The second tankette joined in with cannon and machine-gun fire and then moved past the first tan-kette and sped away down the road. At that point the patrol with-drew to a rendezvous location and directed mortar fire on the road where they had engaged the enemy.

Lieutenant Jones had not finished for the evening. The plan in-cluded a second ambush at a point six hundred yards north of the first site. While moving to this site the advance scouts encountered four enemy soldiers, and the patrol moved into covered positions. They heard much enemy activity while in hiding, including the sounds of digging, chopping, and talking. Lieutenant Jones con-tacted his company commander, Capt. Maurice A. Hunter, and re-ceived permission to withdraw.[9]

The following day, 24 January, a patrol from the 475th's intelli-gence and reconnaissance platoon, under the same Lt. Alton Ship-stead who had rescued the downed aircrew on the march to the Burma Road, crossed that road to scout the area near the village of Loi Kong (not the Loi-Kang hilltop with a similar name). The ob-jective was to determine if the trails in the area were suitable for trucks and tankettes. After engaging an enemy observation point, the patrol returned to report that the trails could not carry vehicles but were suitable for foot soldiers. Another patrol from the 3d Bat-talion also prowled east of the Burma Road, ambushing two squads of enemy soldiers before returning safely.

The following day, enemy pressure against the 2d Battalion in-creased, as did enemy traffic along the Burma Road. Clearly, the en-emy was speeding up its withdrawal while intending to keep the Americans away from the road. A combined patrol of the 3d Squadron's pioneer and demolition platoon and the intelligence and reconnaissance platoon made a daring daylight sortie and de-stroyed an enemy artillery ammunition dump, to the delight of the watching Americans on the hills around the valley.

Lieutenant Lewis B. Mitchell took his platoon from L Company out to scout a known enemy area on 26 January. They ran into a well-prepared enemy position and engaged in a two-hour fire fight with a strong enemy garrison. Despite being severely wounded in the legs and chest, Pfc. Leonard H. Gerow Jr. continued to fire upon the enemy with his automatic weapon until he was ordered to the rear. Rather than be removed from the firing line, however, he refused immediate aid, and he later walked alone to the aid station. He was awarded a Silver Star.[10] Seven Americans were wounded in the fire fight and a reported eight enemy were counted dead.

The Japanese retaliated by shelling the 3d Battalion's perimeter for more than four hours. The enemy paid particular attention to the Americans' 4.2 inch mortar positions, which seemed to anger them more than usual. American Air Corps P-47s continued to strafe enemy positions and any vehicles they could find along the road. Circling over the target area, they would peel off to attack a specific target, dive steeply in the attack, and then return gracefully to the sky to await their next turn. The soldiers on the ground loved the show and cheered the airmen with each explosion. Another highlight of 26 January was that it was the first time since their arrival that the task force had sufficient rations for three meals in one day.

The twenty-sixth of January was a hard day for the Chinese farther along the Burma Road. Late in the afternoon Colonel Osborne received a message from the 114th Regiment commander, advising that its 9th Company had been attacked all night long but had beaten off the attack with nineteen known Japanese casualties. The 8th Company counted twenty-five enemy horses killed in its area, which was the eighty-two-mile marker section of the road. Colonel Ko-Li reported that the "Japs are putting up hard fight to prevent cutting of road."[11]

The next day saw a brief but bloody return to conventional warfare for the 475th Infantry. Supported by the 612th Field Artillery and mortars and machine guns of the 3d Battalion, the 2d Battalion fought all day to secure the rest of Loi-Kang Ridge. That portion, which became known as South Hill, remained an enemy strongpoint at the cost of fifteen casualties to the 2d Battalion. The Japanese counterattacked that night but were equally unsuccessful in trying to dislodge the Americans.

For the 1st Battalion, 475th Infantry, the twenty-seventh of January was memorable for the fresh meat they had that day. Several native cows had mistakenly wandered into their area, providing the entire battalion with fresh meat for their dinner. The only complaint registered in the unit's journal for the day was the enemy fire that continued all night.

The twenty-eighth of January saw another attempt to clear the enemy position that Lieutenant Mitchell and his patrol had attacked two days before. That hill was known as Hill 77, from its location at that mile marker along the Burma Road. It had harassed the positions and patrols of the 3d Battalion since Mars Task Force had arrived. Captain Harold L. Clark led his Company L forward to try to clear the hill. Preparation by air and artillery bombardment had presumably weakened enemy defenses, and the infantry made good progress until they neared the top of the hill. There they ran into a wall of enemy fire from concealed positions. A fierce struggle developed, in which Captain Clark and Lt. Herbert C. Schwarz, the leading platoon commander, were killed along with six enlisted men. First Lieutenant Aaron E. Hawes Jr., the company executive officer, took command and successfully withdrew the company, including all those killed and the sixteen wounded, despite the loss of communications and severe disorganization.

By now the efforts of the 124th Cavalry and the 114th Chinese Infantry Regiment were being closely coordinated. Colonel Osborne and Colonel Ko-Li communicated several times a day, coordinating patrols and artillery barrages. During these messages the task force learned that the 114th Regiment had been joined by the 1st Battalion, 113th Infantry Regiment, on 29 January. They also learned that enemy tankettes had attacked the Chinese at the eighty-one-mile marker and that fierce fighting had taken place while enemy trucks and transport moved past them behind the attacking force.

The following day, 30 January, the brigade headquarters moved forward from Momauk to Ma Wing. At the same time, the NCAC headquarters moved forward from Myitkyina to Bhamo. The Chinese artillery base was heavily shelled by the Japanese during the day as a further cover for the withdrawal. Some Chinese guns were damaged, and hard ground fighting continued along the road.

As January drew to a close, the situation in Burma was moving toward a finale. The Chinese 38th Division, with its 112th and 113th Infantry Regiments, was in position to push down the road to Lashio. The Japanese 56th Infantry Division was conducting a difficult but largely successful withdrawal down the road, partially blocked by the 114th Chinese Regiment and Mars Task Force. The Chinese 30th Division was moving into the same area, pushing

Japanese rear guards back along the road toward the blocking positions. These rear guards had found and were successfully using
the gaps between the Chinese and American blocking positions on
the Burma Road to make their escape. These forces moved around
the Chinese and established themselves on a prominent hill about
one and a half miles north of Hpa-pen village, which was about one
mile northeast of the cavalry position. Hpa-pen was later determined to be the focal point of the enemy line of withdrawal, which
was why its protection was so vital to the Japanese. The hill nearby
blocked the American view of the road to the northeast, and as the
enemy continued to use the road successfully, American attention
turned to securing that area to better observe and interdict the
road. The importance of that area to the Japanese withdrawal was
at the time unknown.

A plan was prepared in which a joint effort by Chinese and American forces would seize the area and establish a position on the hill
overlooking the road. The plan as originally drawn had the 88th
Chinese Regiment, 30th Division, and the 2d Squadron, 124th Cavalry, making a coordinated attack on the hill on 30 January. However, on 30 January the Chinese asked for a one-day postponement,
to which the Americans agreed. On 31 January the Chinese again
postponed, this time until 3 February. Colonel Osborne journeyed
to the regimental headquarters of the 88th Chinese Regiment to
get a commitment from them about the joint attack.

While the cavalry was making plans to improve its positions, the
infantry was defending those they already held. On 1 February the
2d Battalion received intermittent artillery fire all day long. Identified in this incoming fire were 150mm artillery and tank-gun fire.
Late in the day the battalion received three banzai attacks, one each
from the north, south, and west. The attackers were estimated to
number two companies reinforced with mortars and machine guns.
The attacks and the artillery fire were known to be diversionary, to
allow the traffic passing below on the road to continue unmolested.

The battalion noted that traffic was moving both north and south
on the road during these attacks. From their positions the battalion
directed heavy concentrations of 4.2-inch mortars, 75mm artillery
fire, and bazooka shells on the traffic they observed. A patrol sent

out by the battalion fired upon a Japanese road-repair party and then withdrew to the battalion perimeter. The battalion identified an enemy shuttle system designed to move personnel and equipment past the battalion's section of the road. Some later patrols identified "many fenders, headlights, broken glass and other vehicular debris strewn along the Road."[12]

The 3d Battalion spotted an enemy patrol attempting to move between it and the 124th positions nearby and repulsed it with long-range fire, which killed one enemy soldier. The regiment called in three bombing and strafing runs on reported enemy artillery positions during the day in an effort to discourage the continued enemy shelling.

The following day, 2 February, was a quieter day for the 475th Infantry. The 1st Battalion made no enemy contacts. The 2d Battalion, as usual in the heat of contact, had an ambush patrol fire upon an enemy infiltration group. Another of its patrols found an enemy group in a mined area and engaged in a brief fire fight. No casualties resulted from the patrol actions, but enemy artillery fire added two more wounded to the battalion's growing list of casualties. The 3d battalion similarly lost two men to enemy artillery fire, and the 612th Field Artillery had one gun destroyed from an enemy artillery piece firing from the vicinity of Masak.

Enemy artillery fire also continued to harass both the drop fields and liaison strips, hindering both the receipt of supplies and the evacuation of casualties. A flight of fighter planes arrived and was directed to circle over the area. The 475th had noticed that the enemy artillery did not fire when American planes were overhead, for fear of retaliation. During the hour between 1000 and 1100 the fighters circled the area while the evacuees were safely transported to rear-area hospitals by the liaison pilots.

It was on 2 February that 1st Lt. H. G. Garrison, of Company E, received orders that his 1st Platoon, reinforced with a light machine-gun squad, would put in a trail block on the trail between Loi-Kang and the Burma Road. His orders were to move into position at dusk of 2 February, dig in, and hold until ordered to do otherwise. The position had already been reconnoitered by Kachin guides, including five who accompanied Lieutenant Garrison's platoon. At about 1700 hours on 2 February the platoon, led by the Kachin guides, started off down the side of the mountain where the 2d Battalion had its defenses. Using a fifteen-yard interval between each man to avoid harassing enemy artillery fire, the platoon proceeded along a small trail until it reached the foot of the hill. There Lieutenant Garrison noticed three enemy trails marked with white paper for night movement. These he reported over his radio. He also identified eleven new enemy positions dug in the area, fortunately vacant when he found them. These he also reported back to battalion headquarters. The platoon reached the trail it was to block at dusk and after a brief reconnaissance established a perimeter defense with light machine guns placed to cover both directions of the trail. The patrol spent the night with no activity other than one American artillery shell falling within fifty yards of the patrol's position. At 1000 hours on the morning of 3 February the patrol was ordered back to the battalion perimeter. The mission, blocking the trail to prevent enemy retreat or reinforcement from a position to be attacked by the 1st Battalion, was accomplished.

The attack that Lieutenant Garrison's platoon had been placed to support was the result of the continuing fight on Loi-Kang Ridge. The 2d Battalion had been struggling on one end of the ridge while enemy forces held the other end. This caused a constant drain of casualties besides those caused by the constant enemy artillery fire. The strain on the battalion was the most severe of any in Mars Task Force, and as other problems began to be resolved, Colonel Easterbrook determined that this last situation needed to be cleared up. He conferred on 1 February with Colonel Thrailkill and asked if the 2d Battalion wanted to be relieved. Colonel Thrailkill declined and instead asked that his battalion be included in the plan to clear the rest of Loi-Kang Ridge. The matter was referred to General Willey, who approved of the plan to include the 2d Battalion in the operation designed to clear the balance of the ridge.

The plan scheduled the 2d Battalion to draw the attention of the enemy holding the southern end of the ridge, while Colonel Johnson's 1st Battalion moved quietly across the valley that held the Brigade's supply installations and attacked the enemy from the rear. Basically, the 2d Battalion would put in a holding attack from the north while the 1st Battalion attacked from the south. Colonel Thrailkill, however, would not lead his battalion in the attack. During the night of 1 and 2 February an enemy shell hit a 2d Battalion observation post where he was observing enemy positions in preparation for the next day's attack. Colonel Thrailkill and three enlisted men were killed immediately and SSgt. Milton Kornfeld had his leg so badly mangled that the battalion surgeon, Capt. Joseph P. Worley, had to amputate at once and without any anesthetic. The battalion's executive officer, Maj. John H. Lattin, took command.[13]

That the hill needed to be cleared was accepted by all who were in the area. Private First Class Peter J. Faggion was a member of the 1st Battalion Headquarters Company. As a part of Lt. Edwin Rothschild's machine-gun platoon, Faggion had an excellent observation point "overlooking our 2nd and 3rd [Battalion] positions, the Japanese positions of Loi-Kang Ridge and the Japanese motor activities on the Burma Road."[14] Part of this squad's assignment was to protect Battery C of the 612th Field Artillery. Staff Sergeant Charles Finger kept his men busy, but despite their best efforts, enemy fire observed from Loi-Kang Ridge continued to cause casualties and damage to the battery. Faggion remembers in particular 27 January, when with ammunition expended and one gun barrel burned out he watched helplessly as both the gun battery and his squad's position were hammered by the enemy.

> The Japanese were retaliating with much fury and pin point accuracy this day. It crossed my mind at the time that one of those Whiz Bangs had my name on it. This skirmish continued for about one-half hour and they were coming in very close. There was earth/dust flying in the air and I recall seeing my foxhole walls cracking and crumbling all around me from the concussion.[15]

Although the machine gunners survived, this was the day that the C Battery had its greatest losses. Clearly the enemy had to be pushed off the rest of Loi-Kang Ridge.

At midnight of 2 February, Companies B and C moved to a line of departure west of the Nam Maw River. They were to follow a trail that went around the south end of the valley to a village called Ma Sak. This was half a mile south of and below Loi-Kang Ridge. The trail then turned north and went up Loi-Kang Ridge. Colonel Johnson, a veteran Marauder officer, led his two companies forward at 0400 hours on 2 February, escorted by a squad under SSgt. Oral E. Smith. At 0545 hours the 612th Field Artillery joined with the 4.2-inch and 81mm mortars of the 1st Battalion Headquarters Company in laying a fifteen-minute barrage on Loi-Kang. Heavy machine guns joined in the preparation, as did P-47 fighters of the Tenth Air Force. As soon as the barrage lifted, Major Lattin's battalion attacked with two platoons of Company F. The target was a small knoll held by two enemy machine-gun emplacements. The attack was stopped forty yards from the enemy positions by intense enemy fire.

Private First Class Clifton L. Henderson was a member of the attacking platoons. After the attack had failed to dislodge the enemy with mortar and machine gun fire he volunteered to attack the position, which was about thirty-five yards to his front. Dragging his Browning automatic rifle alongside and carrying a hand grenade, he crawled forward alone in the face of heavy machine gun fire. Fire from a flanking enemy machine gun detonated one of the spare grenades he carried on his pack. Despite this, Private Henderson crawled to within four feet of the enemy emplacement and tossed his grenade, destroying the enemy position. His success, however, left him still under heavy fire from the supporting position. He crawled to the rear of this emplacement and set up his automatic rifle. As the enemy garrison of the second position began to run out the rear, he cut down five of them. Then he turned his automatic rifle on the enemy machine gun and destroyed it and the remainder of its crew. These two positions were the key defenses of the knoll, and Company F went on to secure its objective without any further loss. Private Henderson was later awarded a Distinguished Service Cross.[16]

During that battle SSgt. Raymond C. Elm was leading his squad forward when an enemy counterattack stopped the advance and pinned down an automatic rifle team in the open terrain. Sergeant Elm exposed himself to constant and direct enemy fire to use rifle and grenades while covering the withdrawal of these trapped men.

During the exchange of fire, Sergeant Elm was mortally wounded but kept up his covering fire until the trapped men had reached safety. He was posthumously awarded a Silver Star.[17]

Another soldier, Pfc. Martin S. Nagelberg, was unable to stand by and watch while wounded men lay in a crossfire. As a medical aid man, he knew his duty and ran out into the open to aid the wounded. He administered first aid as well as he could under the difficult circumstances until evacuation teams could reach the wounded men. He was killed in action and was awarded a posthumous Bronze Star.[18]

Private First Class Justin J. Rougelot also moved into enemy fire to aid a wounded man. After administering first aid he carried the wounded man to safety. He then repeated his act with a second wounded soldier. He too earned a Silver Star that day.[19]

With the noise of the 2d Battalion's attack to cover their movements, the 1st Battalion moved forward in a column of companies, with 1st Lt. Pete C. McDowell's Company C in the lead. The column bypassed the village of Ma Sak to avoid alerting any enemy garrison within the huts. They moved to a small peak just south of Loi-Kang, where lead scouts Sergeant Smith, Sgt. Dave Pigoni, T5 Leo D. Corn, and Pfc. Robert C. Deyo surprised a party of Japanese, who retreated to a small ravine where they were swiftly eliminated by the battalion's advance elements. Lieutenant McDowell was especially pleased, because the ravine had apparently housed an enemy artillery piece that had caused several casualties in the 1st Battalion's perimeter.

The advance continued undiscovered until it reached the outskirts of the burned-out remnants of the village of Loi Kong. There the men were taken under fire by a well-hidden enemy strongpoint and pinned down. The ridge widened at that point, and additional platoons of Company C were now placed in line for the next advance. As the lead scouts crossed a bare open saddle in the ground, they were taken under fire once again. The 2d and 3d platoons were ordered to withdraw while the artillery observer placed both artillery and mortar fire on the enemy positions. As the enemy opened fire, two sergeants ran forward to draw off the hostile fire and allow the platoons to withdraw. Staff Sergeant David Akui and SSgt. Sylvester G. Garrison made a two-man assault on the enemy, using only their

Thompson submachine guns. Moving in a long-practiced pattern—
one moving while the other one covered with fire—they so distracted the enemy that the platoons withdrew without loss. Both
sergeants successfully withdrew to their company unscathed.

Following closely on the artillery barrage, the 2d and 3d platoons
renewed the assault. They drove off the enemy garrison, and the 1st
Battalion now held the high ground overlooking the 2d Battalion's
positions. Five hundred yards still separated the two units. Rather
than risk friendly fire, Company C went into a horseshoe-shaped defensive perimeter at about 1030 hours. It had suffered only one fatality in the securing of Loi Kong village. Another thirteen had been
wounded and thirty enemy counted dead.

Later that afternoon an attempt to make physical contact with
the 2d Battalion by using two platoons of Company B and one of C
was turned back by heavy enemy fire. Instead of another attempt in
darkness, the official joining of the two battalions was put off until
4 February.

The morning of 4 February found the Japanese gone, and the
contact between the 1st and 2d Battalions, 475th Infantry, was easily accomplished. By 1300 hours the 2d Battalion had fully relieved
the men of the 1st Battalion, who marched wearily back across the
valley to their original positions.[20] Colonel Johnson received a Silver
Star for his leadership, which kept casualties down to two killed,
four seriously wounded, and eleven slightly wounded.

The 124th Cavalry was also busy on those days. Colonel Osborne
had tried and failed to get cooperation from the 89th Chinese Infantry Regiment in a joint attack on the hill, which prevented unobstructed observation of the road by the 124th Cavalry. Still assuming that the Chinese would participate, the cavalry began to
move closer to facilitate cooperation with the 89th Regiment. On 31
January the pioneer and demolition platoon of the 2d Squadron
moved onto a hilltop to construct an observation post for the coming attack. Enemy reaction was swift and deadly. The platoon had to
be pulled back and ordered to another, more protected location.
This one went in undetected, and Major Jordan and his observation
party used it successfully in the coming attack.

The 2d Squadron, the last of the regiment to arrive, had occupied a position between its two sister squadrons. Some of its posi-

tions were in full view of the enemy, and to withdraw the troopers undetected was essential. To ensure that the enemy did not get an idea of the withdrawal of the squadron, men in groups were moved into the perimeter in broad daylight, giving the impression that the perimeter was being reinforced rather than abandoned. Less noticeable, however, was the fact that individual men were moved down the hill throughout the day. By darkness most of the squadron was off the hill. In critical spots, cooks, mess sergeants, supply staff, and administrative personnel held positions and made their presence obvious to deceive the watching enemy.

The 2d Squadron had intelligence reports giving an understrength battalion of about 210 men as the enemy garrison. One company of the 89th Regiment was attached to the squadron as a reserve while the rest of the Chinese unit was to provide fire support. The attack began on 2 February with a heavy barrage from 0600 to 0620 hours. American and Chinese weapons fired upon the target hill, and then the 2d Squadron, led by F and G Troops began to climb the four-hundred-foot-high hill. First Lieutenant Jack L. Knight led F Troop. His first sergeant was his brother, Curtis. Both were original National Guard inductees from Mineral Wells, Texas, two of thirteen original members still with the troop, which was drawn from that town.

As Lieutenant Knight led his troop up the hill, he encountered two enemy soldiers, both of whom he killed. He reached the crest first, and standing fully exposed, he encouraged his troops to join him, shouting "There's nothing up here. Come on!"[21] Under heavy mortar and artillery fire the troop reached the top and prepared to dig in to defend their new home. While his men prepared defenses, Lieutenant Knight moved forward to investigate the southwest slope of the hill. There he found a pillbox, into which he tossed a grenade. Then he found a second and called back to his men to join him in eliminating the enemy defenses. Lieutenant Knight and his troopers had run into a horseshoe defense with themselves in the center. With the enemy on three sides they had to eliminate the entire position in order to secure the objective.

Lieutenant Knight quickly set about destroying each enemy position in turn. Despite being hit in the face by shrapnel from an enemy grenade, he continued to lead the fight. However, he soon ran out of carbine ammunition. He turned to Lt. Leo C. Tynan Jr., an artillery observer and another Texan, who shared his ammunition. Lieutenant Tynan later reported that one of Lieutenant Knight's eyes was shut tight and the other was covered with blood running from his wounds. But he turned back to his men, now taking casualties, and organized them for another attack. Leading from the front, he grenaded another enemy position. Again an enemy grenade wounded him, but he continued in the fight. His brother Curtis saw the wounds and raced to his side but was cut down in the process. Calling to his men to get his brother out of the line of fire, Lieutenant Knight rose and attacked once again. As he raced toward a sixth enemy pillbox, an enemy bullet cut him down for good.

Lieutenant Knight was posthumously awarded the Medal of Honor, the sole Medal of Honor awarded to the infantry in the China-Burma-India theater during the war. Colonel Osborne, who had served on Bataan and with Merrill's Marauders, remarked that "the actions of Lieutenant Knight in leading his troop against a strong enemy will always remain as the finest example of American courage, valor and leadership of any officer I have had under my command. It is officers of Lieutenant Knight's caliber who are winning the war—not colonels and generals."[22]

Private First Class Anthony Whitaker was also attacking the same pillbox that had cost Lieutenant Knight his life. He fired three rounds of bazooka ammunition at the emplacement without any explosions. Tossing away the useless rocket launcher, Private Whitaker attacked the position with his rifle and grenades. He rushed the pillbox and destroyed it at the cost of his own life. He was awarded a posthumous Distinguished Service Cross.[23]

Sergeant Kim Hill jumped into what he thought was an empty foxhole only to come to grips with a live Japanese soldier. The enemy officer jabbed the sergeant in the shoulder with his sword. Sergeant Hill grabbed the sword and used his bayonet on his attacker.

Sergeant Richard M. Hatfield, of Houston, Texas, carried a large Texas flag on his back, determined to raise it on the hilltop. A mortar squad observer who had run out of telephone wire and become a rifleman, Sergeant Hatfield joined a squad of Hispanic Americans under Sgt. Clyde Stockton. When the squad attacked a pillbox with grenades, the enemy threw one grenade back, injuring two Americans. Sergeant Hatfield then used his carbine to eliminate further enemy resistance. After having his wounds treated, Sergeant Hatfield returned to the hill, now secure, to raise his flag. He could not find anything to put it on and was advised that there were many "Yankees" fighting this war, too. The flag stayed in his pack.

Alongside F Troop, Capt. William Wood's G Troop also had attacked a separate part of the deadly hill. His losses were heavy, and he tried to call in artillery fire, only to learn that his artillery observer had been killed. Sending his radio operator to evacuate the wounded men of his command, Captain Wood called in his own supporting fire by moving each round closer to himself until he observed it strike the enemy forces. After the barrage the troopers found minimal enemy resistance and secured their objective. Captain Wood received the Bronze Star.

The story of Pvt. Leonard J. McCord testifies to the efficiency of the medical services in this campaign. Private McCord was in the attack on what became known as Knight's Hill and was wounded in the arm. Falling unconscious, he never felt an enemy soldier rummage through his pockets and take his pocket Bible from his breast pocket. As the enemy soldier fought on, another trooper shot him down. The trooper recovered the pocket Bible with Private McCord's name in it and sent it back to be returned. The Bible chased Private McCord to the aid station, to the portable hospital, and to the liaison evacuation airstrip, missing him each time. He didn't get it back until he was safely resting in a rear-area hospital.

The three troops of the 2d Squadron settled in to defend their gains. Casualties had caused serious gaps in the line, and enemy soldiers continued to try to infiltrate those defenses. Most were simply trying to escape, but fears of a counterattack were very real. Captain Andrew J. Kaeli, commanding the regimental headquarters company, managed to locate the Chinese company held in reserve and tried unsuccessfully to have it move forward and take over a part of the defenses. Major Jordan ordered all troops to hold what they had, and said that if they could get through the night the Chinese would cut the road farther south, relieving them of the pressure they were then under from Japanese forces. In the rear the 49th Portable Hospital conducted 27 major and 116 minor operations on wounded troopers, with a mortality rate of only 1.7 percent. Its surgeons—Maj. Ira Teischer, Capt. Frank Nicholas, and Capt. Frank Rittenhouse—conducted continuous medical service for seventy-two uninterrupted hours. Captain John Buck, the dental officer, administered the anesthetics.

Finally, when most of the firing had died away, Captain Kaeli managed to get the Chinese company to come forward and reinforce the cavalry's perimeter. The battle was over. More than two hundred enemy dead were counted, while an estimated two hundred additional Japanese were seen fleeing the hill. Twenty-two cavalrymen had been killed.

About one mile north of the Battle of Knight's Hill the 3d Squadron had a battle of its own when Troops I and K attacked a nearby hill. Aided by one-man attacks on enemy bunkers performed by Pfc. Bernie W. Beacon Jr. and Pvt. Solomon O. Cureton, the attack was successful in one hour, at a cost of one dead and fifteen wounded. They counted thirty-six enemy dead.

The seizure of Loi-Kang Ridge and the Battle of Knight's Hill marked the end of major combat in Burma for Mars Task Force. The Japanese were now pulling farther back along the road, and the Chinese were present in significant numbers. The British 36th Infantry Division was also in the area, pushing hard against the withdrawing enemy. For the Americans it looked like a time to rest and recuperate. But it wasn't time just yet. The enemy had one last punch left to throw.

Earlier in the month a patrol of the intelligence and reconnaissance platoon of the 124th Cavalry had reported a strong enemy position near the regimental positions. On 4 February the cavalry sent out a combat patrol into that same area with the advice that it was lightly held. Exactly where this intelligence came from was never determined, but the result was nearly disastrous.

The patrol consisted of a platoon from Troop I, under the command of 2d Lt. Burr L. Hughes. Accompanying the patrol but not in command was the troop commander and one of the regiment's most respected "characters," 1st Lt. Hobart "Hobie" T. Kavel. The same officer who had led his troops into its original positions at the start of the battle, he was a veteran Marauder who refused to wear a helmet even at formal inspections, preferring instead his "lucky" cloth cap. Lieutenant Kavel was known and respected throughout the regiment. He accompanied the patrol because there was a chance of combat and he felt he should be nearby should one of his units become engaged. The patrol's mission was to establish contact between the 1st and 3d Squadrons.

The patrol's path lay across some low ground that was covered by the strong enemy positions previously uncovered by the intelligence and reconnaissance platoon.[24] Apparently ignorant of the position, the platoon walked into an ambush. Four machine guns opened fire from concealed positions, cutting down several members of the patrol. After the shock wore off, the platoon attempted to move forward to the attack, but enemy fire was too intense and accurate for an attack. Lieutenant Hughes was among the first to fall. Lying seriously wounded, he turned over command to Pfc. George A. Owen, another Mineral Wells native.

Although wounded himself, Private Owen obtained control of the platoon and directed its defense. He managed to move them forward to within fifteen feet of the enemy position, and his men eliminated one of the emplacements with hand grenades. When it became apparent that the platoon had to withdraw he controlled the withdrawal to ensure that every man was accounted for and that a rear guard was provided. Private Owen was awarded a Distinguished Service Cross for his actions of 4 February.[25]

While the severely wounded Lieutenant Hughes called for help over the radio, one of his squad leaders, Cpl. Pearce W. Moore, was severely wounded in the face and leg by enemy grenades. Despite his wounds and disorientation, Corporal Moore led his squad forward and attacked two enemy machine guns, knocking out both and attacking a third before he was ordered to withdraw. His wounds were so severe that he required four units of plasma at the aid station to survive. He too received a Distinguished Service Cross.[26]

Lieutenant Kavel had been wounded in the hip early in the fight. Despite his painful wounds he moved forward with his radio to direct support for his trapped platoon. To better direct artillery and mortar fire, he deliberately crawled to an exposed position on a ridge. There, under direct fire from enemy machine guns, he called in supporting fire until he was mortally wounded. He received a posthumous Oak Leaf Cluster to his earlier award of the Silver Star.

The episode was ended when two squads from Troop K arrived to cover the withdrawal of the shattered platoon. Second Lieutenant Laurence O. Leonard led his squads forward quickly. He was soon severely wounded but continued to maneuver his men under heavy automatic weapons fire from the ambush positions. Despite his wounds he held his squads in place until all the wounded and dead had been successfully evacuated. He survived his wounds to receive a Silver Star.[27] The ambush had cost the Americans six dead and twenty-four seriously wounded. It had earned the 124th Cavalry two Distinguished Service Crosses, four Silver Stars, and eight Bronze Stars. But it left a bitter taste in an otherwise successful campaign.

After the ambush of the Hughes platoon, combat actions dropped significantly. Patrols and ambushes still were conducted, but heavy combat ceased. During one of these patrols Troop C was struck by enemy fire and Lt. David H. Shephard was wounded. The enemy withdrew, and the patrol prepared to continue. Lieutenant Irving Kofer, of Brooklyn, New York, volunteered to remain with the wounded Lieutenant Shephard until the patrol returned. When the cavalry patrol returned to the site, they found Lieutenant Shephard's body. They also found Lieutenant Kofer's binoculars with the lenses smashed and his maps with burn marks on them. Apparently he had tried to destroy his maps and equipment before being captured by the Japanese. He was the only missing casualty in Mars Task Force. Another 115 men were killed, 7 died of wounds, and 938 were wounded in action. These figures, more than twice the combat casualties of the Marauders, dramatically highlight the differences between a true use of a long-range penetration force and one converted to conventional assignments. A total of 673 enemy dead were buried in and around the Loi-Kang battlefield area.

For the infantry and cavalry, combat in Asia was over.

Epilogue

Mars Task Force remained in the area of Loi-Kang Hill for some time after the Chinese and British troops passed on to the south of them after the retreating Japanese. For American ground forces the war in Burma was over. Movies were set up using abandoned parachutes, and the 511th Medical Collecting Company joined the force and made road evacuation possible, relieving the overburdened liaison planes. Cemeteries were established and deals made with the natives to care for them after the Americans left. Several men who had distinguished themselves in the recent battles received battlefield commissions. Other changes were made as well. Colonel Easterbrook was eligible for rotation back to the United States and was replaced by Colonel Osborne. The latter in turn was replaced by Colonel Pegg, who was promoted to full colonel at the same time.

Generals Sultan and Willey presented awards for bravery at a formal formation of the troops. Men could now walk along the Burma Road in complete safety, aside from careless drivers, and enjoy a day of rest. Passing Chinese troops offered the opportunity for trade and barter. Lord Louis Mountbatten came down to review the troops as well and formally christened Knight's Hill.

However, the war went on elsewhere, and by March all elements of the task force were being withdrawn and flown to China, where they were put to work in various duties. For the 475th Infantry the duty consisted mostly of being assigned to selected Chinese forces under the American Chinese Combat Command. Despite its title this was a training command in which the skills of the soldier were taught to the Chinese by American instructors. The 124th Cavalry followed along later, and by 14 May all were somewhere in China.

They too were soon put to work providing supply, training, and tactical advice to the Chinese.

Although there had been occasional talk of another combat mission for the brigade, none of the rumors passed into reality. So essential were the men of Mars Task Force to the training of the Chinese army that all thought of returning them to combat was put aside. Indeed, General Wedemeyer, under whom they now served, was so certain that they were needed in advisory capacities that on 26 June both regiments were officially inactivated in the China theater of operations. The officers and men were simultaneously transferred singly or in groups to one of the several American-staffed advisory groups such as the Chinese combat command, the Office of Strategic Services, the Service of Supply, or another of the many such organizations supporting the Chinese war effort.

With the inactivation of the two regiments the tale of American ground combat in Burma ceased. Their demise also put an end to the American experiment in long-range penetration tactics for a number of years. Two decades later, however, this concept surfaced again during the Vietnam War. Several units adapted the designation "long-range reconnaissance patrol," or LRRPs. In a manner similar to that of the Marauders and Mars Task Force, they also went behind enemy lines to confuse and destroy enemy rear areas while also gathering intelligence. Although no regiment-sized unit was created for the Vietnam War, company-sized units did participate throughout the conflict with varying degrees of success.

These regiments also lived on in the U.S. Army ranger program. Their lineage as long-range penetration forces was combined with the lineages of the six U.S. Army ranger battalions that fought in Europe and the Philippines in World War II and the ranger companies that fought in Korea. Today the U.S. Army's 75th Ranger Regiment carries on its guidons the list of honors, which include India-Burma and central Burma, one each performed by the 5307th Composite Unit (Provisional) and Mars Task Force. Their heritage is carried forward to Korea, Vietnam, Grenada, the Persian Gulf, and Bosnia by other American soldiers carrying those colors.

Some may question whether the American units that fought in Burma were in fact special operations units. After all, they were

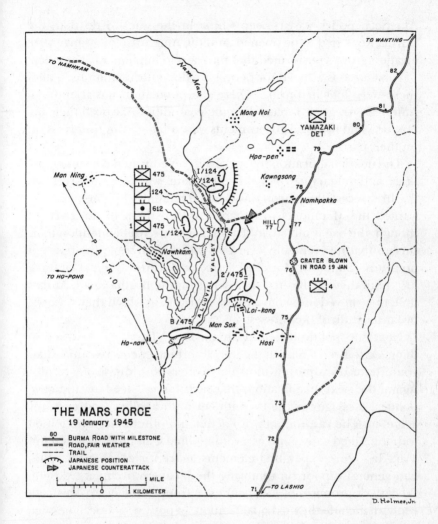

THE MARS FORCE
19 January 1945

80 ⊹ BURMA ROAD WITH MILESTONE
==== ROAD, FAIR WEATHER
---- TRAIL
JAPANESE POSITION
JAPANESE COUNTERATTACK

D. Holmes, Jr.

both rather haphazard groups thrown together with a minimum of training and rushed into combat in a war zone that had minimal value to the overall war effort. Could such a random collection of individuals be truly known as a special operations force?

Recently the Army War College published a study in which the precise requirements for such a qualification were explained. The first of these was a need to "fit the demands of policy." Clearly the

American policy was to keep China in the war. To do that, the Burma Road had to be opened, and the American long-range penetration groups performed that function to implement the policy.[1]

Next listed is a "need for permissive domestic conditions." All of these were met in Burma, where the population was friendly to American irregular forces, the jungle conditions favored their operations, and the local governments were affable to any intercession on their part.

The next qualification for success is "an educated consumer, political and military patrons who appreciate" what special forces can do. In this case the patron was General Stilwell, who knew what he wanted the Marauders to do and enabled them to do it. Here, though, the bag is mixed, in that he became so dependent on their success that he eventually overused their resources to the point of no return. Similarly, Mars Task Force performed as a special force unit until they established themselves on the Burma Road. At that time they moved into conventional warfare, in which they suffered by far the bulk of their losses.

Next is a "politically legitimate mission." This clearly existed in the need to keep China in the war, absorbing enemy resources that could have been moved to other theaters with disastrous results. Again, the next qualification, that such forces "need an attractive political message for the recruitment of local allies" was certainly achieved. The vast number of Kachin and other allies who joined with the Allied cause, and as a result joined with the Marauder and Mars Task Force operating elements, make it clear that the Allies had general support in removing the Japanese occupiers, despite the latter's promises of independence from colonialism. This concept can include the next qualification, "a positive political message for the enemy," whereby thousands of Indian and Burmese allies of the Japanese turned to the Allied cause as the Allies showed their success.

That such forces "need support from regular military forces [it] generally judges likely to win" was another condition met in Burma. It was no secret that the actions taken alone by both the Marauders and Mars Task Force would in no way have chased the Japanese out of Burma. Without the staunch support of regular Chinese, British, and Commonwealth forces as well as the U.S. Army Air Force, anything accomplished by these special forces would have disappeared quickly.

The requirement that these forces have "feasible objectives" is another split verdict. Although both the Marauders and Mars Task Force did in fact capture all the objectives assigned to them, the Myitkyina campaign reveals that the expectations placed upon the depleted Marauders were excessive. These could not be secured without the aid of regular military forces, which were late in arriving and initially poor in execution. The tendency to blame the Marauders for failing to secure Myitkyina upon arrival ignores both the capabilities of a special force and the condition of that force upon arrival at the objective. If blame must be assigned, then it rises to a much higher level than anyone who wore a Marauder shoulder patch.

"Flexibility of mind" is the next qualification. There are numerous examples of such flexibility in both campaigns. General Willey's disobedience of orders in exposing his force to destruction if placed on the Burma Road is one example. The repeated attempts by Colonel Osborne and his 1st Battalion to bypass the opposing enemy on the trail to Shaduzup are another. Both commanders operated independently, making decisions on the best use of their forces while still supporting the goals and objectives of regular military forces. The element of surprise was repeatedly achieved and exploited in nearly every operation of both commands.

The presence of "enemy vulnerabilities" was clear to all concerned with these campaigns, even the Japanese. Knowing that their supply and communication lines were vulnerable, the Japanese did what they could to secure them. Despite the tenacity of such adept commanders such as General Tanaka, these lines were regularly cut by the American special forces. Here, too, the next qualification was met when the Americans took "every advantage that technology can provide." The advent of long-term supply by air was just one such advantage. Many other advantages were taken as well, from medical treatment of the civilian populations, to the novel use of snooper scopes by Mars Task Force.

If "only [forces] skilled in their trade should conduct special operations," then both forces qualify. They learned through training how to fight in the jungles from teachers with prior experience. They exhibited excellent leadership qualities in independent operations from squad to battalion level. Both units were favored with commanders who knew their craft and led from the front whenever practical. Intelligence at the local level was usually good, although we have highlighted some particular intelligence failures that caused difficulties. Plans were made and/or adapted by those who would lead the missions. Skill in the trade was both present and exercised.

A final two qualifications include "a reputation for effectiveness" and "a willingness to learn from history." Both of these were visible in the two campaigns. By the time the Marauders launched their first mission, they had inherited some of the reputation of the first Chindit operation. After Walawbum they had developed their own reputation for effectiveness. Indeed, so concerned was General Tanaka that in the second mission he risked his frontline defenses to ensure the destruction of the more feared American force behind his lines, unsuccessfully, as it turned out. Similarly, at the Burma Road in January 1945 the Japanese had more than two full infantry regiments protecting the road at a time when every Japanese soldier was needed at the front to hold back the Allied tide. Nor did the Japanese command consider destroying the American force on the road as the Americans did with the Japanese, knowing the high cost of such an operation against American troops holding defensive positions. And both forces learned from history. Improvements were constantly made by lessons learned from the British, the OSS, the Kachins, and each other. Improvements in rations, better scouting techniques, and improved weapons and delivery methods were just some of the lessons learned as the campaign moved toward a conclusion. The collapse of the 5307th at Myitkyina was not due in any way to the failure of the special force to learn its lessons, but rather to one of its high command ignoring lessons that had been repeatedly presented to it. Similarly, the rushing of untrained troops directly into a combat situation, as was done with New Galahad, was nothing short of criminal neglect of elementary military precautions justified by military expediency. In fact, some of the severest critics of this episode are surviving Marauders who were the ones intended to benefit most from the action.

Certainly the 5307th Composite Unit (Provisional) and Mars Task Force meet the criteria for special forces, both in their organization and in their operations. As such they are distinguished forefathers of today's elite forces. They also attest to the skill of the average American soldier who with no military background became one of the most effective, skillful, and dangerous jungle fighters of modern times. Without close air support, without artillery support for most of the first campaign, and often with a numerical inferiority, the American soldier in Burma achieved more than was expected of him by anyone other than those he served with from Walawabum to Loi-Kang.

The motto of today's 75th Infantry (Ranger) Regiment is *sua sponte*, "of their own accord." The regiment carries among its honors the Presidential Unit Citation (Myitkyina), won by the 5307th Composite Unit (Provisional) on its standard. Together the two forces trace back to the dank jungles of Burma, when one small American infantry force, on its own, achieved a standard for American infantry that the infantry still achieves today.

Appendix 1: Orders of Battle

AMERICAN ORDERS OF BATTLE

Merrill's Marauders—5307th Composite Unit (Provisional)
Order of Battle—24 February 1944
Brig. Gen. Frank D. Merrill—Commanding
Col. Charles N. Hunter—Second in command
Maj. Edward T. Hancock—Rear Base Supply Officer
Maj. Louis J. Williams—Command Post Group

1st Battalion
Lt. Col. William L. Osborne—Commanding

Red Combat Team
Maj. Edward M. Ghiz (to 6 April 1944)
Capt. Tom P. Senff (from 6 April 1944)

White Combat Team
Maj. Caifson Johnson

2d Battalion
Lt. Col. George A. McGee Jr.—Commanding

Blue Combat Team
Maj. Richard W. Healy

Green Combat Team
Capt. Thomas E. Bogardus

3d Battalion
Lt. Col. Charles E. Beach—Commanding

Orange Combat Team
Maj. Lawrence L. Lew (to 4 April 1944)
Maj. Peter A. Petito (from 4 April 1944)

Khaki Combat Team
Maj. Edwin J. Briggs

Merrill's Marauders—5307th Composite Unit (Provisional)
Order of Battle—Third Mission 27 April 1944
Brig. Gen. Frank D. Merrill—Commanding
Col. John E. McCammon—Executive Officer

· H Force
Col. Charles N. Hunter—Commanding

1st Battalion
Lt. Col. William L. Osborne—Commanding
  Red Combat Team
  Capt. Tom P. Senff
  White Combat Team
  Maj. Caifson Johnson
150th Infantry Regiment
(50th Chinese Division)

K Force
Col. Henry L. Kinnison Jr.—Commanding

3d Battalion
Lt. Col. Charles E. Beach—Commanding
  Orange Combat Team
  Maj. Peter A. Petito
  Khaki Combat Team
  Maj. Edwin J. Briggs
88th Infantry Regiment
(30th Chinese Division)

M Force
Lt. Col. George A. McGee Jr.—Commanding

2d Battalion
Kachin Ranger Detachment

————————

Mars Task Force—5332d Brigade (Provisional)
Brig. Gen. Thomas S. Arms—Commanding (to 31 September 1944)
Brig. Gen. John P. Willey—Commanding (from 31 September 1944)
Col. Willis J. Tack—Chief of Staff

1st Chinese Separate Regiment
Col. Lin Kuan-lsiang—Commanding

124th Cavalry Regiment
Col. Milo H. Matteson—Commanding (to October 1944)
Col. Thomas J. Heavey—Commanding (from October 1944)
Col. William Lloyd Osborne—Commanding (from 10 January 1945)
Col. Loren D. Pegg—Commanding (from 13 February 1945)
Lt. Col Loren D. Pegg—Executive Officer (to 13 February 1945)

1st Squadron
Lt. Col. Earl F. Ripstra—Commanding
2d Squadron
Maj. George B. Jordan—Commanding
3d Squadron
Lt. Col. Charles B. Hazeltine Jr.—Commanding

475th Infantry Regiment
Lt. Col. William Lloyd Osborne—Commanding (to 4 October 1944)
Col. Ernest F. Easterbrook—Commanding (from 4 October 1944)
Col. William Lloyd Osborne—Commanding (from 13 February 1945)
Lt. Col. Arthur K. Harrold—Commanding (from 20 April 1945)

1st Battalion
Lt. Col. Caifson Johnson—Commanding
2d Battalion
Lt. Col. Benjamin F. Thrailkill (KIA 1 February 1945)
Maj. John H. Lattin—Commanding (from 1 February 1945)
3d Battalion
Lt. Col. Arthur K. Harrold—Commanding

612th Field Artillery Battalion (Pack)
Maj. John W. Read—Commanding (to 26 September 1944)
Lt. Col. Richard A. Knight—Commanding (from 26 September 1944)
Lt. Col. Severn T. Wallis—Commanding (from 9 November 1944)

613th Field Artillery Battalion (Pack)
Lt. Col. James F. Donovan—Commanding

Japanese Language Translation and Interrogation Team
Lt. William Swain (to September 1944)
Lt. Kan Tagami (from September 1944)

Japanese Language Translation and Interrogation Team
Lt. Gerald Widoff

Other Assigned Units

8th Veterinary Evacuation Hospital
Lt. Col. Elmer W. Young
42d Portable Surgical Hospital
Maj. Harwood L. Stowe
44th Portable Surgical Hospital
Maj. Daniel E. Egbert(to 15 November 1944)
Maj. William C. King(from 15 November 1944)
49th Portable Surgical Hospital
Maj. Sidney Posner
511th Medical Collecting Company
Capt. Charles H. Ransom (Attached 7 February 1945)
Company B, 13th Mountain Medical Battalion (Attached February 1945)
31st Quartermaster Pack Troop
Lieutenant Hulbert—Commanding
33d Quartermaster Pack Troop
Capt. A. B. Higgins—Commanding
35th Quartermaster Pack Troop
Capt. Ralph H. Hatch—Commanding
37th Quartermaster Pack Troop
Capt. Charles M. Peery—Commanding
252d Quartermaster Pack Troop
Capt. William E. Worrall—Commanding
253d Quartermaster Pack Troop
Capt. Hugh F. Torrence—Commanding
7th Chinese Animal Transport Company
Office of Strategic Services Detachment 101—Kachin Rangers
Detachment, 164th Signal Photo Company

Combat Team Assignments

475th Infantry Regimental Combat Team
475th Infantry Regiment
612th Field Artillery Battalion
44th Portable Surgical Hospital
31st Quartermaster Pack Troop
33d Quartermaster Pack Troop

35th Quartermaster Pack Troop
OSS Kachin Rangers, three platoons
7th Chinese Animal Transport Company, half

124th Cavalry Regimental Combat Team
124th Cavalry Regiment, Special
613th Field Artillery Battalion
49th Portable Surgical Hospital
37th Quartermaster Pack Troop
252d Quartermaster Pack Troop
253d Quartermaster Pack Troop
OSS Kachin Rangers, three platoons
7th Chinese Animal Transport Company, half

JAPANESE ORDER OF BATTLE

Southern Army
Gen. Hisaichi Terauchi—Commanding

Burma Area Army
Lt. Gen. Masakazu Kawabe—Commanding

15th Army (Engaged against the British)
Lt. Gen. Renya Mutaguchi—Commanding

15th Infantry Division
Lt. Gen. Masabumi Yamauchi—Commanding
(Relieved 15 May 1944; replaced by Shibata Ryuichi)
31st Infantry Division
Lt. Gen. Kotoku Sato—Commanding
(Relieved June 1944; replaced by Kawada Tsuchitato)
33d Infantry Division
Lt. Gen. Genzo Yanagida, Commanding
(Relieved 15 May 1944; replaced by Nobuo Tanaka)

28th Army (Engaged against the British)
Lt. Gen. Shuzo Sakurai, Commanding

2d Infantry Division
Lt. General Okazaki—Commanding
54th Infantry Division
Lt. General Katamura—Commanding
55th Infantry Division
Lt. General Hanaya—Commanding
72d Independent Mixed Brigade
General Yamamoto, Commanding

33d Army (North Burma)
Lt. Gen. Masaki Honda—Commanding

18th Infantry Division
Lt. Gen. Shinichi Tanaka—Commanding
    55th Infantry Regiment
    56th Infantry Regiment
    114th Infantry Regiment
49th Infantry Division (from mid-May 1944)
Lt. Gen. Saburo Takehara—Commanding
    106th Infantry Regiment
    153d Infantry Regiment
    168th Infantry Regiment
53d Infantry Division
Lt. Gen. Kaoru Takeda—Commanding
    119th Infantry Regiment
    128th Infantry Regiment
    151st Infantry Regiment
56th Infantry Division
Lt. Gen. Yuzo Matsuyama—Commanding
    113th Infantry Regiment
    146th Infantry Regiment
    148th Infantry Regiment
24th Independent Mixed Brigade
Maj. Gen. Yoshihide Hayashi—Commanding
    139th Independent Infantry Battalion
    141st Independent Infantry Battalion

Appendix 2: Combat Awards

Combat Awards to Members of Merrill's Marauders

Distinguished Service Cross
1st Lt. Melvin R. Blair
Pfc. Marvin H. Dean
Pfc. Willard J. D. Lilly

Pfc. Herman Manuel
Pvt. Howard T. Smith
T5 Russell G. Wellman

Legion of Merit
SSgt. John A. Acker
Capt. Charles E. Darlington
(British army)

SSgt. Roy H. Matsumoto
Maj. (M. C.) Melvin A. Schudmak
TSgt. Francis Wonsowicz

Silver Star
TSgt. Edward C. Ammon
Pfc. Marvin H. Anderson
1st Lt. Paul E. Armstrong
MSgt. James C. Ballard
Pfc. Earnest C. Banks
Lt. Col. Charles E. Beach
Pfc. Paul R. Bicknell
Capt. George G. Bonnyman
1st Sgt. Clarence E. Branscomb
Maj. Edwin J. Briggs
Pfc. Daniel V. Carrigan (P)
SSgt. Ellsworth Dalmus
T4 Lewis Day Jr.
Pfc. Harold E. Dibble
MSgt. Ralph E. Duston
Capt. John R. Fair

1st Lt. William Lepore
SSgt. Earl Little
SSgt. James L. Marsh
Lt. Col. George A. McGee Jr.
Pvt. Paul V. Michael
T4 William H. Miles (P)
1st Lt. Robert C. Newman
Pfc. Lambert L. Olson (P)
Pfc. Leonard G. Porath
SSgt. Salvadore F. Rapisarda
1st Sgt. Worth E. Rector
SSgt. Earnest W. Reid
Sgt. Harold Shoemaker
2d Lt. Winslow B. Stevens
T5 Luther E. Sutterfield (P)
2d Lt. John W. Travis

(P) denotes posthumous award

T5 Joseph N. Gomez
Pfc. Everett E. Hudson
Col. Charles N. Hunter
T5 Emory Jones
Col. Henry L. Kinnison Jr.

Pvt. Clayton A. Vantol
1st Lt. Victor J. Weingartner
2d Lt. Philip S. Weld
1st Lt. Samuel V. Wilson

Oak Leaf Cluster to Silver Star
Lt. Col Charles E. Beach
SSgt Ellsworth Dalmus

1st Lt. Samuel V. Wilson

Combat Awards to Members of the Mars Task Force and New Galahad

Medal of Honor
1st Lt. Jack L. Knight
   124th Cavalry Regiment

Distinguished Service Cross
Capt. Shields A. Brubeck
   5307th Composite Unit (Prov.)
Sgt. Fred N. Coleman (P)
   236th Engineer Combat Battalion
Lt. Col. William H. Combs (P)
   209th Engineer Combat Battalion (second award)
1st Lt. Donald W. Delorey
   5307th Composite Unit (Prov.)
Capt. John J. Dunn
   5307th Composite Unit (Prov.)
Pfc. Anthony S. Firenze
   2d Battalion, New Galahad
Pfc. Clifton L. Henderson
   475th Infantry Regiment
SSgt. Alvin O. Miller
   209th Engineer Combat Battalion
Pfc. Herman Moore
   124th Cavalry Regiment
Sgt. George A. Owen
   124th Cavalry Regiment

Pfc. George C. Presterly (P)
  Combat Engineer Regiment (Prov.)
TSgt. Richard E. Roe (P)
  5307th Composite Unit (Prov.)
Pfc. Anthony Whitaker (P)
  124th Cavalry Regiment

Appendix 3: Medal of Honor Citation

Knight, Jack L.
Rank and Organization: First Lieutenant, U.S. Army, 124th
   Cavalry Regiment, Mars Task Force
Place and Date: Near Loi-Kang, Burma, 2 February 1945
Entered Service At: Weatherford, Texas
Birth: Garner, Texas
General Order Number: 44, 6 June 1945

Citation: He led his cavalry troop against heavy concentrations of enemy mortar, artillery and small-arms fire. After taking the troop's objective and while making preparations for a defense, he discovered a nest of Japanese pillboxes and foxholes to the right front. Preceding his men by at least 10 feet, he immediately led an attack. Singlehandedly he knocked out 2 enemy pillboxes and killed the occupants of several foxholes. While attempting to knock out a third pillbox, he was struck and blinded by an enemy grenade. Although unable to see, he rallied his platoon and continued forward in the assault on the remaining pillboxes. Before the task was completed he fell mortally wounded. First Lieutenant Knight's gallantry and intrepidity were responsible for the successful elimination of most of the Japanese positions and served as an inspiration to officers and men of his troop.

Appendix 4: United States Army Forces, China-Burma-India Theater of Operations[1]

Lt. Gen. Daniel I. Sultan, Commanding
  (from 19 October 1944)
Gen. Joseph W. Stilwell, Commanding[2]
  (from 1 August 1944)
Lt. Gen. Joseph W. Stilwell, Commanding
  (from 9 December 1943)
Maj. Gen. Thomas G. Hearn, Commanding
  (from 19 November 1943)
Lt. Gen. Joseph W. Stilwell, Commanding
  (from 8 June 1943)
Maj. Gen. Raymond A. Wheeler, Commanding
  (from 24 April 1943)
Lt. Gen. Joseph W. Stilwell, Commanding
  (from 4 March 1942)

Services of Supply, India-Burma Theater
Maj. Gen. William E. R. Covell, Commanding
  (from 10 February 1945)
Brig. Gen. John A. Warden, Commanding
  (from 18 December 1944)
Maj. Gen. William E. R. Covell, Commanding[2]
  (from 29 November 1943)
Brig. Gen. William E. R. Covell, Commanding
  (from 15 November 1943)

1. Office of the Chief of Military History, *Order of Battle of the United States Army Ground Forces in World War II, Pacific Theater of Operations.* (Washington, D.C.: Office of the Chief of Military History, Department of the Army, 1959), 217–263.
2. This was a promotion only; there was no change in status.

Maj. Gen. Raymond A. Wheeler, Commanding[2]
  (from 11 March 1942)
Brig. Gen. Raymond A. Wheeler, Commanding
  (from 28 February 1942)

Base Section Number 1 (Karachi)

Brig. Gen. John A. Warden, Commanding
  (from 23 January 1944)
Col. Thomas H. Rees Jr., Commanding
  (from 11 May 1943)

Base Section Number 2 (Mysore)

Col. Robert R. Neyland Jr., Commanding
  (from 13 November 1944)
Maj. Gen. Gilbert X. Cheves, Commanding
  (from 23 January 1944)

Base Section Number 3 (Ledo)

Col. Lewis A. Pick, Commanding
  (from 17 October 1943)
Brig. Gen. John S. Arrowsmith, Commanding
  (from 10 December 1942)

Advance Section Number 1 (Agra)

Col. Robert R. Neyland Jr., Commanding
  (from 28 June 1944)
Col. Lewis P. Jorday, Commanding
  (from 1 February 1944)

Advance Section Number 2 (Assam)

Brig. Gen. Joseph A. Cranston, Commanding
  (from 31 January 1944)
Col. Robert S. Coughlin, Commanding
  (from 8 May 1943)

Advance Base Section Number 3 (Kunming)

Brig. Gen. Paul F. Yount, Commanding
  (from 16 May 1945)
Col. Walter E. Lorence, Commanding
  (from 24 April 1945)

Advance Base Section Number 4 (Kweilin)

Lt. Col. Henry A. Ryroade, Commanding
(from 1 August 1943)
Maj. Charles F. B. Price Jr., Commanding
(from 20 March 1943)

Construction Services, Service of Supply, CBI

Brig. Gen. Thomas F. Farrell, Commanding
(from 15 January 1944)

Services of Supply, Ramgarh Training Area

Lt. Col. W. A. Fuller, Commanding
(from 22 December 1943)
Col. W. H. Holcombe, Commanding
(from 15 August 1942)

Ramgarh Training Center[3]

Col. Raymond R. Tourtillott, Commanding
(from 1 May 1945)
Col. Donald A. Young, Commanding
(from 31 January 1945)
Brig. Gen. Frederick McCabe, Commanding
(from 30 June 1944)
Brig. Gen. William E. Bergin, Commanding
(from 30 April 1944)
Col. Frederick McCabe, Commanding
(from 30 June 1942)

Chinese Training and Combat Command (Ramgarh)

Brig. Gen. Frank Dorn, Commanding
(from 17 November 1944)
Lt. Gen. Joseph W. Stilwell, Commanding
(from 21 January 1943)

The Chinese Army in India

Lt. Gen. Daniel I. Sultan, Commanding
(from 3 November 1944)

---

3. This was an American-staffed and American-operated training center for Chinese military forces.

Lt. Gen. Joseph W. Stilwell, Commanding
   (from 23 October 1942)

Combat Troops, Ledo Section
Brig. Gen. Raymond A. Wheeler, Commanding
   (from 18 February 1943)
Brig. Gen. Haydon L. Boatner, Commanding
   (from 6 April 1943)
Y Force Operations Staff (Kunming)[4]
Brig. Gen. Frank Dorn, Chief of Staff[5]
Z Force Operations Staff (Chungking)[6]
Brig. Gen. Malcolm F. Lindsey, Chief of Staff[7]
   (from 1 January 1944)
Brig. Gen. Thomas F. Timberman, Chief of Staff
   (from 4 September 1944)
Col. Harwood C. Bowman, Chief of Staff
   (from 21 October 1944)
Brig. Gen. Malcolm F. Lindsey, Chief of Staff
   (from 24 October 1944)

Northern Combat Area Command
Lt. Gen. Raymond A. Wheeler, Commanding
   (from 22 June 1945)
Lt. Gen. Daniel I. Sultan, Commanding
   (from 27 October 1944)
Lt. Gen. Joseph W. Stilwell, Commanding
   (from 17 July 1944)
Brig. Gen. Haydon L. Boatner, Commanding
   (from 1 February 1944)

5307th Composite Unit (Provisional)
Col. John E. McCammon, Commanding
   (from 20 May 1944)

---

4. This was created to raise thirty Chinese divisions in Yunnan Province to fight the Japanese troops there.
5. General Stilwell commanded by means of General Dorn.
6. The Z Force was created to raise thirty Chinese divisions to fight the Japanese in eastern China. It was disbanded 17 November 1944.
7. General Stilwell commanded by means of the chief of staff.

Brig. Gen. Frank D. Merrill, Commanding
  (from 26 April 1944)
Col. Charles N. Hunter, Commanding
  (from 29 March 1944)
Brig. Gen. Frank D. Merrill, Commanding
  (from 6 January 1944)

5315th Infantry Training Center (Provisional)[8]
Brig. Gen. Thomas S. Arms, Commanding
  (from 1 November 1943)

American Delhi Military Area Command
Maj. A. T. McHugh, Commanding
  (from 11 August 1945)
Col. S. C. Hilton, Commanding
  (from 19 April 1945)
Col. D. C. Eberson, Commanding
  (from 23 November 1944)
Lt. Col. Mason H. Lucas, Commanding
  (from 15 June 1944)

United States Forces, India-Burma Theater
Lt. Gen. Raymond A. Wheeler, Commanding
  (from 23 January 1945)
Lt. Gen. Daniel I. Sultan, Commanding
  (from 24 October 1944)

United States Forces, China Theater
Lt. Gen. Albert C. Wedemeyer, Commanding
  (from 9 April 1945)
Maj. Gen. Claire L. Chennault, Commanding
  (from 20 February 1945)
Lt. Gen. Albert C. Wedemeyer, Commanding
  (from 31 October 1944)
Maj. Gen. Claire L. Chennault, Commanding
  (from 24 October 1944)

8. Disbanded 25 July 1944.

Services of Supply, China Theater
Maj. Gen. Henry S. Aurand, Commanding
   (from 25 May 1945)
Maj. Gen. Gilbert X. Cheves, Commanding
   (from 12 November 1944)

Chinese Combat Command (Provisional)
Maj. Gen. Robert B. McClure, Commanding
   (from 28 January 1945)
Col. Woods King, Commanding
   (from 14 January 1945)
Col. Albert H. Stackpole, Commanding
   (from 9 January 1945)

Chinese Training Command (Provisional)
Brig. Gen. John W. Middleton, Commanding
   (from 6 January 1945)

Appendix 5: Chronology: China-Burma-India Theater of Operations, 1944–1945

1 January 1944: General Stilwell creates an operations staff for Zebra force.

2 January 1944: Maj. Gen. Daniel I. Sultan arrives at New Delhi to act as General Stilwell's deputy for administrative matters.

6 January 1944: General Sultan advises General Stilwell that SEAC planners want to bypass Burma until Germany is defeated and then mount a major offensive beginning with an invasion of Sumatra. Stilwell responds by sending a mission headed by General Boatner to Washington to present his views.

9 January 1944: The Chinese 38th Division fights for Tanai in Hukawng Valley.

14 January 1944: President Roosevelt, in a message to Chiang Kai-shek, asks that Yunnan forces be committed in Burma, hinting that lend-lease supplies could suffer if his request is declined.

16 January 1944: Chiang Kai-shek replies to President Roosevelt that he will stop providing food and housing to American troops in China after 1 March 1944 unless his request for a billion-dollar loan is approved. Admiral Mountbatten offers British troops to replace the Americans leading Chinese troops in Burma, but General Stilwell instead takes operational control of Galahad for this purpose.

21 January 1944: General Stilwell plans an armored attack with supporting infantry to strike for Walawbum.

25 January 1944: Elements of the Chinese 22d Division enter the fight for Hukawng Valley.

29 January 1944: Attempts by elements of the Chinese 38th Division to place a roadblock along Kamaing Road fail due to the diversion of forces by the division commander.

4 February 1944: The Chinese 22d Division moves to outflank Japanese forces, who retire before Chinese forces can attack.

5 February 1944: British Brigadier General Wingate's special force begins its southward movement from Ledo. Five brigades (77th, 111th,

14th, 16th, and 23d) move behind Japanese lines, supported by the U.S. 5318th Air Unit, under the command of Col. Philip G. Cochran.

7 February 1944: President Roosevelt replies to Chiang Kai-shek that he will study the request for a loan, while China advances the U.S. the cost of U.S. military expenditures for March, April, and May 1944.

8 February 1944: General Stilwell is advised that a major Chinese offensive is about to begin, according to General Headquarters, India.

10 February 1944: Several major units of the British XIV Army are isolated by Japanese attack.

16–18 February 1944: The Chinese 22d Division attempts to encircle an enemy force but becomes lost, permitting the enemy to escape without loss.

22 February 1944: Brig. Gen. Frank Merrill receives oral orders for operation to trap Japanese forces.

24 February 1944: The 5307th Composite Unit (Provisional) begins its march from Ninghyen to Hukawng Valley.

25 February 1944: The first contact with enemy patrols is made by the 5307th Composite Unit (Provisional).

2 March 1944: The 5307th Composite Unit (Provisional), Galahad, crosses the Tanai River. Advance elements of British 16th Long Range Penetration Brigade cross the Chindwin.

3 March 1944: Galahad blocks the road on either side of Walawbum and receives an airdrop near Lagang Ga. The First Provisional Tank Group (Chinese-American) reaches Ngao Ga.

3–6 March 1944: The battle of Walawbum is fought.

11 March 1944: Air insertion of all long-range penetration brigades of the special force is completed.

13 March 1944: The 1st Battalion, Galahad, reaches Nakuy Bum.

18 March 1944: Galahad is ordered by General Stilwell to block approaches to the Tanai Valley from the south.

19 March 1944: Galahad's 2d and 3d Battalions are ordered to block the Kamaing Road near Inkangahtawng while the Orange Combat Team patrols near Janpan.

23 March 1944: Galahad, less the 1st Battalion, is in position to block the Kamaing Road. The Chinese 22d Division moves forward in a flanking maneuver.

24 March 1944: Galahad attempts an attack on Inkangahtawng, but finding opposition too strong, the 2d Battalion withdraws to the Manpin area while the 3d Battalion pulls back to Ngagahtawng.

26 March–9 April 1944: The battle of Nhpum Ga is fought.

3 April 1944: General Stilwell, at a meeting with Admiral Mountbatten and Gen. William Slim, commanding the British XIV Army, agree that two long-range penetration brigades will continue to assist the NCAC in the northern Burma campaign despite the serious situation in the British front at both Imphal and Kohima.

10 April 1944: The British 2d Infantry Division begins clearing operations at Kohima.

14 April 1944: Admiral Mountbatten advises British chiefs of staff that northern Burma campaign should be limited to the capture of Myitkyina.

15 April 1944: Chiang Kai-shek, warned of a coming Japanese air offensive, urges Stilwell to advance cautiously in Mogaung Valley. The Chinese 50th Division is airlifted to Maingkwan.

17 April 1944: The Japanese offensive in Hunan Province, China, begins successfully.

21 April 1944: Task Force End Run is formed for the drive on Myitkyina.

24 April 1944: Galahad's 1st and 2d Battalions begin marching to Naubum in preparation for the drive on Myitkyina.

15 May 1944: Elements of Task Force End Run approach the outskirts of Myitkyina.

17 May 1944: Elements of Task Force End Run seize Myitkyina airfield.

18 May 1944: Galahad assaults Myitkyina town while elements of the Chinese 50th Division seize the railroad station. Elements of the Chinese 30th Division garrison the airfield.

19 May–3 August 1944: The battle of Myitkyina is fought.

27 May 1944: The 209th Engineer (Combat) Battalion reinforces Galahad during the battle for Myitkyina.

30 May 1944: General Boatner replaces Col. John E. McCammon as head of the Myitkyina task force.

1 June 1944: Additional engineer combat battalions are rushed to Myitkyina to reinforce the depleted Galahad remnants.

2 June 1944: Chinese forces at Myitkyina begin formal siege operations, including tunneling toward Japanese positions.

26 June 1944: Brigadier General Theodore F. Wessels takes command of the Myitkyina task force, relieving General Boatner, who has been stricken with malaria.

29 June 1944: Colonel Charles N. Hunter takes command of all U.S. troops at Myitkyina.

27 July 1944: The 3d Battalion, New Galahad, takes the northern airfield and turns it over to the 209th and 236th Engineer (Combat) Battalions for defense.

30 July 1944: The Japanese commander at Myitkyina authorizes withdrawal and commits suicide.

3 August 1944: Chinese troops secure Myitkyina.

7 October 1944: The Chinese 22d Division, which has been training at Myitkyina since its capture, begins the movement to Kamaing.

11 October 1944: Chiang Kai-shek requests that President Roosevelt relieve General Stilwell immediately.

15 October 1944: A general offensive by the NCAC begins to clear northern Burma and open supply routes to China. Included in the attacking forces is Mars Task Force, consisting of the 1st (Chinese) Regiment, Separate; the 475th U.S. Infantry Regiment; and the 124th Cavalry Regiment.

24 October 1944: The China-Burma-India theater is divided into two distinct theaters of operation. The new India-Burma theater will be commanded by General Sultan, and the new China theater will be commanded by Maj. Gen. Albert C. Wedemeyer.

27 October 1944: The 124th U.S. Cavalry Regiment arrives at the training area.

3 November 1944: The Chinese 22d Division reaches and begins to cross the Irrawaddy River near Shwegu.

15 November 1944: The U.S. 475th Infantry Regiment begins their movement to the front to assist the Chinese 22d Division's advance.

30 November 1944: Chiang Kai-shek orders that the 22d Division be withdrawn from Burma for the defense of China.

6 December 1944: The U.S. 475th Infantry Regiment is ordered to relieve the Chinese 22d Division in Mo-hlaing area.

9 December 1944: The 475th Infantry Regiment joins the Chinese 22d Division in retaking positions lost to the Japanese counterattack.

10 December 1944: The 475th Infantry Regiment takes over positions of the Chinese 22d Division to permit that unit to return to China as ordered by Chiang Kai-shek.

13–14 December 1944: The 475th Infantry Regiment repels an enemy attack in Tonkwa area.

16 December 1944: The 124th U.S. Cavalry moves forward from Myitkyina toward Bhamo to assume a position in the front lines.

31 December 1944: Units of Mars Task Force are ordered to assemble at Mong Wi. The 1st (Chinese) Separate Regiment will be held in the NCAC reserve.

2 January 1945: The 475th Infantry Regiment crosses the Shewli River on bridges placed by the Chinese 50th Division.

4 January 1945: The 124th Cavalry searches for a crossing site over the Shewli River while awaiting an airdrop.

16 January 1945: Mars Task Force (less the 1st Chinese Separate Regiment) prepares for an assault on the Burma Road near Namhpakka.

17 January 1945: Mars Task Force clears the village of Namhkam and moves forward to the ridge overlooking the Burma Road.

18 January 1945: Mars Task Force secures Loi-Kang Ridge and prepares to open artillery fire on any enemy forces who are using the Burma Road. The Japanese rush reinforcements to the area.

18–27 January 1945: A battle is fought to open the Burma Road. The road officially opens on 27 January 1945 when the Chinese 38th Division links up with forces from China.

28 January 1945: The first road convoy on the Burma Road to China crosses the border into China.

3 February 1945: The 475th Infantry Regiment opens an attack to clear the rest of Loi-Kang Ridge.

4 February 1945: Loi-Kang Ridge is declared secured. United States forces assume defensive postures.

14 March 1945: The air movement of U.S. forces (Mars Task Force) to China begins. Except for one stronghold, Mandalay falls to the British XIV Army.

Appendix 6: Colonel Hunter's Letter to General Stilwell[1]

25 May 1944

SUBJECT: Galahad Project

TO: Commanding General, USAF-CBI, through the Commanding General Rear Ech. USAF-CBI, APO 885

1. It is desired to bring to the attention of the Commanding General certain facts which, in the opinion of the undersigned, either have not been brought to his attention before, or which are not being given sufficient weight to future planning.

a. Morale: The morale of Galahad has been sustained only because of promises that:

(1) Galahad would not be used as a spearhead for Chinese Troops.

(2) Immediately upon arrival at Myitkyina and the capture of the airfield, its personnel would be flown out for rest and reorganization.

2. Upon arrival in India, Galahad was treated by USAF-CBI HQ as a visiting unit for which the theater felt no responsibility. It was, and still is the opinion that, so far as Combat Hq. is concerned, this attitude has not changed. The following facts bear out the above conclusions:

a. No theater officer met Galahad on its arrival.

b. No adequate preparations were made for its reception.

3. Galahad was debarked at Bombay and moved to the transit camp at Deolali, where the accommodations and food furnished were a disgrace to the British Military authorities. The period of training at Deolali was not entirely wasted, but health and food conditions were such that, in the opinion of the writer, they contributed to the later breakdown in health and morale experienced by personnel from the South and Southwest Pacific Commands.

1. Reproduced in Col. Charles N. Hunter, *Galahad* (San Antonio, Tx.: Naylor, 1963), 192–194.

4. Since Colonel Brink was assigned to the G.S.C. and as such unable to assume command,[2] but by your direction was charged with responsibility for training, organization and administration, many conflicts arose in jurisdiction between the undersigned and Colonel Brink as to the amount of time to be devoted to organization, training, administration, sanitation and basic subjects. Since the unit was to fight shortly, Colonel Brink insisted on, and the bulk of available time was spent on combat training and organization, with a minimum of time being devoted to discipline and other essential subjects of a balanced training program for a newly organized unit, as such simple things as the "issue, marking, care and cleaning of equipment."

5. Galahad was organized as a composite unit which prevented its use of colors, insignia, or other morale building paraphanelia normal to other units. This matter was taken up with Rear Ech. USAF-CBI several times with no apparent results.

6. Very few American officers visited this unit while in training as long as its status was indefinite, and it was difficult to get the normal support with reference to supply, morale, medical, service, and other requirements normal to a unit assigned to the theater. Suddenly General Merrill was assigned to command the unit. Colonel Brink left, and the unit received treatment only comparable to that afforded the prodigal son. American soldiers being of a discerning nature and intelligent, naturally are sensitive to the treatment they receive from higher headquarters. Galahad personnel are all familiar with the conditions and facts outlined above and are gradually growing bitter. This is especially true of the officers whose morale has been adversely affected by the following additional factors:

a. General Merrill's statement that no officers would be promoted until the termination of the operation.

b. Colonel Cannon's reported report that at Nhpum the undersigned was only worried about promotion for officers.

c. The report freely circulated that General Boatner called Major Petito, Captain Bogardus, and L[ieutenan]t Sievers "yellow."[3]

---

2. Colonel Hunter here refers to Colonel Brink's assignment to the general staff corps, which under contemporary U.S. Army regulations prohibited him from commanding a combat unit.
3. This refers to the incident of the early patrol in which these officers were unable to accomplish the mission. Apparently, General Boatner ascribed that failure to personal cowardice. These officers all later distinguished themselves in the campaign, Major Petito commanding from 4 April 1944 the Orange Combat Team, which was heavily involved in the fighting.

d. The unpleasant relationship existing between all Galahad officers and the officers of Combat Hq.

e. The per diem situation now existent in the theater.[4]

7. Repeated reports have been made [in] reference to the health of the command. Apparently these reports are not believed, since no apparent effort has been made to verify this. It can be reiterated again that Galahad is practically ineffective as a combat unit at the present time, and its presence here is rapidly leading to a false sense of security, which is dangerous.

8. Although this unit has been in continuous contact with the Japanese and has performed capably in the field to date, no awards or decorations, no indication of appreciation, and no citations have been received by any personnel of this unit as far as can be determined by the writer, with the exception of the award of the Purple Heart which is routine. This condition can only indicate a lack of interest by higher headquarters or worse, a "don't care attitude" which creates hard feelings.

9. Conclusion: In view of the above the following recommendations are submitted:

a. That on the termination of the present operations, Galahad as an organization be disbanded, and its personnel be reassigned to other units in the theater through the Army Classification Service.

b. That in the future American Infantry Combat Units assigned to this theater be treated in such a manner as to instill in the unit a pride of organization, a desire to fight, and a feeling of being a part of a united effort, and further that every effort be made to overcome the feeling that such units are no better than Chinese Troops, and deserving of no better treatment.

c. That deserved promotions be awarded to officers of this command.

d. That no other theater personnel be promoted as long as officers of this unit are not promoted.

Charles N. Hunter
Colonel, Inf.
Commanding Officer, Galahad

---

4. U.S. Army officers assigned to the China-Burma-India theater were entitled to extra pay of approximately $2.50 per diem. For some reason this rule did not apply to officers assigned to Galahad.

Chapter Notes

Introduction

1. For examples of Stilwell's attitude toward the British and their commanders, see Theodore H. White, ed. *The Stilwell Papers* (New York: William H. Sloane, 1948). This book is filled with the general's diary entries and letters, which contain many derogatory references to most things British.

2. For a full explanation of prewar views on a mainland campaign see Edward J. Miller, *War Plan Orange: The U.S. Strategy to Defeat Japan, 1897–1945* (Annapolis: Naval Institute Press, 1991).

Chapter 1

1. Henry L. Stimson, *On Active Service in Peace and War* (New York: Harper & Bros., 1947), pp. 529–530.

2. Ibid., 530.

3. Quoted in Louis Allen, *Burma: The Longest War* (New York: St. Martin's Press, 1984), p. 58.

4. General Marshall to Field Marshall Sir John Dill, memorandum, 19 March 1942, *The Papers of George Catlett Marshall*, vol. 3, ed. Larry I. Bland and Sharon Ritenour Stevens (Baltimore: Johns Hopkins University Press, 1991), p. 140.

5. James W. Dunn, "The Ledo Road," in Barry W. Fowle, General Editor. *Builders and Fighters: U.S. Army Engineers in World War II.* (Ft. Belvoir, VA.: Office of History, U.S. Army Corps of Engineers, 1992), p. 329.

6. Maurice Matloff, *Strategic Planning for Coalition Warfare, 1943–1944* (Washington, DC: Center of Military History, 1959), chapter 10.

Chapter 2

1. *The Stilwell Papers*, ed. Theodore W. White (New York: William H. Sloane, 1948), p. 219.

2. Military Intelligence Division, U.S. War Department, *Merrill's Marauders, February–May 1944*, American Forces in Action Series (Washington, DC: Military Intelligence Division, U.S. War Department), 4 June 1945, p. 10.

3. Phil Smart, letter to the *Burman News*, November 1994.

4. Charlton Ogburn Jr., *The Marauders* (New York: Harper & Bros., 1959), p. 33.

5. Quoted in Lynn Crost, *Honor By Fire: Japanese Americans at War in Europe and the Pacific* (Novato, CA: Presidio Press, 1994). See also Joseph D. Harrington, *Yankee Samurai: The Secret Role of Nisei in America's Pacific Victory* (Detroit: Pettigrew Press, 1979).

6. This equipment was sent in more than twenty shipments, some of which did not reach India until the Marauders were fighting for their lives at Myitkyina.

7. Lieutenant Colonel John B. George, *Shots Fired in Anger: A Rifleman's View of the War in the Pacific, 1942–1945, Including the Campaign of Guadalcanal and Fighting with Merrill's Marauders in the Jungles of Burma* (Washington, DC: National Rifle Association of America, 1981), p. 419.

8. Stanley Silver, telephone interview with the author, 19 October 1997.

9. Quoted in Olga Gruhzit-Hoyt, *They Also Served: American Women in World War II* (New York: Birch Lane Press, 1995), p. 232.

10. George, op. cit., p. 433.

11. "History of the China-Burma-India Theater," section II, chapter 14 (College Park, MD: National Archives and Records Service), 5–7. Colonel Hunter recalls the date as 1 January 1944 and that the first name was the 5307th Composite Regiment (Provisional), which was changed that same date to the 5307th Composite Unit (Provisional). See Colonel Charles N. Hunter, *Galahad* (San Antonio, TX.: Naylor, 1963), p. 6.

12. Hunter, op. cit., p. 8.

13. Ibid., p. 10.

14. "An Outline of Frank D. Merrill's Life As Remembered by Lucy D. Merrill, Widow," letter to the *Burman News*, February 1996.

15. Barbara W. Tuchman, *Stilwell and the American Experience in China, 1911–1945* (New York: Macmillan, 1970), p. 272.

16. Hunter, op. cit., p. 4. He also mentions General Merrill's "flat feet, a weak heart and a rather subservient attitude toward his superiors."

17. Stilwell, op. cit., p. 276.

18. Quoted in Richard Dunlop, *Behind Japanese Lines with the OSS in Burma* (New York: Rand McNally, 1979), p. 275.

19. James H. Stone, *Crisis Fleeting: Original Reports on Military Medicine in India and Burma in the Second World War* (Washington: DC: Office of the Surgeon General, 1968), p. 296.

20. Dave Richardson, "A Different Kind of Volunteer: Paper Warrior: The Story of a Soldier Correspondent in World War II," *Burman News*, February 1995.

Chapter 3

1. Charlton Ogburn Jr., *The Marauders* (New York: Harper & Bros., 1959) p. 91.

2. Colonel Charles N. Hunter, *Galahad* (San Antonio, TX: Naylor, 1963), p. 31.

3. Dr. James E. Hopkins, "Burma: 15 February–8 June 1944," reprinted in the *Burman News*, May 1991.

4. Colonel Logan Weston, letter to the *Burman News*, November 1992.

5. Charles F. Romanus and Riley Sunderland, *Stilwell's Command Problems: China-Burma-India Theater, U.S. Army in World War II* (Washington, DC: Center of Military History, 1956), p. 36.

6. Ibid., p. 108. The cost took into consideration that as many as fourteen parachutes, at $72 each, were required for dropping one ton of supplies.

7. Ibid., p. 147.

8. Ibid.

9. There are several versions of this engagement from Marauder veterans. None, however, differ greatly except for who was there and who did what.

10. Hopkins, op. cit.

11. Weston, op. cit.

12. Ibid.

13. Hunter, op. cit., p. 37. Lieutenant Weston did not receive a Silver Star for this action. Colonel Beach, who also was recommended by Colonel Hunter for his conduct at Walawabum, eventually was awarded a Silver Star after returning to the United States.

14. As quoted by Sgt. Dave Richardson, "The Dead End Kids," *The Best of Yank, The Army Weekly* (New York: World, 1945), p. 92.

15. Ibid.

16. Ibid., p. 94.

17. Hopkins, op. cit.

18. Hunter, op. cit., p. 38.

19. Takuma Hirose, "Hukawng Operations in Burma War," *Burman News*, May 1990. The history department of the U.S. Army Military Institute, in Carlisle Barracks, Pennsylvania, calls this officer Miyama.

20. Al Fedder, letter to the editor, July 1994, *Burman News*.

21. James H. Stone, ed., *Crises Fleeting: Original Reports on Military Medicine in India and Burma in the Second World War* (Washington, DC: Office of the Surgeon General, 1969), p. 323.

22. Weston, op. cit.

23. Ed King, letter to the *Burman News*, February 1994.

24. Hunter, op. cit., p. 47.

25. Jack Girsham with Lowell Thomas, *Burma Jack* (New York: Norton, 1971), pp. 145–146.

Chapter 4

1. Michael Howard, *Strategic Deception in the Second World War* (New York: Norton, 1990), chapter 10.

2. Field Marshall Sir William Slim, *Defeat Into Victory* (New York: Random House, 1961), p. 202.

3. Quoted in Richard Dunlop, *Behind Japanese Lines: With the OSS in Burma* (New York: Rand McNally, 1979), p. 278.

4. Charlton Ogburn Jr., *The Marauders* (New York. Harper & Bros., 1959), pp. 140–141.

5. Military Intelligence Division, U.S. War Department, *Merrill's*

Marauders, February–May 1944, American Forces in Action Series (Washington, DC: Military Intelligence Division, U.S. War Department, 1945), p. 53.

6. Ogburn, op. cit., p. 171.

7. Ibid., p. 183.

8. Colonel Charles N. Hunter, *Galahad* (San Antonio, TX: Naylor, 1963), p. 53.

9. Quoted in Dunlop, op. cit., p. 283.

10. Hunter, op. cit., p. 54.

11. Ibid. This acquisition makes Galahad the only American combat unit in World War II to employ elephants as a part of its routine combat training.

12. Ibid., p. 58.

13. Ibid., p. 61.

Chapter 5

1. Colonel Charles N. Hunter, *Galahad* (San Antonio, TX: Naylor, 1963), 72.

2. Ibid., p. 73. "Shudmak" refers to Maj. Melvin A. Shudmak, the unit's chief medical officer.

3. James E. T. Hopkins, M.D., Henry G. Stelling, M.D., and Tracy S. Voorhees, "The Marauders and the Microbes," in *Crisis Fleeting: Original Reports on Military Medicine in India and Burma in the Second World War*, ed. James H. Stone (Washington, DC: Office of the Surgeon General, 1969), p. 322. Hopkins and Stelling were battalion medical officers with the Marauders. Colonel Voorhees was an inspector general sent from Washington to investigate medical conditions in the theater.

4. Ibid., p. 328.

5. Military Intelligence Division, U.S. War Department, *Merrill's Marauders, February–May 1944*, 4 June 1945 (Washington, DC: Military Intelligence Division, U.S. War Department), p. 80. "Lew" refers to Maj. Lawrence L. Lew's Orange Combat Team of the 3d Battalion.

6. John ("Red") Acker, "Artillery Comes to the Rescue," *Burman News*, May 1992.

7. Ibid.

8. It should be noted that in some Chindit operations going on

at that time, it became necessary for the Commonwealth soldiers to abandon the wounded in order for most of the unit to survive.

9. Military Intelligence Division, op. cit., p. 83.

10. Dale Abbott, "Nhpum Ga Retold," *Burman News*, November 1993.

11. Military Intelligence Division, op. cit., p. 87.

12. Clarence Branscomb, "Walawbum to Shaduzup to Nhpum Ga," *Burman News*, November 1990.

13. Hopkins et al., op. cit., p. 332.

14. Hunter, op. cit., p. 83.

15. Ibid., pp. 85–86.

16. Ibid., p. 87.

17. Ibid., p. 88.

Chapter 6

1. Charlton Ogburn Jr., *The Marauders* (New York: Harper & Bros., 1959), p. 227.

2. Ibid.

3. Colonel Charles N. Hunter, *Galahad*, (San Antonio, TX.: Naylor, 1963), p. 94. For Lieutenant Ogburn's concerns, see Ogburn, op. cit., p. 131.

4. Ibid., p. 98. Colonel Hunter recalls finally speaking to Colonel Beach and giving him "a lecture on the proper use of the radio . . ."

5. Ibid., p. 99.

6. Charles F. Romanus and Riley Sunderland, *Stilwell's Command Problems: U.S. Army in World War II* (Washington, DC: Center of Military History, 1956), p. 226.

7. Staff Sergeant Clarence E. Branscomb, letter to the *Burman News*, November 1989.

8. Ibid.

9. Hunter, op. cit., p. 109.

10. Ibid., p. 115.

11. Ibid.

12. Theodore H. White, ed., *The Stilwell Papers* (New York: William H. Sloane, 1948), p. 296.

13. Roy S. Appleton, letter to the *Burman News*, May 1999. Mr. Appleton was one of the eight enlisted men on the first plane.

14. Ibid.

15. Stilwell, op. cit., p. 230.

16. Ian Fellowes-Gordon, *The Magic War: The Battle for North Burma* (New York: Scribner, 1971), p. 143.

17. Won-Loy Chan, *Burma: The Untold Story* (Novato, CA: Presidio Press, 1986), p. 59.

18. Quoted in Barbara Brooks Tomblin, *G.I. Nightingales: The Army Nurse Corps in World War II* (Lexington: University Press of Kentucky, 1996), p. 158.

19. James E. T. Hopkins, M.D., Henry G. Stelling, M.D., and Tracy S. Voorhees, "The Marauders and the Microbes," in *Crisis Fleeting: Original Reports on Military Medicine in India and Burma in the Second World War*, ed. James H. Stone (Washington, DC: Office of the Surgeon General, 1969), pp. 346–348.

Chapter 7

1. Shelford Bidwell, *The Chindit War: Stilwell, Wingate, and the Campaign in Burma, 1944* (New York. Macmillan, 1979), p. 260.

2. This is a standard British army designation that refers to the 4th Battalion, 9th Gurkha Rifles (Regiment).

3. Charles F. Romanus and Riley Sunderland, *Stilwell's Command Problems, U.S. Army in World War II* (Washington, DC: Center of Military History, 1955), p. 236.

4. Theodore H. White, ed., *The Stilwell Papers* (William H. Sloane, 1948), p. 298.

5. Colonel Charles N. Hunter, *Galahad* (San Antonio, TX.: Naylor, 1963), p. 125.

6. Barbara W. Tuchman, *Stilwell and the American Experience in China, 1911–1945* (New York: Macmillan, 1971), p. 450.

7. Stilwell, op. cit., p. 300.

8. This unattributed remark appears in several memoirs of the campaign.

9. Hunter, op. cit., pp. 122–123.

10. Colonel Hunter's letter is reproduced in Appendix 6. The question of decorations for bravery is explained by a tale that officers of the 3d Battalion "conspired" among themselves after Walawbum to recommend each other for awards. General Merrill upon

hearing this story ordered that no awards be issued until the end of the campaign. The existence of the "conspiracy" has never been proven.

11. Colonel James D. Holland (Ret.), letter to the *Burman News*, November 1987.

12. Ogburn, op. cit., p. 255.

13. "History of the 236th Engineer Combat Battalion for 1944," 236th Engineer Combat Battalion records, Record Group 407 (College Park, MD: National Archives and Records Service).

14. Ibid. This history includes a list of awards and decorations.

15. For a detailed account of this battle, see Bidwell, op. cit. For the story of another epic British Chindit battle, see John Masters, *The Road Past Mandalay* (London: Michael Joseph, 1961). Brigade Major Masters recounts the fates of wounded men too weak to travel when the block had to be abandoned.

16. Arthur W. Wilson, letter to the author, 21 November 1997.

17. Quoted in the *Burman News*, May 1987.

18. Boatner to Stilwell, letter, quoted in Romanus and Sunderland, op. cit., p. 242.

19. Headquarters, United States Army forces, China, Burma, India, General Orders #78, 20 July 1944 (College Park, MD: National Archives and Records Service).

20. Ibid.

21. Ibid.

22. Headquarters, United States Army forces, China, Burma, India, General Orders #131, 12 October 1944 (College Park, MD: National Archives and Records Service).

23. Ibid.

24. General Orders #78, op. cit.

25. Won-Loy Chan, *Burma: The Untold Story*, (Novato, CA: Presidio Press, 1986), p. 68.

26. Hunter, op. cit., p. 181.

27. Romanus and Sunderland, in the official army history, *Time Runs Out in the CBI*, state that this was Company F. However, the author has located several survivor memoirs that clearly indicate that it was Company G that was destroyed in the ambush.

28. J. T. Tidwell, letter to the *Burman News*, February 1990.

29. Captain Chan reports that the Japanese were dressed in Chinese army uniforms. See Won-Loy Chan, op. cit., p. 71.

30. Headquarters, United States Army Forces, China, Burma, India, General Orders #131, 12 October 1944 (College Park, MD: National Archives and Records Service).

31. Ibid.

32. Chan, op. cit., p. 86.

33. General Orders #131, op. cit.

34. Ibid.

35. Letter from Herbert Harris, H & S Company, 236th Engineers, quoted in the *Burman News*, February 1988. There is some disagreement even among Japanese sources as to exactly where the general died.

36. Louis Allen, *Burma: The Longest War, 1941–1945* (New York: St. Martin's Press, 1984), p. 381.

37. Ibid.

38. Ibid., p. 385.

39. George Hicks, *The Comfort Women: Japan's Brutal Regime of Enforced Prostitution in the Second World War* (New York: Norton 1994), p. 138.

40. Ibid. Most Allied sources give a figure of about twenty comfort women in Myitkyina during the siege. However, no single Allied force encountered all the women after the battle. Several Chinese women surrendered to Chinese forces, who absorbed them into their "camp followers."

41. Ibid., pp. 139–140.

42. Romanus and Sunderland, op. cit., p. 253.

43. Major Hopkins refers to the incident in Sicily when Gen. George S. Patton Jr. slapped two of his soldiers, very nearly ending his military career.

44. James E. T. Hopkins, M.D., Henry G. Stelling, M.D., and Tracy S. Voorhees, "The Marauders and the Microbes," in *Crisis Fleeting: Original Reports on Military Medicine in India and Burma in the Second World War*, ed. James H. Stone (Washington, DC: Office of the Surgeon General, 1969), pp. 46–348.

45. Jack Girsham with Lowell Thomas, *Burma Jack* (New York: Norton, 1971), p. 142.

46. Ibid.

47. Ibid.

48. Interrogation of Lt. Gen. Shinichi Tanaka, commanding general, 18th Japanese Infantry Division, Record Group 407 (College Park, MD: National Archives and Records Service).

Chapter 8

1. Charlton Ogburn Jr., *The Marauders* (New York: Harper & Row, 1959), p. 273.

2. Ibid., p. 275.

3. Ibid., p. 277.

4. Nellis I. Johnson, letter to the *Burman News*, November 1987.

5. Private Clyde Blue, quoted in Mary Pennick Motley, *The Invisible Soldier: The Experience of the Black Soldier, World War II* (Detroit: Wayne State University Press, 1987), pp. 132–134.

6. Louis Allen, *Burma: The Longest War, 1941–1945* (New York: St. Martin's Press, 1984), p. 387.

7. Proposed Outline for Unit History of 475th Infantry, 15 November 1944, Record Group 407 (College Park, MD: National Archives and Records Service).

8. Randall Colvin, "History of the 612th F. A. Battalion (PK)," printed privately, n.d., courtesy Randall Colvin. Mr. Colvin served with the 4th Gun Section. For a complete list of commanding officers see Appendix 1.

9. The units under General Kimura's command at that time were 2d, 15th, 18th, 31st, 33d, 49th, 52d, 54th, 55th, and 56th Infantry Divisions, a tank regiment, and two independent brigades, along with a line of communication and administrative troops.

Chapter 9

1. The 475th Unit History describes the killer as a jaguar.

2. John Randolph, *Marsmen in Burma* (Houston, TX: John Randolph, 1946), p. 48.

3. Ibid., p. 50.

4. Cavalry regiments referred to individual battalions as squadrons, instead of the infantry designation of battalions. They were also based on a differing table of organization that totaled slightly less strength than that of infantry regiments.

5. "Phase #2, Battle for Tonkwa," handwritten report, no author,

n.d., Record Group 407, 475th Infantry Regiment, (College Park, MD: National Archives and Records Service).

6. Randolph, op. cit., p. 96.

7. Captain David B. Lovejoy, infantry, "Commanding: A History of B Company, 475th Infantry, from November 18, 1944 through February 8, 1945," Record Group 407, 475th Infantry Regiment, (College Park, MD: National Archives and Records Service).

8. Randolph, op. cit., p. 100.

Chapter 10

1. Charles F. Romanus and Riley Sunderland, *Time Runs Out in the CBI* (Washington, DC: Center of Military History, 1959), p. 126.

2. Colonel Willis J. Tack, untitled report, 19 December 1944, Record Group 407 (College Park, MD: National Archives and Records Service).

3. John Randolph, *Marsmen in Burma* (Houston, TX: John Randolph, 1946), p. 104.

4. Ibid.

5. Edward Fischer, *The Chancy War: Winning in China, Burma, and India in World War II* (New York: Orion, 1991), p. 201.

6. Ibid.

7. Randolph, op. cit., p. 126.

8. Romanus and Sunderland, op. cit., p. 189.

9. Randolph, op. cit., p. 136.

10. Harold "Chicken" Stringer, letter to the *Burman News*, May 1993. Charlton Ogburn tells almost exactly the same story about one of the earlier Marauder marches.

Chapter 11

1. Platoon Guide Charles F. Cattaneo, "Action of Company F, 475th Infantry During the Attack of January 1945," handwritten report, 13 February 1945, 475th Infantry Records, Record Group 407 (College Park, MD: National Archives and Records Service).

2. Randall Colvin, "History of Btry C, 612 F. A. Bn (PK)," Unpublished memoir provided to the author by Mr. Colvin, p. 17.

3. John Randolph, *Marsmen in Burma* (Houston, TX: John Randolph, 1945), p. 150.

4. 124th Cavalry Regimental Journal, entry 1700 hours 19 January 1945, 124th Cavalry Records, Record Group 407, (College Park, MD: National Archives and Records Service).

5. Ibid., entry of 1815 hours, 21 January 1945.

6. First Lieutenant Richard E. Corvey, "Action of 3d Platoon, G Company, Evening of January 19, 1945, Morning of Jan 20, 1945," handwritten report, 475th Infantry Regiment records, Record Group 407 (College Park, MD: National Archives and Records Service).

7. Lieutenant Colonel Ralph E. Faird, Narrative History 5332d Brigade (Prov.), Kutkai Area, Headquarters, 5332d Brigade. 9 April 1945, Record Group 407, (College Park, MD: National Archives and Records Service).

8. First Lieutenant Ernest W. Caine, "Ambush Burma Road," handwritten memorandum to CO, 2d Battalion, 23 Jan 1945, 475th Infantry Regimental record, Record Group 407 (College Park, MD: National Archives and Records Service).

9. First Lieutenant John W. Jones, Infantry, Company E, "Report: Ambush, Burma Road," 475th Infantry records, Record Group 407, (College Park, MD: National Archives and Records Service).

10. Headquarters, United States forces, India-Burma theater, General Orders #72, 9 April 1945, Record Group 407 (College Park, MD: National Archives and Records Service).

11. 124th Cavalry Regimental Journal, entry 1845 hours, 26 January 1945, Record Group 407 (College Park, MD: National Archives and Records Service).

12. 475th Combat Team, 1 Feb. 1945, Unit Report #1, Record Group 407 (College Park, MD: National Archives and Records Service).

13. Headquarters, United States forces, India-Burma theater, General Orders #72, 9 April, 1945, Record Group 407 (College Park, MD: National Archives and Records Service. Colonel Thrailkill was posthumously awarded a Silver Star for his leadership in his battalion's attack on 19 January.

14. Peter J. Faggion, letter to the *Burman News*, November 1994.

15. Ibid.

16. Headquarters, United States forces, India-Burma theater,

General Orders #72, 9 April 1945, Record Group 407 (College Park, MD: National Archives and Records Service).

17. Ibid.

18. Ibid.

19. Ibid.

20. First Lieutenant Pete C. McDowell, Infantry, commanding C Company, "Unit History, C Company, 475th Infantry," 475th Infantry Regiment records, Record Group 407 (College Park, MD: National Archives and Records Service).

21. Quoted in Randolph, op. cit., p. 197.

22. Ibid.

23. Headquarters, United States forces, India-Burma theater, General Orders #81. 26 April 1945, Record Group 407 (College Park, MD: National Archives and Records Service).

24. The army's official history, Romanus and Sunderland's *Time Runs Out in the CBI*, written in the late 1950s, states that the position was "unknown to the 124th." However, the more contemporary account by John Randolph, op. cit., which was not subject to censorship, clearly recounts the earlier intelligence patrol's findings.

25. United States forces, India-Burma theater, General Orders #72, 9 April 1945, Record Group 407, (College Park, MD: National Archives and Records Administration).

26. Ibid., General Orders #99, 27 May 1945.

27. Ibid., General Orders #72, 9 April 1945.

Epilogue

1. Colin S. Gray, "Handfuls of Heroes on Desperate Ventures: When Do Special Operations Succeed?" *Parameters*, U.S. Army War College Quarterly, 29, no. 1 (spring 1999): pp. 2–24.

Bibliography

Primary Sources

The primary source material for this book can be found in the National Archives and Records Service, located in College Park, Maryland. Record Group 407 contains much original material, including reports, unit journals, maps, and photographs (a separate collection) pertaining to the units involved in the two Burma campaigns.

A source untapped by many historians is the veterans associations, which often provide the most interesting and certainly the most personal stories of any campaigns. In the case of the Burma campaigns, the Merrill's Marauders Association, Incorporated, and its newsletter, the *Burman News*, are essential to any understanding of the human side of these campaigns. President Ray Lyons, a former member of the 5307th Headquarters, has made a conscious effort, with considerable success, to record for history the experiences of his members. Another member, David Quaid, who served as a photographer during the campaign, has an outstanding collection of wartime photographs that are often displayed at memorial occasions. In a similar vein is the *Ex-CBI Roundup* publication by Dwight O. King. Here again the contributions by members can bring events into sharp focus for the historian or the casual researcher.

Secondary Sources

Allen, Louis. *Burma: The Longest War, 1941–1945*. New York: St. Martin's Press, 1984.

Ancell, R. Manning, and Christine M. Miller. *The Biographical Dictionary of World War II Generals and Flag Officers, the U.S. Armed Forces.* Westport, CT: Greenwood Press, 1996.

Barker, A. L. *The March on Delhi*. London: Faber & Faber, 1963.

Bidwell, Shelford. *The Chindit War: Stilwell, Wingate and the Campaign in Burma, 1944*. New York: Macmillan, 1979.

Bland, Larry I., ed. *The Papers of George Catlett Marshall*. Vol. 1. *The Soldierly Spirit, December 1880–June 1939*. Baltimore: Johns Hopkins University Press, 1981.

Bland, Larry I., and Sharon Ritenour Stevens, eds. *The Papers of George Catlett Marshall*. Vol. 3. *The Right Man for the Job, December 7, 1941–May 31, 1943*. Baltimore: Johns Hopkins University Press, 1991.

Bunge, Frederica M., ed. *Burma: A Country Study*. Washington, DC: Headquarters, Dept. of the Army, 1983.

Burns, James MacGregor. *Roosevelt: The Soldier of Freedom, 1940–1945*. New York: Harcourt Brace Jovanovich. 1970.

Butler, J. R. M., and J. M. A. Gwyer. *Grand Strategy*. Vol. 3. London: HMSO, 1964.

Callahan, Raymond. *Burma, 1942–1945*. Davis-Poynter, 1978.

Calvert, Michael. *The Chindits*. London: Ballantine, 1973.

———. *Fighting Mad*. London: Jarrolds, 1964.

Campbell, Arthur. *The Siege: A Story from Kohima*. London: Allen & Unwin, 1956.

Chan, Won-Loy. *Burma: The Untold Story*. Novato, CA: Presidio Press, 1986.

Cornelius, Wanda, and Thayne Short. *Ding Hao: America's Air War in China, 1937–1945*. Gretna, LA: Pelican, 1980.

Craven, Wesley Frank, and James Lea Cate, eds. *The Army Air Forces in World War II*. Vol. 5. *The Pacific: Matterhorn to Nagasaki, June 1944 to August 1945*. Washington, DC: Government Printing Office, 1983.

Crost, Lynn. *Honor by Fire: Japanese Americans at War in Europe and the Pacific*. Novato, CA: Presidio Press, 1994.

Dod, Karl C. *The Corps of Engineers: The War Against Japan*. United States Army in World War II: China-Burma-India Theater. The Technical Services Subseries. Washington, DC: Center of Military History, 1987.

Dunlop, Richard. *Behind Japanese Lines: With the OSS in Burma*. New York: Rand McNally, 1979.

Ehrman, J. *Grand Strategy.* Vols. 5 and 6. HSMO, 1956.

Evans, Lt. Gen. Sir Geoffrey. *Slim As Military Commander.* London: Batsford, 1969.

Fellowes-Gordon, Ian. *The Magic War: The Battle for North Burma.* New York: Scribner, 1971.

Fergusson, Bernard. *Return to Burma.* London: Collins, 1962.

———. *The Wild Green Earth.* London: Collins, 1946.

Fischer, Edward. *The Chancy War: Winning in China, Burma, and India in World War Two.* New York: Orion, 1991.

Fowle, Barry W., ed. *Builders and Fighters: U.S. Army Engineers in World War II.* Ft. Belvoir, VA: Office of History, U.S. Army Corps of Engineers, 1992.

Fuller, Richard. *Shokan: Hirohito's Samurai. Leaders of the Japanese Armed Forces, 1926–1945.* London: Cassell, 1992.

George, Lt. Col. John B. *Shots Fired in Anger: A Rifleman's View of the War in the Pacific, 1942–1945, Including the Campaign of Guadalcanal and Fighting with Merrill's Marauders in the Jungles of Burma.* Washington, DC: National Rifle Association of America, 1981.

Gilmore, Allison B. *You Can't Fight Tanks with Bayonets: Psychological Warfare Against the Japanese Army in the Southwest Pacific.* Lincoln: University of Nebraska Press, 1998.

Girsham, Jack, with Lowell Thomas. *Burma Jack.* New York: Norton, 1971.

Gruhzit-Hoyt, Olga. *They Also Served: American Women in World War II.* New York: Birch Lane Press, 1995.

Harrington, Joseph D. *Yankee Samurai: The Secret Role of Nisei in America's Pacific Victory.* Detroit: Pettigrew Press, 1979.

Hayashi, Saburo, with Alvin D. Coox. *Kogun: The Japanese Army in the Pacific War.* Quantico, VA: Marine Corps Association, 1959.

Hicks, George. *The Comfort Women: Japan's Brutal Regime of Enforced Prostitution in the Second World War.* New York: Norton, 1994.

Howard, Michael. *Grand Strategy.* Vol. 4. London: HMSO, 1972.

———. *Strategic Deception in the Second World War.* New York: Norton, 1990.

Hunter, Charles N. *Galahad.* San Antonio: Naylor, 1963.

Hymoff, Edward. *The OSS in World War II.* New York: Ballantine Books, 1972.

Joslen, Lt. Col. H. F. *Orders of Battle: Second World War, 1939–1945.* London: London Stamp Exchange, 1990.

Kirby, Maj. Gen. S. W., et al. *The War Against Japan.* Vols. 2–5. London: HSMO, 1958–1969.

Lewin, Ronald. *Slim: The Standard Bearer.* London: Leo Cooper, 1976.

Liang, Chin-tung. *General Stilwell in China, 1942–1944: The Full Story.* St. John's University Press, 1972.

Marshall, George Catlett. *Biennial Reports of the Chief of Staff of the United States Army to the Secretary of War, 1 July 1939–30 June 1945.* Washington, DC: Center of Military History, 1996.

Masters, John. *The Road Past Mandalay.* London: Michael Joseph, 1961.

Matloff, Maurice. *Strategic Planning for Coalition Warfare, 1943–1944.* Washington, DC: Center of Military History, 1959.

McKelvie, Roy. *The War in Burma.* London: Methuen, 1948.

Military Intelligence Division, U.S. War Department. *Merrill's Marauders: February–May 1944.* American Forces in Action Series. Washington, DC: 4 June 1945.

Miller, Edward J. *War Plan Orange: The U.S. Strategy to Defeat Japan, 1897–1945.* Annapolis: Naval Institute Press, 1991.

Motley, Mary Pennick. *The Invisible Soldier: The Experience of the Black Soldier, World War II.* Detroit: Wayne State University Press, 1987.

Ogburn, Charlton. *The Marauders.* New York: Harper, 1959.

Owen, Frank. *The Campaign in Burma.* London: HMSO, 1956.

Perrett, Bryan. *Tank Tracks to Rangoon.* London: Robert Hale, 1978.

Phillips, C. L. Lucas. *Springboard to Victory.* London: Kimber, 1959.

Pogue, Forrest C. *George C. Marshall: Organizer of Victory, 1943–1945.* New York: Viking Press, 1973.

Prasad, Bisheshwar, ed. *Official History of the Indian Armed Forces in the Second World War 1939–1945. Retreat from Burma, 1941–1942; Arakan Operations, 1942–1945; Reconquest of Burma, 1942–1945,* 2 vols.; and *Post-War Occupation Forces, Japan and South-East Asia.* Delhi: Orient Longmans, 1954–.

Randolph, John H., *Marsmen in Burma.* Houston: John H. Randolph, 1946.

Romanus, Charles F., and Richard Sunderland. *Stilwell's Mission to*

China. United States Army in World War II: China-Burma-India Theater. Washington, DC: Center of Military History, 1953.

———. *Stilwell's Command Problems*. United States Army in World War II: China-Burma-India Theater. Washington, DC: Center of Military History, 1956.

———. *Time Runs Out in the CBI*. United States Army in World War II: China-Burma-India Theater. Washington, DC: Center of Military History, 1959.

Sawicki, James A. *Cavalry Regiments of the U.S. Army*. Dumfries, VA: Wyvern, 1985.

———. *Infantry Regiments of the U.S. Army*. Dumfries, VA: Wyvern, 1981.

———. *Field Artillery Battalions of the U.S. Army*. Dumfries, VA: Centaur, 1977.

Slim, Field Marshall Viscount William. *Defeat into Victory*. London: Cassell, 1956.

Stanton, Shelby L. *Orders of Battle: U.S. Army, World War II*. Novato, CA: Presidio Press, 1984.

Stimson, Henry L., and McGeorge Bundy. *On Active Service in Peace and War*. New York: Harper & Brothers, 1947.

Stone, James H., ed.. *Crisis Fleeting: Original Reports on Military Medicine in India and Burma in the Second World War*. Washington, DC: Office of the Surgeon General, Dept. of the Army, 1968.

Smith, D. E. *Battle for Burma*. London: Batsford, 1979.

Swinson, Arthur. *Kohima*. London: Cassell, 1966.

Tuchman, Barbara. *Sand Against the Wind: Stilwell and the American Experience in China, 1911–1945*. New York: Macmillan, 1970.

Tomblin, Barbara Brooks. *G.I. Nightingales: The Army Nurse Corps in World War II*. Lexington: University Press of Kentucky, 1996.

U.S. War Department. *Handbook on Japanese Military Forces*. Novato, CA: Presidio Press, 1991.

White, Theodore H., ed. *The Stilwell Papers*. New York: William Sloane Associates, 1948.

Williams, Mary H. *Chronology 1941–1945*. In Special Studies Subseries. United States Army in World War II: Washington, DC: Center of Military History, 1960.

Index

Abbott, Dale, 120–21
Acker, SSgt. John A, 115–17
Air supply, 55–56
Akui, SSgt. David, 245
Alexander, Gen. Sir Harold R. L. G., 17
Allmand, Capt. Michael, 168
Almond, Capt. Edward M., 14
American Volunteer Group (AVG), 32
Anderson, Pfc. Marvin H., 165
Arakan Operation, 19–20, 46
Archer, SSgt. Richard B. 224
Arms, Brig. Gen. Thomas S., 189–90
Armstrong, Col. George E., 177
Armstrong, 1st Lt. Paul E., 125
Arnold, Lt. Gen. Henry H., 12, 34
Arrowsmith, Col. John C., 35
Asensio, Col. Moe, 141

Ballard, TSgt. Jim, 68
Bataan, 2
Beach, Lt. Col. Charles E., 40, 60, 69, 71, 104, 107, 109, 127, 137
Beacon, Pfc. Bernie W., Jr., 250
Berkness, Lt. Norman R., 203
Bhamo, 20, 150, 194, 195, 207, 208
Bissell, Brig. Gen. Clayton L., 33, 34
Blair, 1st Lt. Melvin D., 164
Blocker, Capt. James K., 203
Blue, Pvt. Clyde, 182
Blue Combat Team, 52, 60, 105, 107, 110,
Boatner, Brig. Gen. Hayden L., 153, 155, 160–61, 162, 165, 167, 177

Bogardus, Capt. Thomas E., 107
Bouchard, Lt. Paul E., 204
Braaten, Pfc. Raymond L., 74
Brader, SSgt. William S., 161
Bradley, SSgt. Tim L., 160
Bradley, Gen. Omar N., 14
Branscomb, Sgt. Clarence, 122, 138–39
Bridges, Pvt. Arlie, 223
Briggs, Maj. Edwin J., 61, 63, 68, 72, 114, 115, 126, 136, 137
Brink, Col. Francis G., 39
British Army
  Engineers, 35
  Burma Corps, 17
  King's Regiment, The, 167
  Lancashire Fusiliers, The, 167
  South Staffordshire Regiment, The, 167
  6th Gurkha Rifles, 167, 168
  4th Battalion, 9th Gurkha Rifles, 149–50, 167
  10th Indian Infantry Brigade, 16
  10th Indian Infantry Division, 17
  16th Infantry Brigade, (Chindits), 48
  36th Infantry Division, 147, 150, 204, 205, 210
  69th Light Antiaircraft Regiment, 141
  77th Infantry Brigade, (Chindits), 167
  IV Corps, 17, 46, 186
  XIV Army, 77, 79, 80, 81, 128, 187, 194, 206
  XXXIII Corps, 186
  Morris Force, 149–50, 155

Brooklyn, N.Y., 252
Brown, Pfc. Leroy E., 112
Brown, Col. Rothwell H., 45–46, 61–77, 130
Brubeck, Capt. Shields A., 172
Buck, Capt. John, 250
Burch, Capt. Clarence O., 119
Butler, Lt. Bert, 145
Butner, USS, 191
Burma, 3–5
Burma Defense Army, 5
Burma Independence Army, 5
Burr, 2nd Lt. Othello V., 205

Caine, 1st Lt. Ernest, 231–32
Caldwell, Lt. Meredith, Jr., 91
Calvert, Brig. Gen. Michael, 167–68
Cannon, Col. Joseph, 76, 126
Carbone, Pvt. John P., 112
Chamelas, Lt. Theodore T., 119
Chan, Capt. Won-Loy, 146, 167–68, 171, 174, 178
Chen-yu, Col. Chao, 45
Chennault, Claire L., 10, 15, 17, 27, 33, 34, 193
China Air Task Force, 33
China-Burma-India Theater, 1, 2, 20, 22, 24,, 26, 34, 35, 38, 55, 153, 157, 158, 167
Chindwin River, 3, 21, 78
Chinese Army, 4, 9, 11, 26
  New 1st Army, 210
  1st Chinese Separate Regiment, 187, 190, 192, 199, 215, 218, 225
  1st Provisional Chinese-American Tank Group, 37, 45–46, 61–77, 81, 100–01
  Fifth Army, 17
  6th Pack Artillery Battery, 83
  14th Division, 144
  21st Field Artillery, 37
  22nd Division, 45, 48, 73, 81, 95, 100, 103, 129–30, 132, 194, 195–96, 200, 205–10

30th Division, 126, 208, 210, 239, 240
38th Division, 45, 48, 72, 101, 129–30, 195, 208, 239
42nd Regiment, 144, 161, 167, 169
50th Division, 126, 130, 210
64th Regiment, 73, 100–01
65th Regiment, 48, 61–01
66th Regiment, 48, 100–01, 130, 195, 200–01
88th Regiment, 126, 133, 134, 135, 150, 152, 170, 208, 240
89th Regiment 141, 143, 144, 151, 170, 246
90th Regiment, 208, 210
112th Regiment, 81, 117, 124, 131,
113th Regiment, 45, 72, 73, 81, 83, 85, 90, 94, 95, 101, 207, 239
114th Regiment, 131, 146, 207, 230, 232–33, 235–39
149th Regiment, 130–31, 132
150th Regiment, 126, 140, 143, 144, 151, 161, 162, 166
Chins, 3
Churchill, Prime Minister Winston, 5, 23–24, 142
Clark, Capt. Harold L., 239
Clayton, Sgt. Murray P., 74
Coburn, Lt. Harry B. 88
Cole, Pvt. Robert W., 112
Coleman, Sgt. Fred N., 165
Collins, Gen. J. Lawton, 14
Colorado, 82
Colvin, Pfc. Randall, 224
Combs, Lt. Col. William A., 140, 143, 162, 163
Combat Engineer Battalions, 2, 35
"Comfort Women," 173–75
Coon, Pfc. Barlow, 153
Corn, T/5 Leo D., 245
Cornwall, Lt. Ralph Lee, 214
Corvey, 1st Lt. Richard E., 230
Cox, Maj. Ellis, 146
Cureton, Pvt. Solomon, 250

Curl, Capt. Vincent L., 97, 98
Cytrynowicz, Pfc. Casimir, 158

Darlington, Capt. Charles E., 89
Day, T/4 Lewis E., 165
Davoust, 1st Lt. Albert, 205
"Dead Mule Gulch", 228
Dean, Pfc. Marvin H., 170
Dearborn, USS, 191
Delorey, 1st Lt. Donald W., 172
Denver, Rio Grande & Western
    RR, 35
Deogarh, 39
Deyo, Pfc. Robert C., 245
Dolloff, Phyllis Braidwood, 38
Donovan, Lt. Col. James F., 191,
    212, 227, 235
Donovan, Col. William J., 53–54
Dorman-Smith, Sir Reginald, 17
Doyer, Sgt. Maj. (Later CWO) Joe,
    115, 217
Drolla, Sgt. Frank S., 151
Drum, Lt. Gen. Hugh A., 11–13
Dunlop, 2nd Lt. Paul A., 132
Dunn, Capt. John J., 172

Easterbrook, Col. Ernest F., 194,
    214, 217, 230, 242, 253
Eifler, Col. Carl F, 55, 82, 97
Eisenhower, Brig. Gen. Dwight D.,
    12
Elm, SSgt. Raymond C., 244
Emmerson, John, 171
Evans, Lt. William C., 84–85

Faggion, Pfc. Peter J., 243
Farren, Pvt. Thomas D., 62
Faulkenberg, Jinx, 198
Fedder, Al, 72
Fergusson, Brigadier B. E., 48
Festing, Maj. Gen. F. W., 210
Field, USS C. W., 191
Finger, SSgt. Charles, 243
Firenze, Pfc. Anthony S., 169–70
First World War, 149, 151
Fischer, Capt. Edward, 215, 230

Fisher, Pfc. George, 66
Fleming, Maj. Ian, 79
Freedom Bloc, 5
Fukayama, Colonel, 71

GALAHAD, See 5307th
    Composite Unit (Prov.)
Gardiner, 1st Lt. Robert O., 59
Garrison, 1st Lt. H. G., 241–242
Garrsion, SSgt. Sylvester G., 245
Gerow, Pfc. Leonard H., Jr.,
    237–238
Gates, Maj. Mahlon E., 163
George, Capt. John B., 31, 38, 43,
    117–18
Ghiz, Maj. Edward M., 84, 85
Girsham, Jack, 54, 76, 177
Gordon, Pfc. Chester, 204
Gosho, Sgt. Henry H.
    ("Horizontal Hank"), 30, 63,
    171
Graham, Cpl. Frank L., 114
Green, Pvt. William J., 227–28
Green Combat Team, 60, 108,
    110, 111, 120
Greenlee, Lt. Col. Harold E., 157,
    163, 172
Greer, Sgt. Alfred, 64
Grissom, 1st Lt. William C., 50, 53

Hall, Pfc. Clayton E., 67
Halstead, USS, 191
Hancock, Maj. Edward T., 41, 57,
    58, 126
Hara, Col. Kozo, 207
Harabayashi, Sgt. Grant, 174
Harrold, Lt. Col. Arthur K., 194
Hatfield, Sgt. Richard M., 248
Hawes, 1st Lt. Aaron E., Jr., 239
Hazeltine, Lt. Col. Charles B.,
    199, 218
Healy, Maj. Richard W., 52, 107,
    112
Heavey, Col. Thomas J., 197, 213,
    216
Henderson, Pfc. Clifton L., 244

Hill, Sgt. Kim, 248
Hill, TSgt. Lawrence J., 117
Hill, Sgt. Russell, 31
"Hill 77", 239
Hodges, Maj. Frank C., 143
Hoffman, Sgt. William F., 69
Holmes, 1st Lt. William E., 205
Honda, Lt. Gen. Masaki (Seizai), 47, 157
Honda, Robert Y., 30
Hooper, Cpl. Charles B., 235
Hopkins, Capt. James E. T., 111, 124, 125, 175–77
Horton, T/5 Howard P., 172
Hudson, Pfc. Everett E., 165
Huffine, Maj. Fred, 143
Hughes, 2nd Lt. Burr L., 250–51
Hunter, Col. Charles N., 27, 39, 40, 42–43, 44, 51, 53, 64, 68, 71, 76, 81, 95, 97–99, 101, 103–04, 107, 109, 112–27, 133, 134, 135, 136, 140–48, 151–53, 158, 160, 169, 175, 177, 188
Hunter, Capt. Maurice A., 237
Hyotaro, Lt. Gen. Kimura, 183, 193

Ichimura, Tom, 146
Imphal, 79, 80, 81, 94, 128, 183
Imperial Japanese Army
  Burma Area Army, 46
  Imperial Guards Division, 47
  Southern Army Headquarters, 46
  Yamazaki Detachment, 208–209, 226, 227
  2nd Infantry Regiment, 234
  2nd Infantry Division, 129, 209, 223
  4th Infantry Regiment, 47, 129, 130, 132, 209, 223, 226
  15th Airfield Battalion, 140
  15th Army, 47, 79, 186, 193, 195
  18th Infantry Division, 16, 45, 46, 47, 60, 61, 65, 71, 81, 95, 108, 131, 132, 183, 195, 200, 204, 209
  24th Independent Mixed Brigade, 47
  28th Army, 47, 193
  31st Infantry Division, 46
  33rd Army, 47, 145, 149, 193, 195, 207–09, 210
  33rd Infantry Division, 16, 46
  35th Infantry Regiment, 46
  49th Infantry Division, 47, 193, 209
  52nd Infantry Regiment, 47
  53rd Infantry Division, 129, 149, 167
  54th Infantry Division, 46, 183
  55th Infantry Division, 16, 46, 47
  55th Infantry Regiment, 46, 62, 70, 132, 195
  56th Infantry Division, 16, 46, 47, 178, 184, 204, 209, 210, 222, 234
  56th Infantry Regiment, 61, 62–63, 70, 77, 132, 195
  114th Infantry Regiment, 77, 108, 140, 178
  119th Infantry Regiment, 204
  146th Infantry Regiment, 129, 148th Infantry Regiment, 145
  168th Infantry Regiment, 209
India, 3, 6
India-Burma Theater, 191
India Air Task Force, 33
Infantry School, U.S. Army, 28
Inkangahtawng, 98–99, 101, 102, 104, 106, 130
Irrawaddy River, 3, 150
Iwo Jima, 1

Jones, Lt. John W., 236–37
Johnson, Maj. (Later Col.)
  Caifson, 84, 90–91, 138, 140, 194, 222, 242, 244, 246
Johnson, Lt. Nellis I., 156, 181–82
Johnson, Ambassador Nelson T., 10

Jordan, Maj. George B., 199, 218, 246, 249

Kachins, 3, 54, 88, 256
Kachin Rangers, 54, 82–83, 85, 86, 110, 145, 170, 174, 205, 215, 222, 230
Kaeli, Capt. Andrew J., 249–50
Kai-shek, Generalissimo Chiang, 5, 8, 10, 11, 17, 34, 131, 184–86
Kamaing Road, 47, 48–49, 60, 62, 73, 80, 90, 98, 100, 105, 129, 131
Karens, 3
Katamura, Lt. Gen. Shibachi, 183
Katz, Cpl. Werner, 51
Kavel, 1st Lt. Hobart T., 226, 250–51
Kawabe, Lt. Gen. Masakuzu (Shozo), 46
Kazlousky, Sgt. Aloysius, 112
Kerley, Capt. Thomas L., 143
Keslik, Sgt. John, 111, 117
Khaki Combat Team, 60, 61, 63, 66, 71, 98, 103, 106, 114, 116, 118, 121, 123, 133, 134, 135, 136, 137
King, Sgt. Ed, 75
King, Fleet Adm. Ernest J., 22, 24
King, Maj. William C., 227
Kinnison, Col. Henry L., 126, 134, 135, 136, 137, 138, 143
Knight, First Sgt. Curtis, 247–48
Knight, 1st Lt. Jack L., 247–48
Knight, Lt. Col. Richard A., 197
"Knight's Hill", 247–50, 253
Kofer, Lt. Irving, 252
Kohima, 78, 79, 81, 94, 130, 183
Ko-li, Col. Peg, 232, 238, 239
Kolodny, Capt. Lewis A., 111
Koontz, Capt. Clyde L, 35
Kornfeld, SSgt. Milton, 243
Krueger, Lt. Gen. Walter, 32

Laffin, Capt. William A., 30, 126, 132, 138, 156

Landis, Pvt. Robert W., 52
Landis, Camp, 188–90, 197, 198
Lashio, 6
Lattin, Maj. John H., 201–02, 243, 244–46
Lee, Col. Chin, 51, 68
Leightner, Pfc. Pete, 62
Leonard, 2nd Lt. Laurence O., 252
Lepore, Lt. William, 87
Lew, Maj. Lawrence L., 51, 63–65, 67, 68, 114, 119
Lilly, Pfc. William J. D., 164
Loi-Kang Ridge, 221, 222, 223, 225, 226, 229, 232, 237, 238, 241, 242–244, 250, 252, 253, 259
Lovejoy, Capt. David B., 205
Lowell, 1st Lt. Marlan E., 59
Lurline, SS, 31, 32, 38

MacArthur, Gen. Douglas, 22
Mahoney, Lt. Vern, 217
Maingkwan, 45, 59
Mandalay, 3, 6, 16
Manuel, Pfc. Herman, 94, 171
Marshall, Gen. George C., 12–13, 19, 22–25, 26, 27, 34
Marshall Islands, 78
Marti, TSgt. Alfred T., 225
Martin, SSgt. Amos A., 219
Martin, Lt. William, 138
Maruyama, Col. Fusayusa, 108, 110, 140, 157, 171, 173–174
Matsumoto, Sgt. Roy, 30, 69, 119–21
Matteson, Col. Milo H., 188
Mattina, Capt. John C., 164
Maw, Prime Minister Ba, 5
Maxon, Capt. Robert P., 202
McCammon, Col. John E., 126, 143, 144, 148, 151, 152, 153
McCord, Pvt. Leonard J., 249
McDowell, 1st Lt. Pete C., 245
McElmurray, Lt. John P., 84–85, 89, 93

McFadden, Lt. Alexander, 203
McGee, Lt. Col. George A., 29, 40,
    60, 71, 99, 102, 103–27, 135,
    136, 143, 152, 177
McLogan, Lt., 120
McNutt, Pvt. Guy I., 216
Meachan, Pfc. Norman E., 227
Meade, Fort George Gordon, 154
Merrill, Gen. Frank D., 18, 19–20,
    42–43, 45, 52, 53, 60, 68–69, 71,
    74, 76, 80, 81, 97, 98, 102–04,
    108–09, 126, 127, 132, 136–37,
    141–48, 144, 177
"Merrill's Marauders", 44
Miles, Cmdr. Milton E. 37
Miles, T/4 William H., 165
Miller, SSgt. Alvin O., 164
Mineral Wells, Texas, 247, 251
Ming, Gen. Tu Lu, 17
Mink, Pvt. Walter C., 200
Mississippi, 28
Mitchell, Lt. Lewis B., 203, 237,
    239
Mitsukado, SSgt. Edward, 30
Miyasaki, Herbert Y., 30
Mizukami, Maj. Gen. Genzu, 145,
    151, 168, 171, 172, 173
Monday, Sgt. Broughton, 229
Moore, SSgt. David H., 219
Moore, Cpl. Pierce W., 251
Moore, Pfc. Russell R. 224
Morris, Lt. Col. J. R. (Later
    Brigadier), 149–50, 155
Mountbatten, Adm. Lord Louis,
    24, 128, 142, 185, 253
Mozak, Pfc. George, 203
Mukden, 8
Murphy, 2nd Lt. Patrick E., 235
Murphy, TSgt. (Later Lt.) Patrick
    W., 224
Mutaguchi, Lt. Gen. Renya, 183
Myitkyina, 18, 33, 45, 51, 122, 123,
    126–27, 128–48, 149–79, 184
Myitkyina Task Force, 148, 151,
    178, 227

Nagelberg, Pfc. Martin S., 245
Naiden, Brig. Gen. Earl L., 33
Naka, Lt. Gen. Eitaro, 195–96, 202
Namhpakka, 214–15, 221, 222,
    223
National Guard, 2
Nawkham, 221–22, 227, 229
Nelson, Capt. Willard C. 59
Netzel, Sgt. Wilbert A., 201
Nhpum Ga, 59, 100–127, 175
Nichols, Capt. Frank, 250
Normandy, 1
Northern Combat Area
    Command, 45, 46, 48, 161, 186,
    187
Null, Pfc. William, 220

O'Brien, Pat, 198
Office Of Strategic Services,
    53–54
Ogburn, Lt. Charlton, Jr., 28, 30,
    86, 88, 94, 132, 134, 156,
    180–81
Okinawa, 1
Old, Gen. Donald, 141–42
Operation Longcloth, 20–21, 25,
    28
Orange Combat Team, 51, 60, 62,
    63, 65, 67, 71–72, 98, 109, 111,
    113–16, 118, 121, 123, 134, 136,
    137
Osborne, Lt. Col. William Lloyd,
    29, 40, 61, 84, 85, 87–91, 95, 99,
    122, 126, 134, 140, 177, 188,
    194, 213, 216, 220, 228, 229,
    238, 239–40, 246, 248, 253, 257
Owen, Pfc. George A., 251

Panay, USS, 10
Paquette, Cpl. Lionel J. 62
Parker, 1st Lt. James W., 97
Patriot Party, 5
Patton, Gen. George S., Jr., 15
Pearl Harbor, 10, 11

Peers, Col. William R., 54
Pegg, Lt. Col. 213, 216, 253
Peterson, Col. Vernon W., 75
Petito, Maj. Peter A., 119
Pennsylvania, 31
Pershing, Gen. John J., 12
Phillips, SSgt. Wade, 204
Pick, Col. Lewis A., 36
Pietsch, Pfc. Carter, 74
Pigoni, Sgt. Dave, 245
Ploederl, Ssgt. John L., 114
Poling, T/5 Woodford D., 219
Posner, Maj. Sidney, 229
Presterly, Pfc. George C., 166
Pu, Tharrawaddy U, 5
Pun, Sgt. Lum K., 117
Pun, Rifleman Tulbahadur, 168
"Purple Force", 130
Pung, Sgt. Andrew B., 65–66

Quebec, 8, 22, 24

Rangoon, 3, 6, 15–16, 187
Read, Maj. John W., 190, 197
Rector, First Sgt. Worth E., 165
Red Combat Team, 61, 72, 84, 85,
    87, 88, 90, 93, 138, 140, 143
Red Cross, 37–38
Reed, SSgt. Ernest, 222
Rhoads, 1st Lt. Edwin M., 236
Richardson, Sgt. Dave, 46
Ripstra, Lt. Col. Earl F., 199, 213,
    218
Rittenhouse, Capt. Frank, 250
Robertson, Cpl. Edgar, 114
Roe, TSgt. Richard E., 164
Rogoff, Maj. Bernard, 111, 113,
    125
Romano, Sgt. Anthony, 229
Roosevelt, Pres. Franklin D., 7, 10,
    11, 19, 24, 34, 35, 54, 186
Rothschild, Lt. Edwin, 243
Rougelot, Pfc. Justin J., 245
Royal Air Force, 57
    31st Squadron, 57
    62nd Squadron, 57
    117th Squadron, 57
    194th Squadron, 57

Saidor, 78
Salween River, 3
Sandvall, Lt. Col. Leslie E., 156
Saw, U., 4
Scott, Lt. Charles R., 93
Senff, Capt. (Later Maj.) Tom P.,
    87, 123, 138, 151
Shaduzup, 45, 48, 81–99, 128
Shanghai, 8, 48
Shepley, James, 44
Sheridan, Anne, 198
Shephard, Lt. David H., 252
Shipstead, Lt. Alton M., 202, 237
Silver, MSgt. Stanley, 36–37
Singapore, 23, 46, 47, 154
Sino-Japanese War, 9
Sittang River, 3
Sittner, Lt. John, 213
Slim, Field Marshall William J.,
    16–17, 79, 80, 128, 184–85, 194,
    206
Smart, Phil, 29
Smith, Pvt. Howard T., 162
Smith, Lt. Martin R., 200
Smith, SSgt. Oral E., 244–45
Smith, Lt. Warren R., 104–05,
    111–12
Somervell, Gen. Brehon Burke, 27
Soong, Dr. T. V., 26–27
Southeast Asia Command, 39
Stelling, Capt. Henry G., 111, 175
Stephenson, Maj. William G., 190,
    235
Still, Lt. Col. Daniel E., 39
Stilwell, Gen. Joseph W., 9, 13–15,
    17–19, 23–24, 26, 33, 35, 39,
    42–44, 48, 79, 81, 97, 123, 127,
    128, 133, 142, 147, 150, 151,
    152, 165, 169, 180, 184–85, 256
Stilwell, Lt. Col. Joseph W., Jr., 45,
    130, 209

Stimson, Secy of War Henry L.,
    12–15, 19
Stockton, Sgt. Clyde, 248
Stoneman, Camp, 29–30
Strasbaugh, T/5 Bernard, 67
Stringer, Pvt. Harold "Chicken",
    219
Sugeta, Ben S., 30
Sukup, Pvt. John, 84
Sultan, Lt. Gen. Daniel I,
    184–185, 209, 215, 253
Sumatra, 23
Sun, Gen. Li-jen, 45, 48, 50, 73,
    81, 131, 207, 210
Sweeney, Pfc. Joseph F., 69

Tack, Col. Willis J., 212
Tanaka, Lt. Gen. Shinichi
    (Sumichi), 47, 60, 61, 70, 83,
    94, 99, 122, 123, 129, 140, 142,
    145, 149, 157, 173, 178, 183,
    195, 257
Tanja Ga, 52, 59
Tannenbaum, T5 Joseph, 37
Tanner, Lt. Bob, 145
Tate, Maj. Ferdinand J., 35
Teischer, Maj. Ira, 250
Terauchi, Count Hisaichi, 46
Thailand, 3, 6, 14, 15, 19
Thrailkill, Maj. (Later Lt. Col.),
    Benjamin F., 189, 194, 200,
    242–43
Tice, Capt. James G., 158
Tilly, 1st Lt. James L., 82–83, 85,
    86, 87, 89
"Tokyo Rose", 220
Tonkwa, 195–196, 200, 205, 207,
    215
Transylvania Bible School, 31
Travis, 2nd Lt. John W., 165
Tse-tung, Mao, 8, 10
Tsuji, Col. Masanobu, 173
Tynan, Lt. Leo C., 248
United States Army, 1, 2, 7, 8, 22,
    27
    Americal Division, 31

Base Section Three, Service Of
    Supply, 158
Casual Detachment 1688-A, 29.
    40, 44
Casual Detachment 1688-B, 30,
    40, 44
Corps Of Engineers, 35. 156
GH 770, 154
"H" Force, 126, 132, 133, 135,
    136, 140
"K" Force, 126, 127, 132, 133,
    135, 136, 143
Mars Task Force, 189, 190, 193,
    210, 212, 214–17, 223–52, 253,
    256
Military Intelligence Service, 30
"M" Force, 133, 135
"New Galahad", 155–79
OSS Detachment 101, 54,
    82–83, 96, 138, 170
Ranger Battalions, 254
1st Cavalry, 29
1st Troop Carrier Squadron, 57
2nd U. S. Army, 190
2nd Filipino Regiment, 154
2nd Troop Carrier Squadron,
    57
II Corps, 14
6th Ranger Battalion, 32
7th Bombardment Group, 32
7th Infantry Division, 14
9th Bombardment Squadron,
    33
10th (Mountain) Infantry
    Division, 82
10th Army Air Force, 25, 32, 33,
    34, 35, 54, 191, 207, 225, 244
15th Infantry Regiment, 15
11th Bombardment Group,
    Medium, 33
13th Mountain Medical
    Battalion, 75
14th Army Air Force, 25, 34, 35
14th Evacuation Hospital, 59,
    146–47, 180
16th Fighter Group, 33

20th Station Hospital, 38, 59, 75
22nd Bombardment Squadron, 33
23rd Fighter Group, 32, 33
25th Fighter Squadron, 33
26th Fighter Squadron, 33
27th Troop Carrier Squadron, 57
31st Quartermaster Pack Troop, 41, 194
33rd Infantry Regiment, 29, 154
33rd Quartermaster Pack Troop, 41–42
37th Infantry Division, 31
42nd Portable Surgical Hospital, 148
43rd Infantry Division, 76
44th Portable Surgical Hospital, 227
45th General Service Regiment, 35–36
49th Portable Surgical Hospital, 229, 249
51st Fighter Group, 32
71st (Pack, Jungle) Infantry Division, 154, 190
71st Liaison Squadron, 59
73rd Evacuation Hospital, 75
75th Ranger Regiment, 254, 259
88th Fighter Squadron, 151, 170
98th Field Artillery Battalion, 32, 40, 115
98th Station Hospital, 38
99th Infantry Division, 29
111th Station Hospital, 59
124th Cavalry Regiment (Special), 187–88, 190, 192, 197–00, 212–22, 223–52, 253
151st Medical Battalion, 75
159th Station Hospital, 38
195th Engineer Dump Truck Co., 35
209th Engineer (Combat) Battalion, 36, 148, , 156–58

236th Engineer (Combat) Battalion, 156
315th Troop Carrier Squadron, 57
330th Engineer General Service Regiment, 36, 37
382nd Construction Battalion, 36
413th Field Artillery Group, 190
436th Bombardment Squadron, 33
475th Infantry Regiment (Long Range Penetration), 187, 188–89, 190, 192, 194, 196,199, 200, 205, 212–22, 223–52, 253
491st Bombardment Squadron, 33
492nd Bombardment Squadron, 33
493rd Bombardment Squadron, 33
502nd Military Police Battalion, 41
504th Light Pontoon Company, 144
518th Quartermaster Battalion (Mobile), 57, 182
511th Medical Collecting Company, 253
612th Field Artillery Battalion (Pack), 190–91, 194–95, 197, 212–22, 224–52
613th Field Artillery Battalion, (Pack), 191, 200, 212–22, 224–52
679th Engineer Aviation Battalion, 141
803rd Medical Air Evacuation Squadron, 75
823rd Aviation Engineer Battalion, 36
835th Signal Service Battalion, 41
849th Aviation Engineer Battalion (Colored), 36
898th Heavy Ordnance

Company, 36–37
1883rd Aviation Engineer
Battalion (Colored), 36
3304th Quartermaster Truck
Company, 57
3841st Quartermaster Truck
Company, 57
5303rd Headquarters And
Headquarters Company (Prov.),
38
5332nd Brigade (Provisional),
187, 188, 190, 192, 210
5307th Composite Unit (Prov.),
32, 38, 39, 40–41, 43, 44–45, 48,
50–77, 80, 85–99, 101–27,
128–48, 150–80, 254, 256, 259
5307th Pack Artillery Battery,
126
United States Naval Group,
China, 37

Van Fleet, Maj. James A., 14
Vietnam War, 3, 254
"Vinegar Joe", 14
Virginia Military Institute, 48, 189
Voorhees, Col. Tracy S., 175

Wade, Pfc. Edward A., 32
Walawbum, 49, 50–77, 80, 83
Wallis, Lt. Col. Severn T., 194, 235
Watson, 2nd Lt. James, 144
Wavell, Gen. Sir Archibald, 20
Wedemeyer, Lt. Gen. Albert C.,
184–85, 196, 254
Weingartner, 1st Lt. Victor J.
(Abie), 65–66, 119
Weld, 2nd Lt. Philip S., 90–91,
181
Wellman, T/5 Russell G., 171
Welsh, Lt. Phillip, 203
Wessels, Brig. Gen., Theodore F.,
166, 167, 168
Weston, Lt. Logan, 31–32, 50–52,
75, 104, 105
Whitaker, Pfc. Anthony, 248
White, Pfc. Alpheus W., 160

White Combat Team, 61, 84, 87,
90, 93, 140, 143
Willey, Brig. Gen. John P., 192–93,
214, 215, 217–18, 225, 228, 230,
242, 253, 257
Willey, Sgt. Norman H., 102
Williams, Maj. Louis J., 43
Wilson, Capt. Arthur W., 160–61
Wilson, SSgt. Chester C., 222
Wilson, Lt. Samuel V., 50–54,
63–64, 84, 87, 155–56
Wingate, Gen. Orde, 17, 20–21,
25, 28, 42, 55, 80, 95, 128
Wood, Capt. William, 249
Woomer, 2nd Lt. William E. 64,
121
Worley, Capt. Joseph P, 243
Wright, Pfc. Durad L., 160

Yao-tsiang, Gen. Liao, 48
Yoshimura, Cpl. Akiji, 30, 31

Zokosky, SSgt. John, 74